Bloom's Modern Critical Interpretations

Bloom's Modern Critical Interpretations

Bloom's Modern Critical Interpretations

C.S. Lewis's

The Chronicles of Narnia

Edited and with an introduction by
Harold Bloom
Sterling Professor of the Humanities
Yale University

CHELSEA HOUSE
PUBLISHERS
An imprint of Infobase Publishing

Bloom's Modern Critical Interpretations: The Chronicles of Narnia

©2006 Infobase Publishing

Introduction © 2006 by Harold Bloom

Chelsea House
An imprint of Infobase Publishing
132 West 31st Street
New York NY 10001

Library of Congress Cataloging-in-Publication Data
C.S. Lewis's The Chronicles of Narnia / Harold Bloom, editor.
    p. cm. — (Bloom's modern critical interpretations)
    Includes bibliographical references (p.   ) and index.
    ISBN 0-7910-9310-7
    1. Lewis, C. S. (Clive Staples), 1898-1963. Chronicles of Narnia.
    I. Bloom, Harold. II. Series.
    PR6023.E926C53235 2006
    823'.912—dc22   2006011657

Chelsea House books are available at special discounts when purchased in bulk quantities for businesses, associations, institutions, or sales promotions. Please call our Special Sales Department in New York at (212) 967-8800 or (800) 322-8755.

You can find Chelsea House on the World Wide Web at http://www.chelseahouse.com

Contributing Editor: Amy Sickels
Cover design by Takeshi Takahashi

Printed in the United States of America

Bang EJB 10 9 8 7 6 5 4 3 2 1

This book is printed on acid-free paper.

All links and web addresses were checked and verified to be correct at the time of publication. Because of the dynamic nature of the web, some addresses and links may have changed since publication and may no longer be valid.

Contents

Editor's Note

My Introduction salutes the learned dogmatism of C.S. Lewis, whose *Narnia* abounds in answers, and dismisses all questions, and why not?

Kathryn Ann Lindskoog explains the dualities of *Narnia*'s vision of Nature, after which Charles A. Huttar celebrates the *Chronicles* as Scripture, and why not?

Chad Walsh, another Lewis idolator, praises *Narnia* in a way that insinuates only "ossified grown-ups who have stifled the child within" are excluded. Perhaps, but the child within me happens to be excluded by Lewis's harsh version of Christian dogma.

I find Margaret Patterson Hannay to be more pragmatic in her esteem for *Narnia*, while Donald E. Glover is useful at introducing the pattern of Lewis's fantasies.

Narnia is judged by Lee D. Rossi as Lewis's escape from harsh North Irish familial and political realities, after which Joe R. Christopher finds in *Narnia* the mingled influences of E. Nesbit and Tolkien.

Kath Filmer, a little disenchanted with Lewis, interestingly compares *The Last Battle* to George Orwell's *Animal Farm*, while Colin Manlove clearly establishes that Aslan is Yahweh, opponent of all witches.

Hearty praise is afforded to Narnian storytelling by Lionel Adey, after which Nicole M. DuPlessis provides a balanced ecological view of Lewis as a kind of hierarchial lover of the natural environment.

HAROLD BLOOM

Introduction

Most of the world continues to believe in witches, though the public sport of witch-burning is not so popular as once it was. C.S. Lewis, Christian apologist and allegorist, might seem to have entertained a nostalgia for some of the folkways of what he liked to call Old Western Man. I am charmed to a certain uneasiness by at least one paragraph in his widely admired *Mere Christianity*:

> One man said to me, 'Three hundred years ago people in England were putting witches to death. Was that what you call the Rule of Human Nature or Right Conduct?' But surely the reason we do not execute witches is that we do not believe there are such things. If we did—if we really thought that there were people going about who had sold themselves to the devil and received supernatural powers from him in return and were using these powers to kill their neighbours or drive them mad or bring bad weather, surely we would all agree that if anyone deserved the death penalty, then these filthy quislings did. There is no difference of moral principle here: the difference is simply about matter of fact. It may be a great advance in knowledge not to believe in witches: there is no moral advance in not executing them when you do not think they are there. You would not call a

1

> man humane for ceasing to set mousetraps if he did so because he
> believed there were no mice in the house.

I enjoy the nice edge of this statement, which on my reading hints that Lewis is not just teasing us. A theocratic militarism now governs the United States, whose President proclaims Jesus Christ as his "favorite" philosopher. What other philosophers George W. Bush actually could name is unclear, though even C.S. Lewis was unlikely to name his Incarnate God a philosopher. Witches pervade *The Chronicles of Narnia*, the series of fantasies and not the motion picture, which I have not seen. Narnia indeed might be called Christnarnia, since Aslan is Christ the Lion, who says things like: "You would not have called to me unless I had been calling to you." Lewis is on Aslan's side even if there isn't any Aslan to lead it. One could say that Lewis by far transcended St. Paul's definition of faith. For the author of the *Narnia* books, faith was the substance of things already possessed, the evidence of things perpetually seen. If C.S. Lewis had one singular originality, it was that he was the most dogmatic human being ever to exist. I say this not to malign Lewis, but I am now three quarters of a century old and have read non-stop all my life. Never have I encountered any other writer so dogmatic in temperament and in conviction as C.S. Lewis. Compared to him, John Calvin and Martin Luther were relatively tolerant spirits.

Would that I were being hyperbolical, but I am merely descriptive. For almost a month, in the autumn of 1954, I experienced some seven or eight conversations with Lewis, until both of us decided we could not go on with our acquaintance. We shared a love of great poetry, but I had (and retain still) Gnostic convictions that the God of this world was not benign, and that the Creation and the Fall were one and the same event. As a disciple of William Blake, my manifesto was that great poet's *The Marriage of Heaven and Hell*. One of Lewis's books, *The Great Divorce*, even in its title rejects Blake. In the vocabulary of *The Marriage of Heaven and Hell*, C.S. Lewis was an Angel. Perhaps, if his dogma has proved true, Lewis is now an Angel, and need dispute no longer.

What has all this to do with *The Chronicles of Narnia*? Lewis declined to believe that any poet, even Shakespeare, had created anything. Creation was entirely God's prerogative, and even Shakespeare could only reshuffle the building blocks that God provided. Falstaff, Hamlet, Iago, King Lear, and Cleopatra would seem to defy Lewis's order of priorities, and yet I am a touch remorseful at being ungrateful to a major scholar who dismissed questions and heroically affirmed that he had all the answers, both as to this world and the next.

An aged reader of poetry and of theology, I have forgotten any answers I ever had, and sometimes have trouble remembering the questions. And, pragmatically speaking, my former profession of literary study has been usurped by a rabblement of lemmings, who have answers to everything. New Historicists, ideological Feminists, resentful Neo-Colonialists, gender-and-power freaks, quasi-Marxists, and Sexual Orientationalists all are as dogmatic as C.S. Lewis, while lacking his learning and love for poetry. If the choice is Foucault or Christ, I go elsewhere.

What then of *Narnia*? I tried once, ages ago, to read *The Lion, the Witch and the Wardrobe* to my two little sons, but broke off the process. Neither of the children was greatly disturbed, when we switched happily to Maurice Sendak. I cannot deny *Narnia*'s appeal to hundreds of thousands of children, but that counts for little compared to the worldwide audience of hundreds of millions who respond with total devotion to Harry Potter. Someday, both Aslan and Potter will have been long displaced; Sendak, I believe, will abide, and so will Lewis Carroll's *Alice* books and John Crowley's wonderful *Little, Big*. Dogma may always be in fashion, but even dogmas change. Time's revenges are absolute.

KATHRYN ANN LINDSKOOG

Spoiled Goodness:
Lewis's Concept of Nature

RURAL BEAUTY

Lewis's appreciation of geographical landscape is what one would expect of a Christian romantic—a reverent and insatiable delight. In his personal account, he relates:

> What the real garden had failed to do, the toy garden did. It made me aware of nature—not, indeed, as a storehouse of forms and colours but as something cool, dewy, fresh, exuberant.... As long as I live my imagination of Paradise will retain something of my brother's toy garden.[1]

Lewis's wonder at the fresh exuberance of nature is expressed in his first description of the real Narnia, as the great thaw occurs in *The Lion, the Witch and the Wardrobe*. The sudden rejuvenation of the forest is recorded with great delicacy and sensuous detail. Finally, as the trees begin to come alive, the larches and birches in green, the laburnums in gold, a dwarf stops and announces with horror, "This is no thaw; this is spring" (pp. 97–98).

In contrast to this poignant presentation of nature approached with childlike eagerness is Lewis's short story "The Shoddy Lands," an adult fantasy. The shoddy lands are discovered upon an accidental journey into the

From *The Lion of Judah in Never-Never Land: The Theology of C.S. Lewis Expressed in His Fantasies for Children*. © 1973 by William B. Eerdmans Publishing Company.

mind of a frivolous young woman. There the scenery is extremely vague and dingy, each nondescript feature of the surrounding merely a crude, shabby apology for part of nature. There is no freshness, detail, or clarity, because the woman's mind is jaded and blasé.[2]

Again, at the opposite extreme, the rich profuseness of nature is sensuously exaggerated in Lewis's description of the Wood between the Worlds in *The Magician's Nephew*:

> You could almost feel the trees growing ... a pool every few yards as far as his eyes could reach. You could almost feel the trees drinking the water up with their roots. This wood was very much alive.... It was a *rich* place: as rich as plum-cake.[3]

Here Lewis is apparently reverting to "the older conception of Nature ... tingling with anthropomorphic life, dancing, ceremonial, a festival not a machine."[4] In an early poem, Lewis once said,

> Faeries must be in the woods
> Or the satyrs' laughing broods—
> Tritons in the summer sea,
> Else how could the dead things be
> Half so lovely as they are? ...[5]

Later, Lewis developed this idea in lively prose in his introduction to D. E. Harding's *The Hierarchy of Heaven and Earth*. "We have emptied the baby out with the bath," he states. "In emptying out the dryads and the gods (which, admittedly, 'would not do' just as they stood) we appear to have thrown out the whole universe, ourselves included."[6] According to Lewis, a dryad is the abbreviated symbol for all we know about trees. So is "mind or consciousness" a symbol for what we know about behavior. Rejection of these concepts occurs when the symbol is mistaken for the object.[7]

> At the outset the universe appears packed with will, intelligence, life and positive qualities; every tree is a nymph and every planet a god. Man himself is akin to the gods. The advance of knowledge gradually empties this rich and genial universe: first of its gods, then of its colours, smells, sounds, and tastes, finally of solidity itself as solidity was originally imagined. As those items are taken from the world, they are transferred to the subjective side of the account: classified as our sensations, thoughts, images

or emotions. The Subject becomes gorged, inflated, at the expense of the Object. But the matter does not rest there. The same method which has emptied the world now proceeds to empty ourselves. The masters of the method soon announce that we were just as mistaken (and in much the same way) when we attributed 'souls' or 'selves' or 'minds' to human organisms, as when we attributed Dryads to the trees. Animism apparently begins at home. We, who have personified all other things, turn out to be ourselves mere personifications.[8]

The structure of Lewis's children's books is in direct opposition to the philosophy decried in this introduction.

THE SUPERNATURAL

The Narnian series hinges upon the acceptance of supernatural phenomena:

"Supposing I told you I'd been in a place where animals can talk and where there are—er—enchantments and dragons—and—well, all the sorts of things you have in fairy tales." Scrubb felt terribly awkward as he said this and got red in the face.
    "How did you get there?" said Jill. She also felt curiously shy.
    "The only way you can—by Magic," said Eustace almost in a whisper.[9]

There are, of course, skeptics in these books. In *The Lion, the Witch and the Wardrobe* the children did not accept Lucy's tale about discovering Narnia when they first heard it. They consulted the wise old professor about her strange story. They complained that when they looked in the wardrobe there was nothing there, asserting that if things are real they're there all the time. "Are they?" the Professor said. The time element also bothered the children. During less than one minute, Lucy claimed to have spent several hours in Narnia. "That is the very thing that makes her story so likely to be true," said the Professor. He explained that if there really was a door in his house that led to some other world, it would be very likely that the other world had a separate time of its own so that however long one stayed there it would never take up any time on earth.
    "But do you really mean, Sir," asked one of the boys, "that there could be other worlds—all over the place, just round the corner—like that?" (pp. 39–40).

When the children had had actual experiences with the supernatural, the concept of other worlds was much easier to accept. Once they had been out of their own world, they could conceive of many others with comparative facility. The idea came to Digory in *The Magician's Nephew*: "Why, if we can get back to our own world by jumping into *this* pool, mightn't we get somewhere else by jumping into one of the others? Supposing there was a world at the bottom of every pool!" (p. 30).

The philosophy underlying this structure of multiple natures is clearly explained in a speculative passage in *Miracles* (p. 20). Lewis begins with the supernaturalist's belief that a Primary Thing exists independently and has produced our composition of space, time, and connected events which we call nature. There might be other natures so created which we don't know about. Lewis is not referring here to other solar systems or galaxies existing far away in our own system of space and time, because those would be a part of our nature in spite of their distance. Only if other natures were not spatiotemporal at all, or if their space and time had no relation to our own, could we call them different natures. This is important in Lewis's literary theory:

> No merely physical strangeness or merely spatial distance will realize that idea of otherness which is what we are always trying to grasp in a story about voyaging through space: you must go into another dimension. To construct plausible and moving 'other worlds' you must draw on the only real 'other world' we know, that of the spirit.[10]

The only relationship to our system would be through common derivation from a single supernatural force. Here Lewis resorts to the figure of authorship discussed by Dorothy Sayers in *The Mind of the Maker*.[11] The only relationship between events in one novel and events in another is the fact that they were written by the same author, which causes a continuity in his mind only.

There could be no connection between the events in one nature and the events in another, by virtue of the character of the two systems. But perhaps God would choose to bring the two natures into partial contact at some point. This would not turn the two natures into one, because they would still lack the total reciprocity of one nature, and this spasmodic interlocking would arise, not from within them, but from a divine act. Thus, each of the two natures would be "supernatural" to the other. But in an even more absolute sense, their contact itself would be supernatural, because it would be not only outside of a particular nature but beyond any and every nature.[12]

When this philosophical speculation is geared to a childhood level of interests, delightful possibilities for story situations appear. One of these, the concept of our world being known elsewhere as a myth, is introduced by the prince of Narnia to his young English guest:

> "Do you mean to say," asked Caspian, "that you three come from a round world (round like a ball) and you've never told me! It's really too bad of you. Because we have fairy-tales in which there are round worlds and I always loved them. I never believed there were any real ones. But I've always wished there were and I've always longed to live in one. Oh, I'd give anything—I wonder why you can get into our world and we never get into yours? If only I had the chance! It must be exciting to live on a thing like a ball. Have you ever been to the parts where people walk about upside down?"
>
> Edmund shook his head. "And it isn't like that," he added. "There's nothing particularly exciting about a round world when you're there."[13]

Just as our world bears aspects of a fairy-tale world from the Narnian point of view, so the Narnian world is rich with figures of earthly folklore. For example, there are giants, both good and bad. But they affect us in much the same way. "A good giant is legitimate: but he would be twenty tons of living, earth-shaking oxymoron. The intolerable pressure, the sense of something older, wilder, and more earthy than humanity, would still cleave to him."[14]

In Narnia, giants, centaurs, dryads, fauns, dwarfs, sea serpents, mermaids, dragons, monopods, and pirates live in an environment of castles, caves, magic whistles, golden chessmen, and enchanted gardens. The implication is that all elements of myth as we know them are shadows of a foreign reality. This idea is also demonstrated in Lewis's science fiction trilogy.[15]

THE CORRUPTION OF NATURE

C.S. Lewis is known for opposing the spirit of modern thought with the unpopular Christian doctrines of sin and evil. He considers evil not as a nebulous abstraction but as a destructive immanence which should be openly recognized and not complacently ignored, even though such recognition is disquieting. This principle is the major element in Lewis's otherwise happy concept of nature.[16] In his own words, "We find ourselves in a world of transporting pleasures, ravishing beauties, and tantalising possibilities, but all constantly being destroyed, all coming to nothing. Nature has all the air of a good thing spoiled."[17] In *The Magician's Nephew* original sin enters Narnia: "... before the new, clean world I gave you is seven hours old, a force of evil has already entered it; waked and brought hither by this son of Adam" (p. 121).

Throughout the rest of the series, this element of evil manifests itself in Narnia in various forms, always subjugating and trying to destroy the goodness in nature. In *The Lion, the Witch and the Wardrobe* the leader of evil forces is the White Witch, who has banished spring: "... it is she that has got all Narnia under her thumb. It's she that makes it always winter. Always winter and never Christmas" (p. 14).

In *Prince Caspian* a wise old dwarf informs the Prince of the harm done by evil King Miraz, who has trampled out the natural beauty of Narnia. He assures the Prince that what he had heard about Old Narnia is true. "It is the country of Aslan, the country of the Waking Trees and Visible Naiads, of Fauns and Satyrs, of Dwarfs and Giants, of the gods and the Centaurs, of Talking Beasts"; but the wicked king no longer allows them to be spoken of.[18] This is the situation lamented by Lewis in an early lyric:

> The faerie people from our woods are gone,
> No Dryads have I found in all our trees.
> No Triton blows his horn about our seas
> And Arthur sleeps far hence in Avalon."[19]

In *The Silver Chair* another witch has assumed power, this time by suppression of the glad natural order of the world beneath the surface of the earth, reminiscent of Wagner's Nibelheim.[20] There she enchanted merry dwarfs from the deep land of Bism and brought them up near the surface of the earth to Shallowlands to work for her in a state of glum amnesia. She is planning a great invasion of Narnia. The idea of invasions and battles is basic to those books.

"Enemy-occupied territory—that is what this world is," Lewis plainly states in *Mere Christianity*.[21] Yet he consciously avoids slipping into dualism, which he defines as "the belief that there are two equal and independent powers at the back of everything, one of them good and the other bad, and that this universe is the battlefield in which they fight out an endless War" (p. 33).

In *The Last Battle* the form of the evil power is roughly the shape of a man, but it has the head of a bird of prey with a cruel, curved beak and long bird-like claws. It carries a deathly smell.[22] This creature closely resembles the old Priest of Ungit in *Till We Have Faces*, who looks like a dreadful vulture and bears the evil Ungit smell with him.[23]

"If evil has the same kind of reality as good, the same autonomy and completeness, our allegiance to good becomes the arbitrarily chosen loyalty of a partisan."[24] Lewis makes it clear in *The Lion, the Witch and the Wardrobe* that the power of evil is inferior to the power of good. The power of good is that of the great King:

> "He's the King. He's the Lord of the whole wood, but not often here, you understand. Never in my time or my father's time. But the word has reached us that he has come back. He is in Narnia at this moment. He'll settle the White Queen all right...."
>
> "She won't turn him into stone too?" said Edmund.
>
> "... Turn him into stone? If she can stand on her two feet and look him in the face it'll be the most she can do and more than I expect of her." (pp. 63–64)

The return of spring in this book is one of the many reflections of Norse mythology in the Narnian series. This source was one of the strongest influences upon Lewis's early years. In his long poem *Dymer* he writes:

> And from the distant corner of day's birth
> He heard clear trumpets blowing and bells ring,
> A noise of great good coming into earth
> And such a music as the dumb would sing
> If Balder had led back the blameless spring
> With victory, with the voice of charging spears,
> And in white lands long-lost Saturnian years.[25]

So it is that the return of summer brings inexpressible joy to Narnia, and, the wintry witch having been defeated, "Summer is queen / Summer is queen in all the happy land."[26] Later on, the King himself explains to the children that "though the Witch knew the Deep Magic, there is a magic deeper still which she did not know." Her knowledge went back "only to the dawn of Time."[27]

The limitations of evil are discussed in *Mere Christianity*, where Lewis states, as he does in *The Screwtape Letters*, that wickedness is the pursuit of something good in the wrong way. One can be good for the sake of goodness even when it hurts, but one cannot be bad for the sake of badness. One is cruel for the pleasure or usefulness of it, not for the sake of cruelty itself. Badness cannot be bad in the way that goodness is good, for badness is only spoiled goodness (p. 35).

Spoiled goodness is illustrated in the beginning of sin in Narnia, as related in *The Magician's Nephew*. Digory had been sent to a distant garden to fetch a silver apple. On the gate was written this verse:

Come in by the gold gates or not at all,
Take of my fruit for others or forbear.
For those who steal or those who climb my wall
Shall find their heart's desire and find despair.
                    (p. 141)

Digory was just turning to go back to the gates when he stopped for one last look and received a terrible shock. There stood the Witch, throwing away the core of an apple which she had eaten. The juice had made a horrid dark stain around her mouth. Digory guessed that she must have climbed in over the wall. He began to see the truth in the last line of the verse, because "the Witch looked stronger and prouder than ever ... but her face was deadly white, white as salt" (pp. 141–44).

The King explained the result of this act to the children later. The Witch had fled from the garden to the North of the World, where she was growing stronger in dark Magic. She would not dare to return to Narnia so long as the tree was flourishing there, because its fragrance had become a horror to her. "That is what happens to those who pluck and eat fruits at the wrong time and in the wrong way," the King concluded. "The fruit is good, but they loathe it ever after" (p. 157).

The preponderance of dark magic and witches in Lewis's books gives the impression that he is greatly concerned with demonology. However, the overall tone of his work echoes the glad assurance of St. Paul, "For I am sure that neither death, nor life, nor angels, nor principalities, nor things present, nor things to come, nor powers, nor height, nor depth, nor anything else in all creation will be able to separate us from the love of God in Christ Jesus our Lord" (Romans 8:38).

In contrast to the everlasting quality of God's love, which is his principal message, Lewis reminds us that the physical world is in a process of disintegration. He seems to agree with the concept of Sir James Jeans, that "If the inanimate universe moves in the direction we suppose, biological evolution moves like a sailor who runs up the rigging in a sinking ship."[28]

In Lewis's opinion, the modern conception of progress, as popularly imagined, is simply a delusion, supported by no evidence. Darwinism gives no support to the belief that natural selection, working upon chance variations, has a general tendency to produce improvement. Lewis asserts that there is no general law of progress in biological history. He calls the idea of the world slowly ripening to perfection a myth, not a generalization from experience. He feels that this myth distracts us from our real duties and our real interests.[29]

This attitude is illustrated by the depressing picture of a dying world given in *The Magician's Nephew*:

> The wind that blew in their faces was cold, yet somehow stale. They were looking from a high terrace and there was a great landscape spread out below them. Low down and near the horizon hung a great, red sun, far bigger than our sun. Digory felt at once that it was also older than ours; a sun near the end of its life, weary of looking down upon that world. To the left of the sun, and higher up, there was a single star, big and bright. Those were the only two things to be seen in the dark sky; they made a dismal group. And on the earth, in every direction, as far as the eye could reach, there spread a vast city in which there was no living thing to be seen. And all the temples, towers, palaces, pyramids, and bridges cast long, disastrous-looking shadows in the light of that withered sun. Once a great river had flowed through the city, but the water had long since vanished, and it was now only a wide ditch of grey dust.
>
> "Look well on that which no eyes will ever see again," said the Queen. "Such was Charn, that great city, the city of the King of Kings, the wonder of the world, perhaps of all worlds." (pp. 52–53)

At "The End of This Story and the Beginning of all the Others," in the Wood between the Worlds (Chapter XV, *The Magician's Nephew*), the children learned the fate of Charn and received a warning. They saw a little hollow in the grass, with a warm, dry bottom. Aslan told them that the hollow had been the pool that they had jumped into to go to the dying world of Charn. "There is no pool now. The world is ended, as if it had never been. Let the race of Adam and Eve take warning" (p. 159).

In *The Last Battle* Jill declares, "Our world is going to have an end some day. Perhaps this one won't ... wouldn't it be lovely if Narnia just went on and on ...?"

"Nay," she was answered, "all worlds draw to an end; except Aslan's own country." *Jill* was just replying that she hoped that the end of Narnia was millions of years away, when news came that Narnia was overthrown, with this message from the lips of a dying friend: "... remember that all worlds draw to an end and that noble death is a treasure which no one is too poor to buy."[30]

The destruction of Narnia began with the invasion of commerce and the plunder of nature by greedy men. The idyllic forest was ruthlessly destroyed in a sacrilegious turmoil by crowds of imported workers, before the rightful owners realized what was happening. This is an exact parallel to the development of the near-fatal dangers in Lewis's adult book about Britain, *That Hideous Strength*.[31]

The actual end of Narnia was a dramatic pageant of mythical splendour. It concluded with the moon being sucked into the sun, and the world freezing forever in total darkness. Here Lewis follows the tradition of the North rather than the conventional Christian concept of destruction by fire. Peter, High King of Narnia, was given the key to the door of heaven, and locked out the cold.[32]

Lewis's response to nature, then, is threefold. First is romantic appreciation and idealization. Second is analysis leading to an acceptance of the supernatural and to speculation about it. Third is moral awareness of the force of evil in nature and of the temporal quality of our world. Each of these responses is basic to Lewis's Christian philosophy and is an important influence upon his books for children. Nature is more than a background setting for the action of his characters. "Either there is significance in the whole process of things as well as in human activity, or there is no significance in human activity itself."[33]

NOTES

1. *Surprised by Joy*, p. 14.

2. "The Shoddy Lands," *The Best from Fantasy and Science Fiction: Sixth Series* (New York: Doubleday, 1957), p. 159. Also available in *Of Other Worlds: Essays and Stories*, ed. Walter Hooper (London: Geoffrey Bles, 1966), pp. 99–106.

3. New York: Macmillan, 1955, pp. 25–26.

4. C.S. Lewis, *English Literature in the Sixteenth Century* (Oxford: Clarendon, 1954), p. 4. For Lewis's scholarly analysis of the history and uses of the word *nature*, read "Nature" in his book *Studies in Words* (London: Cambridge, 1960), pp. 24–74.

5. Clive Hamilton [C.S. Lewis], "Song," *Spirits in Bondage* (London: William Heinemann, 1919), p. 73.

6. New York: Harper, 1952, p. 12.

7. *Ibid.*, p. 12.

8. *Ibid.*, p. 10.

9. *The Silver Chair* (New York: Macmillan, 1953), p. 4.

10. "On Stories," *Essays Presented to Charles Williams*, p. 98.

11. *Miracles*, p. 118.

12. *Ibid.*, p. 21.

13. *The Voyage of the "Dawn Treader"* (New York: Macmillan, 1952), p. 195.

14. Lewis, "On Stories," p. 95.

15. *Out of the Silent Planet* (1938); *Perelandra* (1943); *That Hideous Strength* (1945).

16. Walsh, *C.S. Lewis, Apostle to Skeptics*, p. 81.

17. *Miracles*, p. 147.

18. *Prince Caspian* (New York: Macmillan, 1951), pp. 41–42.

19. Hamilton [Lewis], "Victory," *Spirits in Bondage*, p. 16.

20. Richard Wagner, *The Ring of the Nibelung* (New York: Garden City, 1939), p. 38.

21. New York: Macmillan, 1952, p. 36.

22. London: The Bodley Head, 1956, pp. 85–86.

23. Grand Rapids, Michigan: Eerdmans, 1966, p. 54.

24. "Evil and God," *Spectator*, CLXVI (February 7, 1941), 141.

25. Clive Hamilton [C.S. Lewis], *Dymer* (New York: E. P. Dutton, 1926), p. 105.

26. Lewis, "The Ocean Strand," *Spirits in Bondage*, p. 46.

27. Lewis, *The Lion, the Witch and the Wardrobe*, p. 132.

28. Sayers, *The Mind of the Maker*, p. 139.

29. "The World's Last Night," *His*, XV (May, 1955), p. 4. Also available in *The World's Last Night and Other Essays* (New York: Harcourt, Brace, 1960), pp. 93–113.

30. *The Last Battle* (New York: Macmillan, 1956), pp. 92–95.

31. *Ibid.*, pp. 26–27.

32. *The Last Battle*, p. 159.

33. C.S. Lewis, *The Personal Heresy* (London: Oxford, 1939), p. 29.

CHARLES A. HUTTAR

C.S. Lewis's Narnia and the "Grand Design"

This paper is, of necessity, bifocal. One focus is C.S. Lewis's Chronicles of Narnia: I want to contribute to an understanding of Lewis's achievement in this work. My thesis is that the Chronicles must be seen as a literary whole. But how to label this whole I cannot discover in all the lexicon of literary structures. It is not epic, or novel, or any of the commonly known genres. Thus I must offer a new label, "scripture," and not only offer but explain and defend it—which accounts for the other focus.

In the present section I endeavor to explain the notion of "scripture" as a genre; the rest of the paper then may be seen as its defense—not directly, however, but in an effort to apply the notion to the Chronicles of Narnia. To the extent that my analysis "works" I will be able to claim validity for the genre "scripture."

"Scripture" might be taken to mean a canon of traditional utterances, held in especial reverence and embodying the wisdom and ideals of a culture. But this definition emphasizes the accidents of history and culture and has nothing to do with literary form; hence it would be, for our present purposes, misleading.

Let us single out from all the world's "scriptures" those most intimately related to our own culture, the Judeo-Christian sacred writings known as the Bible. Perhaps here we may find clues as to genre. Much recent study of "the

From *The Longing for a Form: Essays on the Fiction of C.S. Lewis.* Peter J. Schakel, ed. © 1977 by The Kent State University Press.

Bible as literature" has been devoted to such inquiries. Recognizing that the Bible consists of many originally separate works, we might explore in some detail the distinctive literary qualities of its varied genres. Or, aware that literary influence results more from how a work is perceived than from what it actually is, we might inquire how our counterparts in earlier centuries perceived those literary qualities; an example would be the fascinating efforts in the sixteenth and seventeenth centuries to elaborate the principles of Hebrew poetics, before the now familiar concept of parallelism was enunciated.[1] We might also investigate the myriad transmutations of biblical archetype and narrative and doctrine and phrase into independent works of literature, all the way from the biblical idioms of *Piers Plowman* through the plot framework of Peele's *David and Bathsheba* and the symbolic patterns of *The Dunciad* to the elaboration of the Joseph story by Thomas Mann and the Pauline allegory of Christopher Fry's *A Phoenix Too Frequent*.[2] Another approach would be to study how the genres particularly associated with the Bible—psalm and parable and apocalypse, for example—have left their stamp on modern literary forms.

But none of these is what I have in mind. Beyond all the piecemeal study of the Bible's component parts it is possible to see the Bible as a whole in structural terms. It may seem strange to say this, when the word itself by derivation reminds us that it is a collection of materials widely separated in time, kind, intent, and sophistication. Yet it is certainly as a whole, more than as separate parts, that the Bible has had its greatest impact on the Western mind; may this be true not only of dogma but of literary form? I find literary justification for thinking of the Bible as a single work; it is not merely historical accident that compels us to do so. For this reason our choice of the Bible, out of all the world's "scriptures," is justified not merely because it is the most intimately related to our culture, but even more, because it is unique. Its uniqueness is a corollary of the unique Judeo-Christian incarnational view of history, in which Time is seen as linear and directional.

Surely the earliest biblical authors had no grand artistic scheme, shaping a massive outline for later writers to fill in. Still, the Bible is unified, by common strands of theme and imagery running throughout, and especially by the feature I have already mentioned, the idea of history as a meaningful succession of stages in a story that runs from the beginning of the world to its end. The later biblical writers saw themselves to be part of this ongoing process and deliberately wrote as continuers of a tradition; steeped in the older writings, they took traditional imagery and used it in a new way, unfolding its implicit meanings as the continuing process of history made these meanings become apparent.[3] The unity and structural arrangement of the Bible are matters of hindsight.

But it would be wrong to refer to the process of history as if it were something impersonal and mechanical. It is rather the concept of history as divine activity that imparts new depths of meaning to the traditional images, and structure to the work as a whole. The underlying pattern of the Bible is not just discovered by its writers in the course of history: it is history. The beginning with Genesis and ending with Revelation and the basic division of Old and New Covenants illustrate how the whole structure is built on a foundation of history. Of course, the beginning recedes into prehistory and the end goes on into posthistory; both are necessarily mythographical. But if we think of "history" as the totality of events, and not limit it to events that have been recorded or might ever be recorded,[4] we shall see that Genesis and Revelation are not substantially different from the rest. Conceptually, the uniqueness of the Judeo-Christian scriptures lies in their refusal to draw a sharp line of demarcation between myth and history.

The beginning is light conquering darkness, the creative Word overcoming Chaos, followed quickly by the reappearance of the threat of Chaos in the Fall. The end is the final resurgence of Chaos, and then the destruction of destruction itself, and a new creation. In between, the whole story, reduced to its skeletal form, is redemption history. In this the Incarnation, Passion, and Resurrection of Christ are central and paradigmatic, but practically everything else is brought somehow into the pattern. The whole story is what Jonathan Edwards referred to as "the grand design of God"[5]—almost as if to designate God himself as the artist responsible for the original conception, which would mean that the basic structure of the scriptures is more something perceived by the human authors than something they invented; and that has deep implications for the nature of any artistic activity.

Be that as it may, the genre "scripture" in the sense that now concerns us seems to me to have these essential qualities: it is comprised of varied material loosely unified, it is a blend of mythography and realism, and its structure is that of the "grand design"—Creation and Fall, Redemption, and Eschatology.

How this genre has left its stamp on modern literary form is a question we might trace from the medieval cycle plays on down. Rather than taking that line now, let us look at a single recent work which strikingly reflects the characteristics just listed for the genre "scripture."

But some may wonder whether the Chronicles of Narnia can properly be thought of as a single work, especially as one deserving serious critical consideration. It has three strikes against it already. It came out in series form, and quite clearly the first book was written without any plan for a larger work; second, it is a collection of tales for children; and third, it has become immensely popular. Nevertheless, Lewis's invention of Narnia has been hailed as a major achievement of the mythographic imagination, and some think that Lewis's place in history will owe as much to the Chronicles as to anything else he wrote. As for the unity, the example of the Bible shows us that retrospective structuring can convert what began as a loose collection into a literary whole.

Each of the seven books in the Chronicles of Narnia began, Lewis tells us, "with seeing pictures in my head." He wrote a few pages around the start of World War II but "at first ... had very little idea how the story would go."[6] Lewis turned to other matters—indeed, to the most productive period in his life. The popular theological writings (*The Problem of Pain*, *The Screwtape Letters*, the books that were later to become *Mere Christianity*, and *Miracles*) all appeared in the period 1940–47. At the same time he was producing *Perelandra* and a nonfiction work closely related to it, *A Preface to Paradise Lost*; then *That Hideous Strength* and its companion, *The Abolition of Man*; and finally, in quick succession, *The Great Divorce*, the George MacDonald anthology, and the long essay "On Stories." To list the major themes of these works, and especially those they share in common, would be to anticipate what was preoccupying Lewis's mind during the period of writing the Chronicles of Narnia, 1949–53. Without seeming to claim for the Chronicles any exalted position beyond their due, we may say that in a way, all through this period, Lewis's mind was unconsciously preparing itself to return to the Pevensie children. By the late forties he was "talk[ing] vaguely of completing a children's book which he [had] begun."[7] Scarcely two years later, the first five books in the series were finished. What had happened? "Suddenly Aslan came bounding into it," he tells us. "Once He was there He pulled the whole story together"—this is the one that became *The Lion, the Witch and the Wardrobe*—"and soon He pulled the six other Narnian stories in after Him" [*Of Other Worlds*, p. 42].

But even this appears to me to be a highly condensed account of what the actual process must have been. We can infer from the meager surviving manuscripts that even after *The Lion, the Witch and the Wardrobe* Lewis didn't yet know where his inspiration was leading him.[8] During that intense period when the first five books were composed the scheme was growing in Lewis's mind, so that by the time publication of *Lion* was under way he was able to give the book's illustrator instructions for a map that contained references to *Prince Caspian* and *The Silver Chair*.[9] Further, these books occasionally cross-reference one another. Yet they still are more a series than a unified whole. Like the Bible, they contain material that is incidental to the main historical line: folktale (*The Horse and His Boy*) and voyage literature. The two books that frame the story of Narnia chronologically, *The Magician's Nephew* in which Narnia is created and *The Last Battle* in which it is destroyed, were the last to be written, and they didn't come as quickly as the others. After a year's work on *The Magician's Nephew* (among other things, of course, such as the *Oxford History of English Literature*), Lewis still was only three-quarters finished with it, and *The Last Battle* took him another year and a half. Only then could he sit down and write, for the record, a summary chronology of Narnian history from beginning to end[10]—not in itself evidence of literary unity, but still some indication of his interest in having the story of Narnia viewed as a whole. I conjecture it was mainly in late 1950 or early 1951, when all but the last two books in the series were completed, that the overall design of the Chronicles took firm shape in Lewis's mind. And it is these last two books that make of the whole collection a unified literary work, a panoramic survey of a world's entire existence, centering on the themes of creation, sin, redemption, and apocalypse: a sort of Bible for a Bibleless age.

In chapter viii of *The Magician's Nephew* four humans, a horse, and the witch Jadis find themselves in "an empty world" where there is no light, no wind, no sound. Then creation begins. There follows what must surely be one of Lewis's greatest achievements as a mythmaker. Those familiar with traditional accounts (I have chosen two for comparison, those in Genesis 1 and *Paradise Lost*) will notice a few echoes, and perhaps some hints as well of Lucretius or Ovid [*De rerum natura*, V.772–836; *Metamorphoses*, 1.32–44, 69–75]; but on the whole, here is no scissors-and-paste job but a magnificently evocative new myth. The pagan critic Longinus had long since recognized the sublimity of Genesis, but the story is told there very rapidly, even summarily; indeed, the sublimity arises in part from the brevity. Milton offers considerably more detail—fascinating to follow, tracing out his classical and scientific and moralistic allusions. In Lewis we find both the detail and the sublimity, a sense of the numinous that Milton's Raphael, in his highly didactic conversation with Adam, is not permitted.

Two things account for the difference. First, Milton's description is almost entirely visual, while in Lewis, though visual imagery abounds, the other senses are also brought into play, and most of all the auditory. Second, Lewis is writing for children; therefore he need not stand on his dignity nor follow the grand style. He can risk a phrase such as "grassy land bubbling like water in a pot"; he can include "the first joke." For humor is no bar to true "solemnity," as Lewis taught us in *A Preface to Paradise Lost* to understand the word.[11] On the contrary, his evocation of the numinous is aided by the recurring element of play, which is closely allied to joy. Milton, taking a hint from Job 38:7, had the angelic choirs celebrate the creation with song, both at the end of the first day and again (accompanied by all the constellations in their Pythagorean harmony) as the Son returned to heaven, his work of creation complete. But such celebration fails to enter into his account of creation itself. Lewis, however, manages it. Traditionally it is by God's *word* that creation is accomplished, as in Psalms 33:6 and in the first creation story in Genesis. By the time of John 1:3 that Word has been identified as the second Person of the Trinity. Lewis's imagination goes one step further, making Aslan's creative voice a singing voice. Variations in the music communicate his commands and call forth responses—from the ground, life; from the spectators, fear, hatred, or joy. And when the stars join in harmony, they too are a part of the creative activity.

When the animals burst full-grown from Narnian soil, Lewis has several touches probably borrowed from Milton. In Lewis, "the humps moved and swelled till they burst, and the crumbled earth poured out of them, and from each hump there came out an animal" [p. 113]. In Milton "the grassy clods now calved" [*Paradise Lost*, VII.463], and the great cats "the crumbled earth above them threw / In hillocks" [468–69]. Lewis mentions specifically: moles, dogs, stags ("at first Digory thought they were trees"—p. 114), frogs (which immediately jumped into the river), panthers, leopards "and things of that sort," birds, butterflies, bees, and an elephant. In Milton's list, which follows in full, there are several suggestive parallels: "the wild beast," cattle, lion, ounce, libbard, tiger ("as the mole / Rising"), the stag (with "branching head"), the elephant, the flocks, amphibious creatures (hippopotamus and crocodile), insects, worms, ants, bees, serpents. Milton's lion is "pawing to get free / His hinder parts"; Lewis's dogs are struggling as if to get through a hedge, and his great cats "wash the loose earth off their hind quarters." Milton's cattle fall at once to pasturing; Lewis's dogs, frogs, panthers, and bees all begin immediately their characteristic behavior. Most of these resemblances are far too tenuous to support any assertion that Lewis consciously borrowed from Milton, though doubtless the whole Miltonic passage was stored in his mind somewhere, along with a great deal else, and might have unconsciously furnished a detail here or there.

But the differences are much greater. Milton, of course, follows the order of creation given in Genesis, which is why birds aren't included in the passage just cited from *Paradise Lost*: they already existed. The traditional order of creation, you remember, was light, the firmament, dry land with grass and trees, the sun and moon and stars, fish and birds, animals, and finally man, whose creation is set apart stylistically and to whom is committed dominion over all the rest. Lewis has his visitors standing on dry land from the outset; when Aslan sings the stars appear first, all at once, and singing; then a light in the sky as of approaching dawn, against which the hills are silhouetted, together with a light wind (a suggestion of the divine spirit?); then the sun comes up, revealing a whole landscape, but without vegetation; then come the grass, trees, and flowers; and finally, the animals, including birds. Two steps in the process remain, the creation and the commissioning of man.

Man is already in Narnia and needs not to be created anew; in the light of what we shall soon observe regarding the Fall, it would be confusing if he were. The creation of man in Genesis is paralleled in Lewis by the elevation of selected animals to be Talking Beasts. At this moment, one of the climactic scenes in the whole Chronicles of Narnia, the stars burst forth again into song. With his breath and with "a swift flash like fire"—two symbols of the Holy Spirit—Aslan awakens the chosen animals to love, to think, to speak, to know. And he proceeds to appoint them a place in the hierarchy:

> Creatures, I give you yourselves.... I give to you forever this land of Narnia. I give you the woods, the fruits, the rivers. I give you the stars and I give you myself. The Dumb Beasts whom I have not chosen are yours also. Treat them gently and cherish them but do not go back to their ways lest you cease to be Talking Beasts. For out of them you were taken and into them you can return. [p. 118]

There are echoes here of two passages in Genesis—both things said to man: first, that all the plant kingdom has been given to him and to the beasts for food, and he is to have dominion over all the animal kingdom [128–30]; second, *after the Fall*, that man will "return unto the ground; for out of it wast thou taken; for dust thou art, and unto dust shalt thou return" [3:19].

Echoes—but just as important are the differences. The Talking Beasts do not fully occupy in Narnia the place given to man on Earth. Though man is not created in Narnia, he has a role there—a paradoxical role of rulership and service. Frank and Helen (for like Milton's Adam, who asks "In solitude / What happiness?" [*Paradise Lost*, VIII.364–65], the Cabby is allowed to send for his wife) are to be king and queen, but the reason is that "Adam's race shall help to heal" the harm brought into Narnia by humans. Their responsibilities are delineated. They are to name the animals, as Adam does in *Paradise Lost*, VIII.350, *where they appear before him two by two* (a detail Lewis incorporated earlier, when Aslan selected out the Talking Beasts). They have other responsibilities too, ones that would be inappropriate at the parallel place in Genesis, for that world was not yet fallen. They are to rule, do justice, protect from enemies, prevent oppression.

What are we to make of these differences? Is Lewis deliberately heterodox, is he simply enjoying imaginative freedom, or does he have reasons that lead him to deviate so much from the traditional creation myth? The form in which I have put the question hints strongly at my answer. In creating his mythical world of Narnia Lewis is consistent with principles he followed in his other imaginary worlds, in the space trilogy (published 1938–45). And these principles embody a theological point of no little importance.

Most of us take for granted the continuity of earthly experience with experience throughout the universe. Our age long ago adopted empiricism and uniformitarianism as working presuppositions, necessary to the endeavors we hold most valuable; the result by now, not surprisingly, has been to forget that they are no more than working presuppositions. Just as the speed of light and the atomic structure of silicon are constant throughout the universe, we easily assume that less tangible aspects of our own experience are constant as well—that our observations in the moral and spiritual realms are valid universally. It is a case, I think, of contemporary popular attitudes reduplicating those prevalent among professional thinkers a century ago. The professionals, meanwhile, have moved on. The Newtonian "law" of gravity may be adequate for mundane purposes, but ever since Einstein the world has been served notice that it may not simply project earthbound observation on a universal scale.[12] Such developments should prompt us to a certain skepticism about our assumptions, but they don't seem to have filtered down to the popular mind. Some scientists and some science-fiction writers may have the imagination to speculate of intelligent beings in other than human form, of whole life systems based on silicon instead of carbon; or, with even greater freedom, of a color spectrum or sense organs with no parallel in earthly biology, or social relationships following no human model. But such habits of thought are rare. Further, to imagine things outside our experience in the moral and spiritual realms is still more difficult.

As an example, let us consider the notion that only by a knowledge of evil can we fully appreciate the good. Since our whole experience bears witness to this obvious truth, it takes a great effort of the imagination, assisted perhaps by rigorous logic, to consider the possible existence of beings on this or any other world who might know and fully savor good per se, alone, by itself. Milton observed, in *Areopagitica*, how "involved and interwoven" is the knowledge of good with that of evil, and in how "many cunning resemblances hardly to be discerned." But then he went on to speculate that perhaps this was the meaning of the fruit of Adam's tree, the knowledge of good and evil: "That is to say, of knowing good by evil." For the central meaning of the Judeo-Christian doctrine of the Fall is that there are aspects of "human nature" as we have always experienced it that are at variance from "human nature" as it was meant to be and potentially is. When that idea is embodied in a myth which narrates that change actually taking place, it clashes head-on with the much more modern idea—equally mythical, in one sense of the word—of uniformitarianism.[13] But without the effort to get back behind Lyell and all he symbolizes, we shall miss the whole point of certain cruxes in *Paradise Lost*.

And we shall also fail to understand what Lewis was up to in the Chronicles of Narnia. For what Milton (and Christian tradition at large) saw as a radical break *within* the history of the human race,[14] Lewis projected into his imaginary worlds as a difference from earthly experience as we know it. His Malacandra is an unfallen world; realizing that fact is one of the major adjustments Ransom has to make when he visits it. Perelandra is also unfallen, differing, however, in that a temptation occurs there, but unsuccessfully. These two worlds differ also in the role played by humans. On Malacandra they are just visitors having no permanent impact, but on Perelandra they come to perform tasks that are crucial to overcoming the temptation; only then do they leave. How does Narnia compare with these worlds? The Fall is not a part of Narnian history; in this Narnia resembles Lewis's two imagined planets. Still, Narnia is in many ways like our fallen world. An evil force (a devil-figure) resides there permanently for most of Narnia's history; fallen children of Adam enter from time to time, some of ahem staying there and having descendants; and, for both these reasons, individual Narnians can fall (cf. Aslan's warning to the Talking Beasts quoted above, paralleled by a postlapsarian passage in Genesis). But there is no Fall as a racial event in Narnia, comparable to the Terran myth. The role of humans in the Chronicles needs to be described carefully. Unlike the otherworld visits in Lewis's space trilogy, the visits of humans to Narnia have no effect on earthly affairs, except insofar as they improve the character of a few children. But the converse is not true. Humans play an essential role in Narnian affairs: they are responsible for the entrance of evil in the very hour of creation, they influence the course of Narnian history with all their potential for both good and evil, and the true monarchs of Narnia are human.

This leads us to a further subtlety in Lewis's scheme. In addition to the truths he considered applicable only to Earth and its peculiar situation (the "silent planet" as he called it)—and the inability to know good per se is only a single example—he held to another class of principles, those truly universal. Two examples, especially germane to the part of the Chronicles presently under consideration, would be the principle of Hierarchy and that ultimate moral law which Lewis designated the "Tao."[15] Another would be the existence and the nature of God, including such attributes as his creative power, love, transcendence, and participation in human history. The high point of that participation is the Incarnation, which to Lewis meant a permanent union of the human with the divine."[16] Thus the humanity of God, though coming about through an event in mere earthly history, becomes a part of his nature and therefore of universal significance throughout all the worlds. It is for this reason that, though the intelligent life Ransom encounters on Malacandra has various bodily forms, on Perelandra, a younger planet, the King and Queen are in human shape. As the Green Lady explains, "Since our Beloved became a man, how should Reason in any world take on another form?" [*Perelandra*, p. 62].

To digress for a moment, we have now before us an interesting array of ways to view the universe. First there was the pre-Copernican view in which it all moved about Earth; this was sometimes accompanied by the anthropocentric idea that all the universe exists *for man's sake*. Concerning this idea two mistakes are often made: (1) that it is part of Christian theology,[17] (2) that it was stamped out when the new astronomy triumphed. On the contrary, it is still with us in a selfish, degenerate form today, and has borne fruit in our present ecological crisis. It also accounts in part for the energy with which space exploration has been pursued, and in this connection one of its most vigorous challengers has been C.S. Lewis. Furthermore, the scientific revolution quickly led in its turn, ironically enough, to a second kind of anthropocentricity, the attitude described above that human experience is the measure of all things. This too Lewis opposed, on the commonsense ground of Hamlet's remark to Horatio, "There are more things in heaven and earth ... than are dreamt of in your philosophy." But his speculations on the subject, as we have seen, led him around to still a third sort of anthropocentric view, that it is both the glory and the tremendous burden of the human race to have been made the unique vehicle for God's identification of himself with his creatures.

Perhaps it would be well at this point to remind ourselves that these thoughts *were* speculations and that Lewis's other worlds are frankly imaginary. On the question whether other inhabited worlds actually exist he was (inevitably, one is tempted to add) agnostic. But if they should exist, he wanted to lay alongside the nineteenth-century anthropocentric view, which would in no case lack for champions, an alternative, perhaps an equal, possibility. Other "possibilities" may spring to mind as well: other *fallen* worlds; other, nonhuman, Incarnations. Presumably one might also build imaginative works on these speculations. Lewis was so habituated to using Occam's razor that he wasn't interested in doing so.

We now have the necessary framework for understanding Lewis's departures from Genesis in his Narnian creation. (1) According to Lewis's "Outline of Narnian History" the creation of Narnia took place A.D. 1900.[18] But the creation of the entire universe—the Genesis tradition—had obviously taken place long before; Lewis saw this as fact and, by definition, among those truths that have universal validity. The creation of Narnia, then, turns out to be quite a different sort of thing from the creation presented in Genesis. A major imaginative conception in Lewis is that of a world existing *in potentia* from the beginning, with land and water topography, but lifeless, waiting for the instant when it should be "turned on"—for that is the best way to describe the sudden appearance all at once of the stars, as the darkness and silence of this "empty world" in an instant give way to light and music. A similar effect is achieved in the sunrise which follows, as if the new world were set in motion at the flip of a switch, initiating the process (familiar to us) of the gradual coming of dawn. That "turning on" is not, strictly speaking, creation; all Aslan actually creates are the various forms of life on Narnia.

(2) Another difference is that the "breath of life" is imparted to beasts, not man. This is inconsistent not only with the Genesis tradition but with the principle Lewis set forth in *Perelandra* concerning Reason in human form. But Lewis had no choice: Talking Beasts are not only one of the hardiest conventions of children's literature, but they had also been a part of this world from the first book. This seems to support our conclusion that when he began the Chronicles Lewis did not anticipate the form it would finally take. Having given these chosen beasts Reason, Lewis must (in accord with another of his universal principles) find them a new place in the hierarchial Chain of Being. That is why they are given dominion over the dumb animals, which in Genesis is given to man.

(3) Still, man has a role in Narnia too. Ultimate rule (under Aslan) belongs to him. This is in keeping with the Green Lady's observation, and it holds true from the first book, where Sons of Adam and Daughters of Eve are required in order to set matters right. But the humans who receive the throne are already fallen. That is why Aslan asks Frank, "Can you use a spade and a plough and raise food out of the earth?" So, too, things said to man before and after the Fall in Genesis are telescoped into this one scene at the finish of creation, concluding with the somewhat Abrahamic promise to Frank and Helen which ends chapter xi.

We must now try to rephrase more accurately the description of the Chronicles of Narnia as "a sort of Bible." The term is accurate enough as a label of the genre: a loose collection of varied material structured to highlight the climactic events of world history, beginning, middle, and end. But the history is not that of our world. If Lewis finally conceived of the Chronicles as a Bible, it is a Narnian Bible. Narnia's 2,555 years occupy less than half a century of human time and have no effect on human history. *Indirect* relationships may exist insofar as universal truths (e.g., hierarchy, moral law, the identities good/creation and evil/destruction, the interplay of transiency and permanence) produce similar situations in the two worlds. But in no way may the climactic events of Narnian history be equated with those of Earth. This is what Lewis meant by insisting that he was not writing allegory. Narnia's history resembles ours because the universe is truly a universe; when they, differ, there is a reason—not some supposed allegory "breaking down."

The importance of this point becomes clear as we move to the next major biblical theme, how one man's disobedience "brought death into the world, and all our woe." In Narnia that does not happen. Nevertheless there are some points of tangency. For the concept of moral law, anywhere, implies the possibility of choice, and that in turn opens the door to temptation. Like Milton, and for the same reason just given, Lewis returned again and again in his writing to temptation scenes. The Chronicles of Narnia contains at least five, in which a number of significant biblical and Miltonic parallels may be noted. I do not propose to treat these in detail, offering instead just a list and some comments.

(1) Digory's temptation in Charn [*The Magician's Nephew*, ch. iv]. As in *Paradise Lost*, the man and woman quarrel and a part of the temptation's appeal—here, the major part—is to curiosity.

(2) Digory's temptation by the Witch [*The Magician's Nephew*, ch. xiii]. Here the parallels are numerous. There is a walled garden atop a lofty mountain [cf. *Paradise Lost*, IV.131–47]. The only proper access is through an eastern gate, though Jadis leaps over the wall instead [cf. 178–93]. The garden is deliciously fragrant [cf. 156–66] and in the very center is a tree of life with silver fruit [cf. 218–20, golden fruit]. The Witch's attempt to persuade Digory to eat the fruit has much in common with the temptation of Eve in *Paradise Lost*, Book IX.

(3) Edmund's defection to the Witch [*The Lion, the Witch and the Wardrobe*, ch. iii–ix]. He is led astray first by greed—in this case, a boyish hunger for Turkish Delight—and then by appeals to his ego.

(4) Lucy reading the Magic book [*The Voyage of the "Dawn Treader,"* ch. x]. The appeal is to forbidden knowledge.

(5) The temptations of Rilian and the others [*The Silver Chair*, ch. xi–xii]. The Prince's enchantment reminds us of the temptation scene in

Comus. Both *Comus* and *Paradise Lost* are in the background of the next scene, in which a serpentine temptress of dubious parentage casts a rhetorical spell, obtruding false rules prankt in reason's garb.[19]

We may also note that when Digory returns from the garden, faithful to his promise, Aslan greets him with "Well done!"—the same greeting given Abdiel in *Paradise Lost* when he forsakes the rebel angels and returns to the camp of the faithful [VI.29]. Poggin the dwarf, who alone of the dwarfs fights on Tirian's side in *The Last Battle*, is also an Abdiel figure—a resister of temptation.

The next climactic event in human history is the Redemption. But like the Fall which made it necessary, this event is not universal but peculiar to Earth. There is no need to repeat in Narnia the full pattern of Christian redemption.

This will seem at first difficult to believe, there are so many obvious resemblances between Aslan and Christ. Each is the Son of the Highest and his emissary to the world; each possesses great power linked with immense self-control; each knows sorrow; each is killed as an innocent substitute for the guilty, and then returns to life.[20] But Aslan dies for Edmund alone, not for the whole world. The Atonement of mankind is a doctrine unique (so far as we may suppose) to Earth.

The principle of voluntary self-sacrifice on another's behalf, however, is one that is valid throughout the universe. Often it takes the form, in Narnian as well as in earthly myth, of a descent into the underworld, a journey to danger and death, to perform a rescue. Aslan, who submits silently to the Witch's knife, going for all he knows on a journey from which he will not return—this point is important[21]—is only one among many in the Chronicles who enact this archetypal descent. Lucy venturing into the Magician's room to free the Monopods from invisibility; Caspian sailing to the world's end to break the spell on the three sleeping lords; Jill and Eustace and Puddleglum journeying underground to rescue Prince Rilian—all these also exemplify the pattern. Digory offers an example too, but with differences: he journeys to Paradise, not Hell, and does it in obedience to Aslan, and only secondarily to save his mother from death; but once there, he faces a temptation that threatens to destroy him. All these are Christ figures; but none mean the same thing to Narnia that Christ means to human history, because Narnia is not Earth.

In *The Last Battle* the history of Narnia comes to an end. Lewis's invented eschatology resembles these features of scriptural eschatology: Antichrist, Armageddon, final judgement, destruction of the world, the end of time, and the new paradisal creation.

It is all done, of course, as befits the audience, with a light touch. Puzzle, the lovable ass, dressed in a lionskin that he has fished out of the pool, is a far cry from the beast emerging from the sea in Revelation 13, with its ten crowned horns and seven heads marked with blasphemous titles. But the parallel is there. A false Aslan is set up—very pointedly, an anti-Christ— and all are made to worship him, all save a small remnant who are true to the old Narnia traditions. Compare Revelation 13:9–10: "If anyone has ears to hear, let him listen: Captivity for those who are destined for captivity; the sword for those who are to die by the sword. This is why the saints must have constancy and faith" [Jerusalem Bible]. The fate of the remnant reflects the persecution of Christians under Nero and his successors, as St. John identifies contemporary political evil with the unseen principalities that war against the faithful. It is in the spirit of this tradition that Lewis, in narrating the machinations of Ape and Cat to promote the false Aslan, attacks the demagoguery and false rationalism that characterize corrupt political activity in our own century.

Compared to the terrible image of Armageddon [Revelation 14:18–20; 19:17–21], the last battle of Narnia doesn't amount to much; perhaps again we have what is suitable in a book for children. Yet the central importance of this scene is underscored by Lewis's choice of it for his book's title. And the next event in the scriptural eschatological vision is likewise paralleled in *The Last Battle*. In Revelation 20:12–13 the entire harvest of the dead comes before God to be judged. A fuller description of this impressive scene is found in Matthew 25:31–46, where the sheep and goats are separated for everlasting punishment or life eternal, according to the way they treated "the least of these my brethren." This passage has furnished many details for what is surely one of Lewis's most unforgettable scenes. The world of Narnia is coming to an end. Driven almost as in a stampede, all the Narnians pass before Aslan and, according to whether they can look upon him with desire or hatred, they go by on his right hand or his left. Even one devotee of the wicked god Tash finds himself in Aslan's country, thus proving the principle in the Matthew passage that God may be truly served even by those who do not know Him to call by name.

In the same discourse Matthew records Jesus as saying that "heaven and earth shall pass away" [24:35]. This is very much a part of New Testament apocalyptic tradition; we find it also in 2 Peter 3:10, which speaks of destruction by fire, and Revelation 20:11, where fire from heaven is part of the context but the immediate cause of heaven and earth ceasing to be is simply the removal from them of the divine sustaining power. This is closer to the way Lewis does it. Unhampered by any rainbow promise to Noah about how the earth will or will not end, Lewis has his "other world" overwhelmed by the rising sea: what was dry land becomes chaos once again underneath the waves [ch. xiv]. Essentially the process of creation as we saw it in *The Magician's Nephew* is, step by step, undone. Already the sky is black as at the beginning: there are no stars, for "Aslan had called them home" [p. 151]. Once the land has been drowned, our attention is turned to the dying sun (reminiscent of that weak luminary at the end of the world of Charn, in The Magician's Nephew) in whose rays "the whole waste of shoreless waters looked like blood." The vivid sensory images of Revelation have entered into Lewis's mind and are coming out at other places in the story—yet still as powerfully evocative parts of a whole picture, a Gestalt, that is in the apocalyptic tradition. There is a final Johannine touch as the giant Father Time throws "his horn into the sea" [cf. Revelation 18:21]. Time has ended; eternity is begun.

For the end of Narnia is the beginning of a new Paradise which turns out to be, in fact, the true Narnia—a notion very close indeed to the New Testament vision of a new heaven and new earth [2 Peter 3:13; Rev. 21:1]. But the image that dominates the last two chapters of Revelation is that of the city, the new Jerusalem, and Lewis prefers the garden. I find him much less Hebraic here, and owing more to Plato and Milton—and Wordsworth, for in Aslan's country a splendor has truly returned to the grass [p. 171]. The way the Narnians float effortlessly *up* a waterfall reminds me of Milton's concept that human bodies eventually could "turn all to spirit" and "winged ascend"—lines on which Lewis had particularly remarked in *A Preface to Paradise Lost* [p. 68]. But this, of course, is fully in keeping with those cryptic New Testament accounts of the resurrected body of Christ, and with Christian belief in the mystery of bodily resurrection. So too in Aslan's country everyone has his physical being at its prime; age, pain, and stiffness are vanished. And this is only the beginning of new experiences. Over and over the motto is repeated, "Further up and further in." Lewis owes much here to the Christian Platonist views of the fourth century, which he says went into the making of the "Medieval Model": the view that "we are creatures of the margin."[22] As the Professor in *The Last Battle* sputters, "It's all in Plato" [p. 170]. That is the true "sunlit" country, to which Earth as we know it, and Narnia too, are mere "Shadow-Lands" [p. 183]. Earlier in the Chronicles of Narnia, Lewis's embodiment of similar ideas at some length in *The Silver Chair* shows how deeply Plato's myth of the cave affected his imagination. But as we've already seen in Lewis's emphasis on the body, he is too materially minded to go all the way with Plato. His Paradise is filled with delicious odors and "fruits such as no one has seen in our world." The first thought of the humans in the story is that fruit so tempting must be forbidden—but this is "the country where everything is allowed" [p. 137].

Lewis's church admonishes its adherents to think about the "last things," a phrase which includes, alongside the last judgement and the joys of heaven, death. This represents to us a common duality in the concept of time. The "time" of which we are abstractly aware is the whole of history, the world's time; but another "time" of which we are immediately aware is our own, individually, from birth to death. In one sense, within a scriptural context we know time as a reality that ends in apocalypse of the sort we have been speaking of; but in another sense, equally valid, we know time as a reality that is coextensive with our own life. This duality too is reflected in the Chronicles of Narnia. A familiar image of personal nightmare is evoked in *The Last Battle* when the stable door through which the heroes are thrown is described as "a grim door ... more like a mouth" [p. 128]. As the newcomers move on to Aslan's country they meet the Phoenix, perennial symbol of resurrection, and they find the old Narnian heroes there to greet them. These, having died much earlier, have already come into their eternal Paradise. At the end of *The Silver Chair* we witness Caspian's resurrection and rejuvenation by a drop of Aslan's blood. Still earlier in the Chronicles, at the end of *The Voyage of the "Dawn Treader,"* comes (significantly, "when the third day dawned") a vision of Paradise in the Utter East, and one of the adventurers chooses to go on there. (Incidentally, the ease with which we find ourselves cross-referencing to other parts of the Chronicles, almost in the manner of a Bible expositor, is perhaps another result of Lewis's following Scripture as a generic model for his work.)

I have said that underlying the structure of the genre "scripture" is a concept of history as linear and directional. Something of this dynamic quality rubs off on the way the story is told. Lewis was able to do things in *The Last Battle* that he could not have done earlier, because it is the eschatological close of the work. In thinking about Creation, Fall, and Redemption in Narnia we had to pay attention to the many ways they differ from Earth's story as the Scriptures give it. What strikes us about the last things, and especially about Lewis's vision of heaven, is how little it differs. There is a reason. When the Children in *The Last Battle* get far enough in and high enough up, they discover that not Narnia alone but England too, in its ideal form, is a part of Aslan's country. All roads point toward the Center. The various worlds, real and imaginary, may be quite different at the beginning, but the end is one.

NOTES

1. See Israel Baroway, "The Bible as Poetry in the English Renaissance: An Introduction," *Journal of English and Germanic Philology*, 32 (1933), 447–80, and other articles by Baroway on related subjects in *JEGP*, 33 (1934), 23–45; *Modern Language Notes*, 49 (1934), 145–49; and *ELH* [*Journal of English Literary History*], 2 (1935), 66–91; 8 (1941), 119–42; and 17 (1950), 115–35.

2. Stanley Wiersma, *Christopher Fry: A Critical Essay* (Grand Rapids: Eerdmans, 1970), pp. 19–20.

3. See Austin Farrer, *A Rebirth of Images: The Making of St. John's Apocalypse* (London: Dacre Press, 1949), reissued in a completely revised version as *The Revelation of St. John the Divine: Commentary on the English Text* (Oxford: Clarendon Press, 1964).

4. See Lewis's essay on "Historicism" (1950), in *Christian Reflections*, ed. Walter Hooper (London: Geoffrey Bles, 1967), pp. 100–13.

5. See C. A. Patrides, *The Grand Design of God: The Literary Form of the Christian View of History* (London: Routledge and Kegan Paul, 1972), p. 119. Patrides's footnotes provide a full bibliographical guide not only to the history of this idea but also to modern studies of the Judeo-Christian concept of history.

6. "It All Began With a Picture...... in *Of Other Worlds: Essays and Stories*, ed. Walter Hooper (New York: Harcourt, Brace and World, 1966), p. 42.

7. Chad Walsh, *C.S. Lewis: Apostle to the Skeptics* (New York: Macmillan, 1949), p. 10.

8. Walter Hooper, "Past Watchful Dragons: The Fairy Tales of C.S. Lewis," in *Imagination and the Spirit: Essays in Literature and the Christian Faith presented to Clyde S. Kilby*, ed. Charles A. Huttar (Grand Rapids: Eerdmans, 1971), pp. 301–09.

9. Hooper, "Past Watchful Dragons," pp. 310–11.

10. Hooper, "Past Watchful Dragons," pp. 297–301.

11. *A Preface to Paradise Lost* (London: Oxford University Press, 1942), pp. 15–16.

12. Parallel difficulties exist in attempting to project *recent* observation (i.e., within the history of man) on a time scale of billions of years. Discoveries in radio astronomy have led German scientist H. von Ditfurth to at least entertain the antiuniformitarian hypothesis "that *other laws* governed the universe when it was young"—*Children of the Universe: The Tale of Our Existence* (New York: Atheneum, 1974), p. 41 [original italics].

13. For the general idea of this paragraph, see "Religion and Rocketry" (1955), in *The World's Last Night and Other Essays* (New York: Harcourt, Brace and World, 1960), pp. 83–92.

14. In *A Preface to Paradise Lost*, pp. 65–69, 113, 118, Lewis cites Augustine as a locus classicus for this idea.

15. On Hierarchy see *A Preface to Paradise Lost*, ch. xi; on the Tao, *The Abolition of Man* (London: Oxford University Press, 1943).

16. Cf. the classic statement of this doctrine in the Athanasian Creed: "He is God and man, ... not two but one Christ. He is one, however, not by the transformation of his divinity into flesh, but by the taking up [*adsumptione*] of his humanity into God"—J. N. D. Kelly, *The Athanasian Creed* (New York: Harper & Row, 1964), p. 21. The doctrine of Christ's Ascension also points to the permanence of the divine–human union.

17. Man's "dominion" over the rest of creation can only be understood in conjunction with his participation in and responsibility to the created world. For a typical statement see D. Bonhoeffer, *Creation and Fall* (New York: Macmillan, 1959), pp. 39–40. The author of the Epistle to the Hebrews (2:5–9) sees man's "dominion" as not yet fulfilled, except prototypically in Christ, the God-Man.

18. Hooper, "Past Watchful Dragons," pp. 310–11.

19. See *Comus*, l. 758; *Paradise Lost*, II.226: IX.549ff., 670ff.

20. For a full discussion of these and other parallels, see Hooper, "Past Watchful Dragons," pp. 325–32.

21. Cf. Mark 15:34. See C. A. Huttar, "Samson's Identity Crisis and Milton's," *Imagination and the Spirit*, p. 157.

22. *The Discarded Image* (Cambridge: At the University Press, 1964), p. 58.

CHAD WALSH

The Parallel World of Narnia

Lewis's first book for children, *The Lion, the Witch and the Wardrobe*, was published in his early fifties. For seven years, at the rate of one a year, the Narnia books came off the presses. Readers accustomed to adult fare found themselves puzzled by this sudden alteration in his focus.

The shift is easier to comprehend if one takes a second look at Lewis's childhood, when he and Warnie played in the roomy attic. Their principal activity was composing adventure tales set in such imaginary locales as Animaland, India, or Boxen. Lewis continued this activity up to his early teens, as in a story probably written around 1912—"Boxen: or Scenes from Boxonian City Life."[1] This tale, never published in book form, begins as follows:

I

Night was falling on the Bosphorus as the town guardsman sighted a small but tidy schooner tacking up to Fortessa. Forward stood a young Fracity Chessary Pawn and at the tiller a sturdy thickset knight stolidly smoking his pipe. With a little deft maneuvering he brought her up a secluded, rocky creek and

From *The Literary Legacy of C.S. Lewis.* © 1979 by Chad Walsh.

dropped anchor about 200 yards from the shingle. He called the assistance of the Pawn to lower his solitary boat, which soon was lying under the schooner's counter, and several vigorous strokes sent him to the beach. Mooring the boat he stepped out and in the dusk descried two athletic figures walking along a short distance away.

"Why! Your Majesties!"

They turned. "Macgoullah."

"At your service. What are you doing here?"

"Oh," said the 'Jah. "Learning Turkish."

"Alone?" inquired the knight.

"No. Big's here," answered Buny.

"At the inn?"

"Yes."

The three friends walked together to the postern gate, where the guard admitted them for a small fee. A few hundred yards brought them to the inn. Through the door into the dinner room Macgoullah caught sight of a stout frog in evening dress.

"I'll stay in the Outer," he observed.

The boys walked into the Inner. It was a small room crowded to overflowing. Round the table sat Puddiphat, Goose, Quicksteppe, and the Little Master.

"Boys, where have you been?" asked the Frog.

"Oh, nowhere special," returned the 'Jah with characteristic vagueness. Big gulped and continued bisecting a portion of cod. All present were Boxonians except one Prussian who sat in a far corner silent and morose, unnoticed by all: true, there was a cautious look in Quicksteppe's grey eyes, but no one observed it. The company bent over their meal and conversation and quietly the Prussian slipped into a curtained cupboard. Big looked up.

"Are we alone?"

"Yes, my dear little Master," said Goose.

"Now Goose, tell your tale."

"Yes. Gentlemen, I have just found that the whole Clique is threatened by Orring, one of the members for 'the aquanium—'"

"Come, my good bird," cried Big. "What does that mean?"

"For Piscia, my good Frog," Big gulped, "has determined to throw all the present clique out of office, and is bribing right and left."

One touch of the future scholar is seen in the story's footnotes. Two occur in the passages just quoted. The first explains that "The kingdoms of Boxen, although united in Parliament, retain their monarchs, the Rajah of India and the King of Animaland." The other fills in background: "'Little Master' was the speaker of the Parliament, and had many powers, including that of being the constant guardian and adviser of the Kings. The present one, Lord Big, exercised much influence over King Benjamin and the Rajah, as he had been their tutor in their youth: in private he neglected all the usual formulae of address to a prince...."

One hopes that some day a selection of Lewis's juvenilia will be published, both for scholars and the simply curious. Meanwhile, the portions quoted from "Boxen" give some idea of Lewis's writing as he entered his teens.

A reader coming on "Boxen" might first leap to the conclusion that here is the ancestry of the Narnia tales, but he would quickly learn that the resemblance is superficial, amounting to little more than a cast that includes talking animals. These characters seem like normal men dressed up for a masquerade. The profound difference is in atmosphere. Narnia is a kind of fairyland, and even its political and military events have an otherworld quality. In "Boxen," one is plunged into a tale of cliques and conspiracies and countermeasures. The everyday Tellurian world is very much with us. One seems to hear in the background the voice of Lewis's father, declaiming political opinions. Or one senses the influence of cheap adventure and mystery books in which such sinister characters as a Prussian lurk in curtained cupboards.

In short, "Boxen," despite its vocal animals, represents one side of Lewis: the realist. From this book he could have evolved into a realistic novelist, determined to present the earthly condition in all its photographic concreteness.

This was not the road he took, and yet in minor ways "Boxen" foreshadows things to come. Even if the animals act completely human, still they are animals and they do talk. The theme of inner and outer circles, so important in Lewis's later work, is already here, as is the conviction that government must function as a kind of conspiracy. There is a keen eye for small, specific details. Most of all, perhaps, even at this early age we have a smooth narrative style.

More typical of the later Lewis is "The Quest of Bleheris," written two or three years later after he had fallen under the magic spell of the Arthurian legends. Here instead of talking animals there are knights and fair ladies. It begins:

THE QUEST OF BLEHERIS

CHAPTER I—Of the City of Nesses
and of certain that dwelt therein

As I sate in the garden in summer time, when the sun had set and the first stars were trembling into light, and while the ghostly, little bats were bleating above me, it came to me in mind to write for you, Galahad, somewhat of the life and dealings of this Bleheris; for—in my conceit—since he was surely not unlike yourself, it seemed that you might have pleasure in hearing of his life and his death, that fell so many years ago. Know then, that in the old days, when this world was still young and full of wonders, there lay a little country that men called The Land of Two Nesses: for there was a wide bay, and on either side of it stood great, bold nesses where the rocky hills sank down into the sea, and between them was a beach of fair, golden sand.... Now from out of the heights that were thereabouts came a swift and deep stream, called Coldriver, that ran through the valley-land, and out into the bay beyond, on the which stood the City of the Nesses: the same was a very fair city of stones, with five bridges over that stream, and good wharves for many ships of the merchants that lay by them, and towers and palaces and rich halls as fair as might be....

For in that city was a rich old knight, a worthy man who had done great deeds of arms in his day, driving back rovers that came to harry them from over the seas, and riding at all adventure in the ill lands beyond the pass of which I told you.... Now the whole prop and stay of this old knight, and all his pride and glory was [his daughter] for she was the fairest and most virtuous maiden as at that time alive: and her hair was more yellow than corn and her feet and her breasts more white than—But, in truth, my friend, there is little need to tell of such matters: for I believe well that you, who have read so deep in old books, must have heard this same lady spoken of ere now....

Now the fame of this lady was very great in the land, inasmuch as all squires and knights, yea and barons and great kings wooed her to wife: but she would have none of them.... But though many said that they would, yet it is not known that any man died for love of her: nay, some even were so ungentle that they went

afterwards and wed others, and lived merrily all their life days. ...
But let us go forward: now, as might be looked for, this young
knight [Bleheris] would be no worse than his fellows either in
love or in war or in any other thing, so that he too sought the
favour of Alice the Saint, and wrote verses upon her and jousted
for her, and sighed piteously and altogether deemed that he was
no less sorely smitten in love than Lancelot or Palomides or any
of the knights of old song. None the less, he forebore not to eat
lustily, to ride to the chase with a good heart, and to sleep sound
of nights.

So far the tale shows Lewis wavering between complete
commitment to his story and a schoolboyish debunking tone. He makes
Alice the Saint a frigid maid, and as we have seen, comments on her
conventional beauty with tongue in cheek. As the story goes on, Lewis
falls more under its spell and develops a series of visionary scenes, some
of which are powerful. For instance, the death of Wan Jadis, a companion
of Bleheris (Chapter XI):

... now nothing was left of Wan Jadis, above the marish, but only
his head and his arms stretched out desperately to the landwards.
And, whereas his helmet was off (for in his haste he had left it
hanging by the saddle), Bleheris could see the beautiful, sad face
strained and drawn with loathing and the agony of death: it
seemed that he strove to speak, but in that moment the slime and
mud rose to his white lips, and the evil creeping things crawled
over the fair skin, more delicate than porcelain. His eyes cast one
more look upon Bleheris: and then the marish closed over his
head, and thus Wan Jadis died.

"Bleheris" is full to overflowing with marvelous sights and strange
adventures. It is that form so beloved of Lewis, the quest story, but not a
Christian one; indeed there is an antichurch tone and Christianity is treated
as a superstition. At times the description of scenery reminds one of *The
Great Divorce* and the variety of symbolic episodes suggests *The Pilgrim's
Regress*. The turning point in Bleheris's quest is the death of Wan Jadis, which
is one event he cannot take half frivolously.

Lewis's mature talent represents a merger of the fanciful and the
realistic, the quest and the intrigue. In "Boxen," despite its talking animals,
one sees the realist at work, and there is even a foreshadowing of the future
logician and satirist. "Bleheris," by contrast, explores mysterious landscapes

where the soul is challenged to know itself; realms of deadly perils but also occasional hints of "Joy."

Lewis was not a man who consorted much with children. Then how did he learn to depict them so well? The answer may be the obvious one, that like almost all effective writers, he both grew up and stubbornly refused to grow up. As a small boy he was fascinated by never-never lands. He never lost this interest. Advancing years merely gave him the courage and skill to exploit the abiding dreams of childhood.[2]

Though Lewis speaks of the influence of Beatrix Potter, he seems to have been more familiar with the stories of E. Nesbit. On the whole, however, he appears not to have read vast quantities of children's stories in his early boyhood but he devoted a good deal of time to producing his own.

The adult Lewis was haunted by a mental picture of a faun carrying parcels in a snowy wood, a picture that went back to about the age of sixteen. Eventually, when around forty, his imagination began to play with the recurrent picture. This appears to have coincided with the arrival at Lewis's home of some schoolgirls who had been evacuated from London in fear of air raids. Perhaps, one can speculate, their presence aroused and intensified his long-standing interest in children's stories. It is not certain that he did much actual writing on the project at the time. I recall that in 1948 when I first met Lewis, I asked him what he intended to write next, and he said something rather vague about completing a children's book he had begun "in the tradition of E. Nesbit." By this time he was beginning to see more pictures, including a "queen on a sledge" and perhaps Aslan.

Another catalyst may have been a still unpublished tale by his former pupil, Roger Lancelyn Green, *The Wood That Time Forgot*. A reader coming on it today would be sure it derived heavily from *The Lion*, but the truth is if anything the opposite. Green told Lewis about the fantasy he was writing; Lewis asked to read it and tried, unsuccessfully, to find a publisher for it. The tale concerns three children and an undergraduate friend who stumble into a wood where time is suspended. There they find a girl who is a kind of succuba; she is pursued by a bad angel. With the aid of the children, she and the undergraduate finally meet, and by saving each other, save themselves. Several parts of the story have a strong Narnia flavor. When the children visit Agares in his home, he seems a jolly and innocent old man, and they do not suspect the drink, a sort of raspberry cordial, which lures one of the children to side with the forces of evil. This instantly brings to mind the White Witch's temptation of Edmund by the use of magic Turkish Delight. It is, however, not so much individual episodes as the total feeling of the wood that brings most strongly to mind the enchanted world of Narnia. Lewis's cavalier disposal of his own manuscripts makes it impossible to determine how detailed an impact Green's book had on him but, at the very least, we know he was greatly excited about it.

As Clyde Kilby has pointed out in his excellent discussion of the Narnia tales in *The Christian World of C.S. Lewis*, the order of publication of the tales does not correspond to the chronology of events inside the sequence. *The Magician's Nephew* should come first, *The Lion, the Witch and the Wardrobe* next, and *The Last Battle* of course last.

All seven of the stories are rich in Christian symbolism. Three, however, carry major themes. *The Magician's Nephew* presents the creative act by which the divine Aslan sings Narnia into existence. *The Lion, the Witch and the Wardrobe* dramatizes the crucifixion and the resurrection, as Aslan first dies at the hands of the White Witch and then triumphs over the bonds of death. *The Last Battle* is, as its title indicates, the account of how the earthly Narnia comes to an end and the heavenly Narnia takes its place.

The remaining four stories are by no means lacking in theological themes, but they are less conspicuous. It is as though these books correspond not to the key events in the Bible but the quieter events and dimensions of everyday life. Aslan, it is true, weaves in and out of the four books, but not as centrally as in the three key tales. The chapter in Kilby's book, "The Kingdom of Narnia," points out the many ways that these four other stories embody Christian themes: In *The Silver Chair* Jill must pass close to Aslan in order to drink of the sparkling water she craves. Aslan will not promise to leave her untouched if she moves toward the water; at the same time He tells her there is no other source for the kind of water she seeks. In *The Voyage of the "Dawn Treader"* a lamb gives the children fish, an ancient Christian symbol, and then reveals Himself as Aslan. In *The Horse and His Boy*, which Kilby rightly singles out as the tale having the fewest explicit Christian echoes, we find Aslan insisting that the skeptic Bree touch Him and know from experience that Aslan actually exists.

Some critics have asked whether the symbolic dimensions of the seven tales are handled in such a way as to make the stories more effective works of literature. Or rather, do Christian doctrines seem dragged in by their heels, converting the stories at their most theological moments into sugarcoated Sunday school instruction? Perhaps those best able to answer this question are the people who read Narnia as children. I have had the chance to talk with many of them, particularly as they move on into college and perhaps seek counsel on additional Lewis books they might read. I find two things: the first is that children almost always recognize a second level in the tales. This in no way obstructs or engulfs the primary level, which is simply a series of good stories. But they become alert to characters and events operating on two levels. This is rarely taken as the sly attempt of an older and pious man to sneak in religious propaganda. Children know from fairy tales and science fiction all about "willing suspension of disbelief." They enter into the game. They welcome Aslan as a special kind of talking animal and the focus of luminous meaning. Second, this acceptance of Aslan and the whole other level of the stories may or may not take an explicitly Christian form, depending on what sort of religious background the young reader has. The one who has been brought up as a Christian instantly recognizes Aslan as a kind of Christ for the talking animals and begins to see parallels with specific events in the life of Christ. The child lacking this background sees in Aslan something awesome and compelling, however he may put it in words. It is interesting that often readers of both backgrounds single out the most theological events of the tales as the most effective episodes. This suggests that the firm theological themes running through the tales may be a literary asset rather than otherwise.

Another factor is at work here. If the Chronicles of Narnia were a straight allegory, in the manner of *The Pilgrim's Progress* (or *The Pilgrim's Regress*) the reader would expect every event to have a precise correspondence with some proclamation of Christian doctrine. In Narnia, life simply goes on. It has its occasional epiphanies and revelations, but it also has long stretches in which the characters have interesting but rarely definitive adventures. The realism and detail of these routine experiences help to make the high points stand out more sharply.

Since a full treatment of Narnia would require a book the length of this one,[3] I shall concentrate on the three major tales which are central from both a literary and a religious viewpoint.

In *The Magician's Nephew*, the land of Narnia is sung into existence by Aslan. The actual creation comes rather late in the book. This is partly a way of building toward a climax, but it also represents a way of dealing with fantastic material. We saw the same strategy earlier in the interplanetary tales, all of which commence with realistic, indeed prosaic details, thereby winning the reader's confidence, and preparing him for a gradual movement toward the unexpected and incredible.

The earthly setting is a line of Victorian row houses in the time of Sherlock Holmes. Polly, a young girl living in one of the houses, gets acquainted with Digory, who later—in *The Lion*—reappears as an adult, Professor Kirke. Digory lives in the adjoining house; his father is away in India on some imperial mission; his Aunt Letty and eccentric Uncle Andrew Ketterley are more or less taking care of him, while concentrating their attention on his gravely ill mother. The uncle is something of an amateur magician, and is perfectly ready to use the children as guinea pigs in his experiments.

Digory and Polly play in the connected attics and explore Uncle Andrew's study. There they find yellow rings and green ones, which—they accidentally discover—have the power to transport them to other worlds and to bring them back.

The uncle has the trademark of Lewis upon him. He is a little like Weston, a little like Devine, but more absurd than either. Andrew defends the practice of magic as a prerogative of superior persons. He recalls how his godmother, Mrs. Lefay, who helped inspire his passion for magic, had given him a box of magic before her death and instructed him to burn it unopened; he did not carry out her instructions. Digory is shocked at this betrayal, but his uncle explains:

> ... Oh, I see. You mean that little boys ought to keep their promises. Very true: most right and proper, I'm sure, and I'm very glad you have been taught to do it. But of course you must understand that rules of that sort, however excellent they may be for little boys—and servants—and women—and even people in general, can't possibly be expected to apply to profound students and great thinkers and sages. No, Digory. Men like me who possess hidden wisdom, are freed from common rules just as we are cut off from common pleasures. Ours, my boy, is a high and lonely destiny.[4]

This sounds like Weston proclaiming the higher morality that could justify the extinction of the Malacandrans if the deed would advance the Tellurian destiny. Later, in a conversation with Jadis the Witch, Digory hears her make exactly the same defense of her destruction of the city of Charn. "You must learn, child, that what would be wrong for you or for any of the common people is not wrong in a great Queen such as I. The weight of the world is on our shoulders. We must be freed from all rules. Ours is a high and lonely destiny."[5]

If the White Witch, alias Queen Jadis, represents pure, metaphysical evil, Uncle Andrew in his eager and bumbling way is trying hard to catch up with her but will never make it. She attracts; she terrifies; she never amuses. Uncle Andrew's grand gestures are more often comic than lordly in their consequences.

The plot of the tale is built around a series of adventures in other worlds with return visits to the earth. Digory and Polly travel by means of the magic rings. One world they visit is Charn, obviously the victim of some vast destructive force. Here they first encounter Queen Jadis. She discovers the children are from a newer world and instantly resolves to conquer it. The children hastily touch their rings to return to London, but Jadis goes along by touching the children. The queen and Uncle Andrew meet in London and he finds himself spending his last penny to entertain her in proper queenly style. Their night on the city ends in a wild hansom cab ride and the beginnings of a local riot, with Uncle Andrew humiliated almost to the point of losing his elevated dignity.[6] The children manage to touch the queen with their rings and then find themselves in the Wood between the Worlds, from which they enter the world of nothing. With them are Jadis, Uncle Andrew, the cabbie, and his horse.

Up to this point the story has been a rather relaxed adventure tale, spiced with magic. The one serious metaphysical theme is the nature of good and evil, simplified and indeed almost oversimplified into the contrast between the Witch and the naturally good and kind cabdriver. Another theme running through the story is health and illness, life and death. One gets the impression that Digory's mother has some lingering and probably fatal illness. She is constantly on his mind, and he yearns to find, perhaps in "another world," a cure for her.

These themes begin to draw together when Aslan starts singing. High, heavenly voices join in harmony with His deep notes; the black heavens suddenly gleam with countless stars. Out of nothing, hills emerge and take shape. Grass springs up and trees grow tall before their eyes. Flowers pierce the air. A new earth stands in its first perfection. Animals now appear. Aslan wanders among them, picking out certain ones and giving them the gift of speech, almost as though the image of God were being planted in them. The Witch futilely opposes him. The evil she represents may have eventual consequences in Narnia and require strange and even hideous remedies, but for the moment she is defeated.

The great lion sends Digory to the mountains of the Western Wild to pluck a particular kind of apple and bring it back uneaten. The cab horse, now turned into a winged Pegasus, carries the two children on his back. Arrived there, they discover Jadis eating an apple, and she almost persuades him to follow her example. Obedient to Aslan, Digory resists the temptation, and he brings the apple back intact. A new tree springs up from its seeds and Aslan gives Digory an apple to take back for the healing of his mother. Meanwhile, the new tree will protect Narnia from the Witch for many years, though not forever.

Back on earth, Digory buries the core of the apple that cured his mother in his back yard, and with it the magical rings, to prevent future harm. What he does not know is that the tree that grows from the core still has some of the magic of Narnia, and that when later he fashions its wood into a wardrobe, it will prove an entryway to Narnia.

These magic apple trees seem to serve a double role in the story. Depending on who uses them and under what circumstances, they can be trees of the knowledge of good and evil (with all those fateful possibilities) or trees of life, incarnating in their quieter way the overwhelming abundance of life that Aslan has sung into beautiful existence.

The Magician's Nephew provides a theological and metaphysical background for the other tales. The theme of the apple trees is less convincingly depicted than that of creation. It is almost as though Lewis were here guided more by theological necessities than literary imperatives. This episode lacks the freshness, the sense of "So this is what the legend is all about," that a reader of *Perelandra* experiences when he suddenly realizes what the fixed land symbolizes.

The Magician's Nephew has relatively few clanging swords and bloody tumults compared to some of the other tales. With the exception of climactic moments, it moves quietly, as one adventure fades into another. Thus, even the creation of Narnia has a more lyric and less epic tone than one might expect. Aslan quietly goes about His business, and His fullness of life, expressed through His singing, brings forth a universe and its inhabitants. For all its quietness, it is one of the great creation myths. Few readers will quickly forget the rapid stages of Narnia's creation, and such startlingly effective pictures as the little hillocks out of which all varieties of animal burst forth into the splendor of existence. Abundance is the word for all Aslan's creative deeds; He has come into the world of nothing and made it something, gloriously alive and fertile.

The distinction between good and evil, as has been suggested, is brought to a point in the contrast between Queen Jadis and the cabbie and his wife. No explanation is ever offered of why the Witch is evil. After all, who can give a genealogy for a metaphysical absolute? It is not that she is filled with evil. She is evil, and anyone who is locked in combat with her is battling demonic forces. The cabbie and his wife are simply plain, good people. They have come from the innocence of the countryside into teeming London, driven by the necessity to earn a living. When Aslan names Frank and his wife the first king and queen of Narnia, they represent everything that is lacking in the glittering but utterly evil Witch.

Aslan's song, to Uncle Andrew, is unrecognizable as song; His attempts to communicate with animals fail. They are puzzled by Him—is He an animal, a tree, or what? In a scene reminiscent of the dunking in cold water that Weston endures at the court of Oyarsa, the animals decide He is a tree and try to plant Him in the soil, with great squirts of river water delivered from an elephant's capacious trunk.

In Aslan, Lewis has created a highly effective objective correlative to Christ. Bestiaries are not a favored literary form today, but popular assumptions about the nature of animals still color metaphorical speech. A fox is automatically assumed to be clever and crafty, a snake is sneaky, a wolf (despite all the zoologists may say) is bloodthirsty, and so it goes. The lion is the noblest of the beasts, formidable in his power to destroy but regal in that very power. At the same time, a lion looks remarkably like a magnified kitten. The lion, Aslan, can roar with the authority of the universe and advance into battle with fierce face and gleaming teeth. But at other times, and with no loss of leonine dignity, He takes children riding on His back, or tussles with them in a montage of flailing limbs and teeth. He is ultimate power, ultimate gentleness, ultimate goodness, even ultimate cuddlesomeness. Without Aslan, we would have simply stories of cute talking animals with a few human beings scattered in. They would be superior tales, more vivid and convincing than most in their genre, but not fundamentally different. The presence of Aslan introduces and sustains the additional dimension that makes the Chronicles of Narnia more than a series of adventures and marvels; Lewis infuses them with the spirit of great myth. One suspects this is the largest element in the near-universal appeal of these stories, which introduce the reader not merely to strange lands and odd creatures, but into that holy land of the unconscious where the mighty archetypes dwell, and both sacred and demonic figures act out their ritual dramas.

These archetypes never die in our consciousness, no matter how rigidly modern and reductionist the mind may fancy itself. They are waiting in the shadows, to transform a familiar landscape. Lewis, through Aslan and the events he sets in motion, challenges the reader to say yes or no to what is already affirmed in his innermost soul. Thus it is that the religious (or mythological) strand of the tales is the source of their greatest power, and that the three most theological (or mythic) stories are the ones that last longest in the memory and reverberate with the most resonance. They take us to where we already are in our inwardness.

The relatively quiet tone of *The Magician's Nephew* helps make it a good contrast to the tale immediately following in the Narnian chronology. In this story the dark prophecies of Aslan come true, and He plays a more central role, acting out his passion and resurrection. Once again, Lewis is careful to create a matter-of-fact, prosaic setting for the beginning of the tale:

> Once there were four children whose names were Peter, Susan, Edmund and Lucy. This story is about something that happened to them when they were sent away from London during the war because of the air-raids. They were sent to the house of an old Professor who lived in the heart of the country, ten miles from the nearest railway station and two miles from

the nearest post office. He had no wife and he lived in a very large house with a housekeeper called Mrs. Macready and three servants.[7]

Like Polly and Digory in *The Magician's Nephew*, they set out to explore the more than ample house. Lucy, more curious and venturesome than the others, goes into a huge wardrobe, not knowing it is built of magic wood from the apple tree that Digory (now Professor) Kirke planted many years ago. Suddenly, she finds that the coats hanging there have disappeared, and she is standing in a dark woods with snow falling. As she looks around she notices a faun carrying an umbrella and some brown-paper parcels. He is described in realistic detail, as though it were important to distinguish one faun from another. The meeting of beings from two worlds is initiated courteously; the faun exclaims a conventional "Good gracious me!" and well-bred Lucy says, "Good evening." The faun picks up the packages he has dropped, makes a belated bow and tactfully inquires whether she is a "Daughter of Eve." When she looks puzzled, he explains, "a girl." She accepts the label. He then asks how she got into Narnia and where she is from, but their lack of geographical knowledge about the other's country makes communication vague and unclear. Finally, he suggests a cup of hot tea to ward off the winter chills, and Lucy—worried about what people will be thinking back at the professor's house—agrees, but says she can't stay long. He takes her arm and holds the umbrella over both of them, and they walk to his tidy cave, inside of which a wood fire is cheerfully burning. He lights a lamp with a piece of blazing wood, and puts the tea kettle on to boil. Something of a "beauty and the beast" intuition stirs her in a gentle way— the meeting of the human and the nonhuman.

Tumnus the faun is a troubled soul. He bursts out sobbing and disjointedly reveals that he is in the pay of the White Witch. Then he escorts Lucy as far as the wood from which she can see the wardrobe door, and in fear and trembling says goodbye to her. She soon finds the other children in the old house and is astounded to learn that no time has elapsed. Her story of strange adventures falls on deaf ears; they think she is attempting an obvious hoax.

Tumnus is destined to reappear in the tale. When the children finally enter Narnia as a group, they go to his cave and find a notice nailed to the floor proclaiming that "The former occupant of these premises, Faun Tumnus, is under arrest and awaiting his trial on a charge of High Treason against her Imperial Majesty Jadis ... also of comforting her said Majesty's enemies, harbouring spies and fraternising with Humans."[8] Later they learn that he has been taken to the queen's house, where doubtless he will join the group of stone statues she has created by her magic of ossification. Mere human power cannot save him; only Aslan is equal to that task.

In the group of four brothers and sisters there is a Judas, by name Edmund. At first, his leaning toward the side of the enemy seems trivial, almost harmless. It begins with his passion for Turkish Delight. The Witch lures him by promising an infinity of this delicacy. What he does not know is that the confection is habit-forming. The witch offers to bring him up as a prince, and when she is gone, he will reign with a golden crown on his head and eat Turkish Delight from morning to night. He is still not a complete scoundrel in his heart, but he is weak and unable to resist temptation. The plight of the repentant Tumnus and the traitorous Edmund both cry out for supernatural rescue. The case of Edmund is particularly grave, for by the rules of the Deep Magic of Narnia, traitors belong to the White Witch, and only a terrible deeper magic can release them.

The movement of the story is a leisurely progress from yearning for Aslan to rumors of His return and His actual appearance. Some of the episodes, such as the visit with the cozy beaver family, seem deliberately prolonged for perhaps two purposes: to create a sense of ordinary life in Narnia going on as best it can, and to allow sufficient time for tension to build up as the world turns more and more demonic. Long before Aslan appears, He is firmly planted in the reader's imagination as a messiah, the only one who can save the suffering folk of Narnia.

The White Witch's downfall comes about very gradually—as two things happen, closely connected. Rumors of Aslan's return combine with the empirical fact that in the south a thaw is setting in and there are signs that the long winter is drawing to an end. Lucy asks if Aslan is a man. Mr. Beaver emphatically replies in words that suggest the Divine becoming incarnate: ... "Certainly not. I tell you he is the King of the wood and the son of the great Emperor-Beyond-the-Sea. Don't you know who is the King of Beasts? Aslan is a lion—*the* Lion, the great Lion."[9]

Further conversation makes it clear that Aslan is good but not safe—as one person after another in the tales puts it, "He is not a tame lion." Mr. Beaver also explains that the four children are the first humans to come to Narnia, and that their arrival and the simultaneous arrival of Aslan is no coincidence. An old Narnian saying has it that when the four thrones at the palace of Cair Paravel are occupied by two Sons of Adam and two Daughters of Eve, it will mean the end not only of the White Witch's reign; it will also mean her death. No wonder, then, that the Witch is implacably pursuing the earthly visitors, whose survival can mean her destruction. Through Mr. Beaver, the children learn that Aslan has summoned them to meet Him at the ancient Stone Table. Aslan is on the move, Aslan is on the move. The phrase begins to be a kind of drumbeat, building up in intensity each time it is uttered. Some revelation is at hand.

Mr. and Mrs. Beaver and the three children continue their journey to the Stone Table, as commanded by Aslan's message, and come to the top of a long hill. In the middle of the open hilltop is the Stone Table. A great crowd of creatures is assembled, among them Tree-Women and Well-Women (Dryads and Naiads) who are playing stringed instruments. In the center of the throng stands Aslan. It is an overwhelming experience of the numinous. Aslan is both ultimate good—the goal of all truly seeking hearts—and awesome. No one is willing to approach him. Finally, Peter advances, salutes with his sword, and says, "We have come—Aslan."[10] Lucy begs Aslan to do something to rescue Edmund, and Aslan promises all possible help, but explains that the task may be more difficult than they think.

The climax of the book, the Passion and Resurrection of Aslan, now approaches. Here Lewis achieves one of his most remarkable reimaginings of a familiar biblical theme. He undertakes a thorough process of translation. The human figure of Christ is replaced by the noblest of the animals. A Witch becomes the concentrated embodiment of all the converging forces of evil that brought Christ to His death. In Edmund is symbolized the self-serving self-deceptions of ordinary life, which have their inevitable consequences and can be redeemed only by the deepest magic of all.

It is not enough, in the economy of the divine Magic, to slay the Witch and rescue Edmund. A price must be paid for the affront to the *Tao* (the term Lewis uses in *The Abolition of Man*). The moral foundations of the Narnian universe have been undermined. Mere fleshly strength cannot rebuild them. But what Lewis dramatizes is not simply the price but the glory of the price, as new life is released into a redeemed world.

Despite the profound theological overtones at this point, the reader does not find the story heavy. Aslan catches us with our guard down. And He is not merely an animal objective correlative to Christ. He is, in some ways, a vegetation god in addition to all else; where He stands, there is abounding life, not just of the spirit but also of the very earth with its teeming manifestations of vitality.

The action of the tale speeds up once Aslan appears. The desperation of the Witch increases. She is frantic to accomplish the death of Edmund, to make sure only three children are left to reign at Cair Paravel. What the Witch does not know is that in her own completely evil way she is moving the course of Narnian history toward a good greater than any the land has ever known.

Later, Aslan and Edmund have a private, heart-to-heart talk. Edmund goes to his brother and two sisters and tells each of them, "I'm sorry," and

they all reply, "That's all right."[11] Meanwhile, the Witch's Dwarf
approaches and arranges a conference between Aslan and the Witch. She
soon appears in an eddy of cold air and takes her place face to face with
Aslan. The two confer with a circle of humans and talking animals
eavesdropping as best they can. The Witch summarizes the Deep Magic
that is written on the Stone Table. All traitors belong to her and death is her
prerogative. The fact that no treason was committed against her personally
is irrelevant. Unless she has blood as the law commands, Narnia will perish
in fire and water.

The great Lion denies none of this. He orders the group to fall back
while He and the Witch continue talking in low voices. Finally, He summons
the multitude and tells them the Witch has renounced all claims to Edmund's
life. What he does not reveal is that Aslan has agreed to take Edmund's place.
This is the deepest magic of all.

The climactic moment is near. The death of Aslan at the hands of the
Witch is one of the most compelling Passion stories. It achieves its power
partly by a process of selection. Many events from the biblical story are
repeated here, suitably modified for a Narnian setting. Jesus had a large and
loyal following of women; likewise, on Aslan's last night it is the two girls
who accompany Him to the Stone Table and try to comfort Him. The tone
of this scene is like that on the Mount of Olives; Aslan, the very channel
through whom God's creative energy has brought Narnia into being, is
weary, sad, desolate.

When they reach the Stone Table, a vast concourse is there:[12] the
Witch, of course, and multitudes of "Ogres with monstrous teeth, and
wolves, and bull-headed men; spirits of evil trees and poisonous plants,"
not to mention "Cruels and Hags and Incubuses, Wraiths, Horrors,
Efreets, Sprites, Orknies, Wooses, and Ettins." Aslan is spat upon, and His
mane shaved off. The hideous creatures pluck up courage to mock him:
"'Puss, Puss! Poor Pussy,' and 'How many mice have you caught to-day,
Cat?' and 'Would you like a saucer of milk, Pussums?'" The Witch whets
her knife, as Aslan—quiet but unafraid—looks up at the sky. Then, before
she stabs him to death, she bends down and speaks her words of triumph
into His ear:

> "And now, who has won? Fool, did you think by all this you
> would save the human traitor? Now I will kill you instead of him
> as our pact was and so the Deep Magic will be appeased. But
> when you are dead what will prevent me from killing him as
> well? And who will take him out of my hand *then*? Understand
> that you have given me Narnia forever, you have lost your own

life and you have not saved his. In that knowledge, despair and die."

It is a moment when Aslan might well cry out, "My God, my God, why hast Thou forsaken me?" But Lewis knew better than to overwork the parallel.

At dawn the children discover that Aslan is gone and the Stone Table is cracked in two. A mighty voice calls from behind them. They turn. There, gleaming in the sunrise, even larger than they remember him, stands Aslan, shaking His mane, which is now fully restored in all its splendor. The risen Lion explains that the Witch's magic goes back only to the dawn of time. If it had extended farther back, she would have known that when an innocent victim took a traitor's place on the Stone Table, the table itself would crack, and Death would begin working backward. Moment by moment, new life flows into Aslan. He then commands the girls to climb on His back and they begin the most glorious of bareback rides, lasting almost till noon, when they come to the Witch's castle. With His breath Aslan restores the stone statues to life. He then organizes a search of the castle to find any more prisoners, and in the course of this operation liberates the poor faun, who is none the worse for having been a statue. After a pitched battle, Aslan slays the Witch. He then knights Edmund, who has behaved with great heroism.

The children gradually signalize their new adult and royal status by adopting a style of speech reminiscent of *Bleheris*—for example, King Peter to Queen Susan:

> ... never since we four were Kings and Queens in Narnia have we set our hands to any high matter, as battles, quests, feats of arms, acts of justice, and the like, and then given over; but always what we have taken in hand, the same we have achieved.[13]

The purpose is obviously to dramatize their metamorphosis from ordinary British school children to monarchs with golden crowns. Some critics, including the author of children's books Jacqueline Jackson, have found this sudden linguistic shift jolting. Perhaps it is a little too cute, seeming to introduce a note of condescension toward the young which is otherwise blessedly lacking in the book.

The rest of the story moves swiftly. The four children are solemnly installed on the four thrones of Cair Paravel. Great multitudes cheer, and there is the sound of mermen and mermaids singing close to the castle in honor of the new queens and kings. Aslan quietly slips away; no one knows when He will return, but that is His way. The children grow up, prove excellent rulers.

The Magician's Nephew and *The Lion* have some elements in common. Each is full of talking animals acting remarkably like ordinary children and adults. Each has Aslan as the central character. Each succeeds in making a never-never land convincing. Where they differ is in intensity. Aslan's supreme deed in the earlier book is that of creation, which He accomplishes so easily that it seems the by-product of a song. But in *The Lion*, His great deed is one that Christians refer to with such words as propitiation, redemption, and salvation. The whole moral landscape darkens from one tale to the other. Uncle Andrew fraternizes with evil; Edmund is shown moving steadily toward absolute complicity. When in *The Lion* Aslan pays the price to rescue Edmund, there is a depth of feeling that one does not find in *The Magician's Nephew*. At the same time, Aslan's resurrection evokes deeper joys and more spontaneous gaiety.

The Magician's Nephew has the more casual structure. It moves along from one adventure to another. When the great act of creation comes, it appears almost as offhand as the other marvels of the tale, suggesting that the creation of a world, while impressive to mortals, is all in a day's work for the Aslans of this universe.

The Lion has a more tightly organized structure, built around the Witch–Edmund relation, and the coming of Aslan. These two strands interweave and finally coalesce. The tempo of the tale is carefully controlled, so as to move from faint rumors of Aslan to signs of his activity (like the melting snow) to his final manifestation. In the same way, by slow and measured stages, Edmund gives himself into the hands of the Witch. With the intersection of these two strands, there is the image of the cross. Only by Aslan's sacrifice can Edmund the traitor be saved.

The firm framework of the three key Narnia tales is theological, reaching from the creation of Narnia to last things, when the old Narnia ceases to exist. If one thinks of the biblical perspective as involving a cosmic five-act drama, the parallel becomes clear:

BIBLE	NARNIA
I Creation of universe	Creation of Narnia
II Struggle of good and evil	Aslan vs. the Witch
III Death and resurrection of Christ	Death and resurrection of Aslan
IV The present world, with its confused struggle of good and evil, though	Aslan intermittently reappears

good has already
triumphed in principle

V	The "end of the world"	The end of the old Narnia
	and the emergence of a	and the coming of the new
	new world	Narnia

The four tales that, by Narnian chronology, belong between *The Magician's Nephew* and *The Lion* at one end, and *The Last Battle* at the other, are episodes from Act IV of the Narnian drama. Lewis's fantastically fertile imagination, so well stocked with all the conventions and traditions of fairy tales, and so free in reshaping them and supplementing them by pure products of his own imagination, pours forth one set of adventures after another. We see earthly children restoring Prince Caspian to his throne. We experience one of the most haunting of myths, the land of eternal youth, when a group of children sail into clear seas and find the water is fresh and filled with white waterlilies, while the sun is much larger than they remember. In another story we encounter a prince always in danger of turning into a serpent. In yet another, a queen must be rescued before she is compelled to marry a man she detests. In all these tales, Aslan weaves in and out, supplies advice, sometimes crucial aid, but does not perform any of the grand, cosmic deeds such as those in *The Magician's Nephew* and *The Lion*.

Although relatively marginal, the role of Aslan in the four tales critically affects the reader's response to the total myth of the seven chronicles. If Lewis had written only the three most theological stories—or if he had contrived to pack more theology into the other four—there might have been a stronger sense of the swift rush of divine events. But at the same time, the portrayal of daily life would have been out of balance; Heaven, so to speak, would have engulfed earth.

Finally comes *The Last Battle*. This is surely one of the most astounding children's stories ever written. Such tales do not ordinarily end with the death of all the characters. But as Ransom was told in *Out of the Silent Planet*, Maleldil creates new worlds but not one of them is meant to last for ever. So it is with Narnia. It has served its purpose; it is time now for the heavenly Narnia, on the other side of death, to take its place.

The Last Battle begins quietly. There is first of all Shift, an old ape, clever, selfish, malicious. He notices a strange object in the water and commands his companion, the dull witted donkey, Puzzle, to pull it out. It is a lion's skin. Always eager for mischief, especially when it can advance his own comfort and power, Shift makes a garment to put on Puzzle so that he will look, more or less, like a lion. He wants Puzzle to pass himself off as

Aslan and thus gain control over the inhabitants of Narnia, who desire
nothing so much as the return of their leonine ruler. Poor Puzzle is pushed
into the role of being a fake messiah, receiving the adoration of the people.
Shift promises Puzzle that he will tell him what to say. The donkey,
dimwitted but right-minded, protests.[14] "It would be wrong, Shift. I may be
not very clever but I know that much. What would become of us if the real
Aslan turned up?" Shift has an answer for every objection: "Probably he sent
us the lion skin on purpose, so that we could set things to right. Anyway, he
never *does* turn up, you know. Not now-a-days." As usual, Lewis does little to
reshape the traditional symbolism associated with animals. Apes are clever
and crafty, donkeys are stubborn but not intellectual giants.

After the prologue of the ape and donkey, the scene quietly shifts to
King Tirian at his hunting lodge, in conversation with his beloved friend,
Jewel the Unicorn. The king is in a state of euphoria as he recounts all the
reports he has heard of Aslan's return. They are joined by Roonwit the
Centaur, who bluntly tries to destroy their dream. No matter what gossip-
mongers may report, the message of the constellations is a clear negative.
Not only do they deny the rumors about Aslan's return; they prophesy
unspecified but terrible events for Narnia. The tone of the story, still very
quiet, is becoming more somber and foreboding. Next they hear a voice,
Cassandra-like, crying out, "Woe for my brothers and sisters! Woe for the
holy trees! The woods are laid waste. The axe is loosed against us."[15] The
speaker appears, a tall tree-spirit or Dryad. She explains that the talking
trees are being felled. In his fury, the king and Jewel rashly set out to find
the axemen and stop them. Soon they encounter a Water Rat on a raft and
he explains that Aslan has given orders to fell the trees and sell them to the
barbaric, dark-skinned Calormenes. The king and Jewel are bewildered.
Could this be possible? After all, as Jewel points out, Aslan is not a tame
Lion. Presumably his thoughts are not always their thoughts. A terrible
ambiguity has entered their lives. They want to serve and obey Aslan, but
first they must find out if this rumored lion is Aslan. Uncertain whether
they are doing the right thing, and heavy-hearted, they continue on their
way and soon hear the sound of axes on tree trunks. A great crowd of
talking animals and human beings is at work. The men were "... not the
fair-haired men of Narnia: they were dark, bearded men from Calormen,
that great and cruel country that lies beyond Archenland across the desert
to the south."[16]

The mention of the Calormenes and their complexion is worth a
moment's pause, as an indication of how readily Lewis accepted conventional
symbolism. In the space tales he uses the contrast of light and darkness for
good and evil. To anyone ever caught in a cave, it might perhaps seem an

inevitable association. The reference to the dark skins of the Calormenes evokes the British Empire at the height of its civilizing zeal when clean-cut blond young men went to darkest Africa to suppress the Fuzzy Wuzzies. Darkness (to blond people) suggests aliens, probably dark within as well as without. European fairy tales and romances of the Middle Ages prefer blonds.

Lewis was less bothered by these matters than a modern liberal would be. He simply took his symbols where he found them. And as we will see later, Lewis could depict a noble, dark-skinned Calormene who turned out to be a true servant of Aslan without knowing it. This, however, is a cause for much astonishment as well as rejoicing.

When Tirian and Jewel the Unicorn discover two Calormenes savagely whipping a Narnian talking horse as he strains at a heavy log, their fury knows no bounds. They plunge in and slay the aliens. The king leaps on the unicorn's back and they quickly make their escape. Tirian is then smitten by pangs of conscience. They have slain two men without challenging them—and furthermore, can they be sure that the felling of the trees is *not* being done at the command of Aslan? More by tone than explicit exposition, the story increasingly conveys the feeling of a moral order falling apart; no one is any longer sure what is right and what is wrong. If Aslan has become an ambiguity, then the center cannot hold.

Tirian and Jewel walk back and give themselves up to the Calormenes. "Then the dark men came round them in a thick crowd, smelling of garlic and onions, their white eyes flashing dreadfully in their brown faces."[17] The captors lead them to a small stable, outside of which Shift the ape is eating. He is dressed in odds and ends of fancy clothing like some savage who has raided a wrecked passenger ship, and the main thing on his mind is nuts. In the name of Aslan he commands the squirrels to bring a better supply. From the ape's rambling oration it becomes clear that he is in alliance with the king of Calormen and is using the prestige of the false Aslan to sanctify such activities as the felling of talking trees.

The general situation is like a fairy-tale version of the opening of *That Hideous Strength*, when the forces of progress, represented by the N.I.C.E., move in on the university. The land of the Calormenes is a modern results-oriented society advancing and taking over. Most of the Narnians are uneasy and miserable, but they believe, more or less, that everything is at the will of Aslan—though Aslan seems to have changed His values since the Narnians last saw Him. The Ape assures the talking animals that they will learn the value of hard work, dragging things and working in mines. All in all, the Ape's rambling discourse is a classical description of imperialist capitalism on the march, spreading civilization and gaining profit. This is accompanied by theological warfare, as the invaders coin the portmanteau word, Tashlan, to express the belief that Tash and Aslan are really the same god.

King Tirian finds himself thinking about the long history of Narnia, and how when things are at their worst, a rescue expedition is always mounted by earthly children in alliance with Aslan. In despair he cries out the name of Aslan and asks that Narnia be saved though its king may die.

His prayer is answered by a vivid dream in which he makes spectral contact with seven humans in a lighted room. Two of them, a man and a woman, are very old; the others are children. They see him faintly and exclaim. One of the children is Peter the High King, who commands Tirian to explain his mission. Tirian tries to, but his lips make no sound. The vision fades, but not until some sort of contact has been made with earthlings who may prove of help.

In fact, two children shortly appear from nowhere. They are Eustace Scrubb and Jill Pole, who in an earlier adventure had rescued a Narnian king from a long enchantment. They cut the king's bonds and sate his hunger with six sandwiches. The children, back on earth, had been traveling on a train when there was a terrible crash, and immediately thereafter they found themselves talking with King Tirian. What they do not know until later is that they are dead. From this point on, the distinction between the living and the dead becomes blurred.

It is not necessary to follow the military operations in detail. The king and his little following of children and talking animals put up valiant rearguard resistance to the massed forces under the Calormene banner, but it is almost as though this struggle were being fought to keep the record clean rather than in any real hope of victory. The basic problem is not a military one; rather, a question of morale. The lies about the false Aslan and the new doctrine of the universal god, Tashlan, have eaten away at the moral and psychological integrity of the Narnians. Even when the fakery of the false Aslan is finally revealed, many of the Dwarfs draw the conclusion that everything, including also the real Aslan, is propaganda, and impartially fight both the Calormenes and the Narnians.

King Tirian now has another vision—or is it simple reality? He sees seven kings and queens in their crowns and glittering garments. One of them is Jill, another is Eustace, both fresh and clean and splendid in their attire. Tirian himself is no longer battle-stained; he is dressed as though for a great feast at Cair Paravel. The other monarchs all turn out to be previous participants in the annals of Narnia.

Soon the air turns sweeter and a brightness flashes. Aslan, the true Aslan, has returned. Tirian flings himself at the divine feet, and the great Lion commends him for standing firm at Narnia's darkest hour. From now on, it becomes harder and harder to say who is living and who has passed through death. All this is eloquently dramatized in Chapter XIV, "Night Falls on Narnia." Father Time wakes from his long sleep and blows a strangely beautiful melody on his horn. At once, the stars of the sky begin to fall by the hundreds, and soon not a star is left. Great companies of living beings, both animals and humans, begin streaming through the stable door. They are being called home. As each comes close to Aslan he is impelled to look Him straight in the eye. Those whose faces mirror fear and hatred disappear to the left of the doorway. Those who gaze upon Him with love do not disappear. In the mirror of Aslan's eye, each creature finds out what he is.

Dragons and giant lizards denude the landscape; the sun enlarges and begins to die. As Jewel the Unicorn said earlier in the tales, all worlds draw to an end. This one ends with a surrealist landscape: enormous red sun, the moon in the wrong position, a great tide of water that washes away the mountains. The moon and sun come together; masses of fire drop into the sea; steam rises. The giant reaches out one arm and squeezes the Sun as though it were an orange. Utter blackness everywhere. The story of Narnia is over. Aslan commands Peter the High King to shut the door.

But the new Narnia is beginning. The children find blue sky now above them, flowers, and laughter in Aslan's eyes. While they yet mourn for all that was good and beautiful in the old Narnia, Aslan summons them to come further in, come further up. It is while exploring the paradise in which they now find themselves that they meet a wandering Calormene, Emeth, who tells his story. He has long been a true devotee of Tash, and has yearned to meet him face to face. He was one of the disguised soldiers sent into Narnia. This pleased him, for he hated Aslan and felt that by defeating the Narnians he would be striking a blow against a false god. When the Ape had invited people to enter the stable to meet Tashlan, Emeth accepted the invitation, hoping the true Tash would be there. Once through the door, he found himself in a land of grass and flowers, and set out to find Tash. Suddenly, Aslan appeared in his path, terrible in His gleaming beauty. Then followed a dialogue in which Aslan explained that Emeth had sought Him all along.

> ... the Glorious One bent down his golden head and touched my forehead with his tongue and said, Son, thou art welcome. But I said, Alas, Lord, I am no son of Thine but the servant of Tash. He answered, Child, all the service thou hast done to Tash, I account as service done to me.... Therefore if any man swear by Tash and keep his oath for the oath's sake, it is by me that he has truly sworn, though he know it not, and it is I who reward him. And if

any man do a cruelty in my name, then, though he says the name Aslan, it is Tash whom he serves and by Tash his deed is accepted. Dost thou understand, Child? I said, Lord, thou knowest how much I understand. But I said also (for the truth constrained me), Yet have I been seeking Tash all my days. Beloved, said the Glorious One, unless thy desire had been for me thou wouldst not have sought so long and so truly. For all find what they truly seek.[18]

The episode of Emeth is one of the few places where one may feel that for the sake of theological completeness Lewis has inserted what is more an essay than part of a story. It is disproportionately long for the pace of the narrative, but its beauty is so great one cannot really regret that it is included. In fact, as *The Last Battle* ends, it is on the verge of bursting the narrative bonds and becoming a great hymn of praise. Narnia, which in book after book has dramatized the ways of God with man, is pointing beyond all symbols and allegories to Him who is not a symbol but sheer being.

The Last Battle has a particular wealth of symbolism which serves not merely to convey ideas but to create moods. It is a darkening world; the human enemies ranged against the world of Aslan show it in the very color of their skin. Ordinary, decent life itself is under attack. The talking trees are being felled, the talking beasts whipped into slavery. The gift of speech that many of the animals possess seems to be a symbol of "the image of God" (or image of Aslan) that was, originally breathed into them, for when any of them reject Aslan at the end they simply lose this gift and become ordinary animals. The god Tash is not an illusion. He symbolizes brute evil and thus is the opposite of Aslan. The one is like a hideous vulture with cruel beak and flailing arms to grasp and tear, the other glorious in his golden mane and justly hailed as the king of the beasts. The remaining characters are the spectrum of mortal possibilities in between, pulled this way and that, but in the long run making their choice between the two absolute alternatives. That choice is made as they pass through the narrow door of the stable and read in Aslan's eyes their decision.

All this vast cosmological drama is firmly buttressed by details of ordinary realism. The Ape is real as any selfish schemer. The Donkey reacts in a dimwitted way human readers can consider plausible. King Tirian is believable as one who has lost hope but finds honor still worth dying for. The invasion of the Calormenes is as carefully organized as any imperialist expedition, complete with psychological warfare and the manipulation of religion. Much of the action and many of the incidental details in *The Last Battle* are perfectly convincing from the purely terrestrial viewpoint; at the same time the reader never forgets that eternal and ultimate forces are locked in conflict, and that, as Lewis liked to say, things are coming to a point.

The charge most frequently leveled against the Narnia tales is that they cash in on "stock responses," particularly to the high points of the Christian tale. Nearly two thousand years of psychic history have engraved these pictures in our imagination. Thus—so the criticism runs—Lewis could achieve an easy victory by presenting this cultural heritage under a transparent disguise. A half-truth is involved here. Western man does indeed carry within himself this storehouse of significant images, but they would not have gripped him so powerfully in the first place if they had not seemed the fulfillment of still older images living immortally in the unconscious mind. The earliest converts to Christianity already knew that a self-sacrificing God is needed to resolve the contradictions of existence. When Lewis evokes Christian parallels, he is at the same time profiting by racial memories older than Christianity.

Tolkien, a devout Roman Catholic, was himself troubled by the Narnia stories. In part, it may have been a feeling that the stories came too easily. Lewis could write seven books quicker than Tolkien could write one. But he also disapproved of the obvious Christian correspondences. He was attempting a different kind of imaginary world, one overwhelming in its own integrity and relying less on resemblances to the earth and its familiar beliefs. Where Lewis redramatizes the decisive moments of the Christian story, Tolkien slowly, stroke by stroke, builds up a world that is heroic and tragic, more akin perhaps to *Beowulf* and the Icelandic sagas than to the relative cheerfulness and hopefulness of a believing world that beholds its salvation in a Christ or an Aslan.[19]

By the time Lewis began writing Narnia, his mind was uniquely filled with usable images and symbols. He knew his Germanic, Celtic, and classical mythology. He commanded the literature of Western Europe, at least through the Renaissance period. He had already created many symbols in his own writing, particularly in *The Pilgrim's Regress* and the space tales. With the freedom that seems to characterize a major writer, he was willing to draw on his own private store as well as from the public symbology that he shared. He used talking animals in *Out of the Silent Planet* and used them again in Narnia. His Weston corresponds in his early stages to a more impressive Uncle Andrew, and in his later Unman stages he would be a suitable mate for the White Witch. As early as *The Pilgrim's Regress*, varied landscapes of mountains, hills, and well-watered valleys had been symbols of the heart's desire, paradise, the new Narnia, Heaven. Symbolism of light and dark runs through his books. Speech itself is a symbol of rationality and the kind of relation with God that only rational beings can experience. In his use of animals, Lewis was like the author of a medieval bestiary. Of a given animal, he is less interested in "What is this animal good for?" (still less its exact biological classification) than in "What does this animal stand for?" Thus, it is no surprise when Lewis chose a Lion for his central character; the bestiaries would have certified the choice. Even Lewis's use of cold as a symbol of evil has its precedent in the bottom circle of *The Inferno* where the worst of sinners lie perpetually congealed.

In a way, the mature Lewis (maybe apart from his literary criticism) had one main theme, which is to reveal and justify the ways of God to man. This did not prevent him from writing books which can be thoroughly enjoyed by a reader as atheistic as the Great Knock. It emphatically does not mean that the literary merit of his books is a kind of disguised religiosity. No, from a literary viewpoint, the religious themes of his books are like the moral themes of Dickens or the sociological themes of Ibsen. They are part of the structure of a given book, and must be evaluated not by whether they will get you to Heaven, but by whether they are doing their literary job.

It is an irony of literary history. This man, who wrote the most glittering religious apologetics of his time, and who was a major literary historian, may well have created his most lasting work in seven fairy tales nominally for children. All theories of literary determinism and influence falter at the thought. He had no children of his own; the tales were launched before he acquired stepsons. It is said that a fetal ape looks more human than a mature one, and some have suggested that humanity arose through a process of arrested development. A writer sometimes succeeds as much from his limits as from his unlimited outreach. By remaining a boy as well as becoming a man, Lewis was able to speak in a language which is simultaneously the tongue of the fairy tale and the epic; he speaks to the adult, the child, and the child within the adult. He speaks to everyone, except to those ossified grown-ups who have stifled the child within.

NOTES

1. Quotations from Lewis's juvenilia ("Boxen" and "Bleheris") are courtesy of The Trustees of the Estate of C.S. Lewis, and are copyrighted by the Estate.

2. Anyone wishing a fuller account of the genesis of Narnia should consult Chapter X of Green and Hooper's *C.S. Lewis: A Biography*, which lays out the background in great detail. In the present book I am concerned more with the finished works than with their evolution.

3. An interesting start, mainly theological in emphasis, is provided by Kathryn Ann Lindskoog, *The Lion of Judah in Never-Never Land* (Grand Rapids, Michigan: W.B. Eerdmans, 1973).

4. *The Magician's Nephew* (New York: Collier Books, 1955, 1970), p. 18.

5. P. 62.

6. As Clyde Kilby points out, this is one place where a direct literary influence is obvious; the ride and near-riot are inspired by a similar scene near the end of G.K. Chesterton's *The Man Who Was Thursday*.

7. *The Lion, the Witch and the Wardrobe: A Story for Children* (New York: Collier Books, 1950, 1970), p. 1.

8. P. 55.

9. P. 75.

10. P. 123.

11. P. 136.

12. Pp. 148, 150, 152.

13. P. 184.

14. *The Last Battle* (New York: Collier Books, 1956, 1970), p. 10.

15. P. 16.

16. P. 21.

17. P. 25.

18. Pp. 164–65.

19. A short but valuable comparison of Tolkien's and Lewis's imaginary worlds is contained in Charles Moorman, "'Now Entertain Conjecture of a Time'—The Fictive Worlds of C.S. Lewis and J.R.R. Tolkien," published in Mark R. Hillegas, editor, *Shadows of Imagination* (Carbondale, Illinois: Southern Illinois University Press, 1969), pp. 59–69. See also Richard Purtill, *Lord of the Elves and Eldils* (Grand Rapids, Michigan: Zondervan, 1974).

MARGARET PATTERSON HANNAY

Further Up and Further In:
Chronicles of Narnia

Lewis began *The Lion, the Witch, and the Wardrobe* in 1939 while four children were evacuated to his house during the air raids: "This book is about four children whose names were Ann, Martin, Rose, and Peter.... They all had to go away from London suddenly because of the Air Raids, and because Father, who was in the army, had gone off to the War and Mother was doing some kind of war work. They were sent to stay with ... a very old Professor who lived by himself in the country."[1] In this first draft he drew on stories he had loved as a child, particularly "The Aunt and Anabel," in which a child enters a magic world through "Bigwardrobeinsparoom." The story was then set aside for almost ten years.

In March of 1949 he read the complete story to his friend Roger Lancelyn Green. Green recalls that Lewis then spent some time on a sequel, beginning a story about Digory and his fairy godmother Mrs. Lefay, which was to tell of the beginnings of Narnia. That fragment still exists, opening with Digory's ability to talk to trees and animals, a gift he lost when he sawed off a branch of his friend the oak in order to avoid the taunts of a playmate, Polly. Then the fascinating Mrs. Lefay enters, assuring Digory "Don't be afraid you're going to have to kiss me ... I'm too ugly for that and ten to one you don't like snuff. I do, though."[2] Although elements of this story survive in other places—Digory and Polly, the red squirrel Pattertwig—it was

---

From *C.S. Lewis*. © 1981 by Frederick Ungar Publishing Co., Inc.

apparently never developed further. Instead, Lewis thought of an immediate sequel to the first book, *Prince Caspian*, and completed it by the end of 1949. *The Voyage of the Dawn Treader* and *The Horse and His Boy* were written in 1950, *The Silver Chair* in 1951. *The Magician's Nephew*, which had begun with Mrs. Lefay, went through many revisions, including the removal of a long story about Digory's visit with a farmer and his wife in the dying world of Charn; it was not completed until early in 1954, several months after *The Last Battle* was written.[3] So the order in which the books were written is not the same as that in which they were published or that of events in Narnia. Walter Hooper says that Lewis told him they should be read in the following order: *The Magician's Nephew, The Lion, the Witch, and the Wardrobe, The Horse and His Boy, Prince Caspian, The Voyage of the "Dawn Treader", The Silver Chair, The Last Battle.*[4]

Not until the stories were completed did Lewis chart out the history of Narnia as a whole, including events and characters which had never appeared in the seven chronicles. Because of the difference in times between our world and Narnia, the entire history of Narnia takes 2555 Narnian years, but only fifty Earth years. Narnia is created in 1900, when Digory is twelve and Polly is eleven. The Pevensies arrive in 1940, which is the year 1000 in Narnian time. Professor Digory Kirke, who seems ancient to the children, is fifty-two, about Lewis's age when he wrote the story. In 1941 the children return to Narnia to aid Prince Caspian, discovering that 1303 Narnian years have passed and all their old friends have died. But by their next visit, in 1942, only three Narnia years have elapsed, so they travel with Caspian on the *Dawn Treader*. Fifty Narnian years go by before Eustace and Jill rescue Prince Rilian later in 1942. And then no one from our world visits Narnia until 1949, when the railway accident sends all the friends of Narnia into that world for the last battle (2555 Narnian time). In between come stories about characters Lewis never wrote up—Moonwood the Hare, Queen Swanwhite of Narnia, Ram the Great, the outlaws who move into Lantern Waste.[5]

It is easy to find parallels to Lewis's life in the Narnia books. After all, he began a story about four children evacuated to a professor's house in the country at a time when four children were evacuated to his house. We know that he owned wardrobes somewhat similar to the one he described. (One of his wardrobes is now on display in the Wade Collection at Wheaton College.) The house the children explore, with its unexpected rooms and piles of books, is like his childhood home, Little Lea. The children visit Narnia when they are exploring inside because of the rain—Lewis remembers his own childhood as being mainly indoors, out of the Irish rain. The attic which Digory and Polly explore is similar to that of Little Lea, which was full of tunnels. Perhaps more significantly, Digory's mother is lying very sick, probably dying, when he goes to Narnia. We could say it is the most obvious sort of wish fulfillment for Digory to bring back the silver apple that makes his mother well; of course Lewis wanted to make his mother recover from cancer. But we should also notice that Aslan cries with Digory over his mother, that he is even sadder than Digory about it, and that Digory is not allowed to use unlawful means to make his mother well.

It is also pertinent that there are few scenes where children meet with their parents. Mr. and Mrs. Pevensie come into the story only by waving to the children in *The Last Battle*, after they, too, have died. In *Prince Caspian*, Caspian's father and mother are dead, and he is at the mercy of his uncle, who usurped the throne. At the beginning of *The Silver Chair*, Caspian, an old man whose wife has died, sets sail; his son, Rilian, does not meet him until the end, when he is carried ashore on a stretcher. Even that scene we see from a distance, watching (with Jill and Eustace) Caspian raise his hand, as he dies, to bless Rilian. Jill and Eustace later meet Caspian on Aslan's mountain, but Rilian does not. In *The Horse and His Boy* Shasta's abusive "father" turns out to have found him after a shipwreck; when Shasta is finally reunited with his true father, King Lune, his mother is already dead. And both of Tirian's parents are dead before the last battle. Lewis himself had so little experience of family life that he was no doubt wise (if it was a conscious choice) in avoiding those scenes.

Because *The Lion, the Witch, and the Wardrobe* has obvious affinities to the passion and resurrection of Christ, many readers assume that Lewis began with Christian truth, then thought of a story to sugarcoat it. That is almost the opposite of what he says happened. He says he saw pictures, pictures which began to join up into patterns: "a faun carrying an umbrella, a queen on a sledge, a magnificent lion. At first there wasn't even anything Christian about them; that element pushed itself in of its own accord."[6] Once he had the images, he had to search for a form, a literary type, which was appropriate. Because the story had no love interest and no deep psychological probing, the fairy tale suggested itself. And the more he thought about the fairy tale, the more he was intrigued by its brevity, its restrained descriptions, and its traditions.

After he had the pictures and a form to fit them, he had to ask himself if the story was worth writing. He says he began to realize that a fairy tale "could steal past a certain inhibition which had paralysed much of my own religion in childhood. Why did one find it so hard to feel as one was told one ought to feel about God or about the sufferings of Christ? I thought the chief reason was that one was told one ought to." But if the story were set in an imaginary world, one might be able to "steal past those watchful dragons."[7] Walter Hooper believes Lewis was successful. "By degrees which are often unnoticed by even the most cautious atheist, we progress from a love of Narnia, to a greater love of Aslan himself, to a sharp regret that there is no Aslan in this world, to a sudden recognition which makes the heart sing that there is an Aslan in this world—and then, if my own experience is any guide—Narnia and this world interlock and Aslan and Christ are seen as one."[8]

Yet any summary of the books makes the Christian parallels more obvious than they are in context; many people simply read the books for the story, unaware that there is any theological parallel. The closest Lewis ever comes to direct theological comment in the stories is at the end of *The Voyage of the Dawn Treader* when Aslan tells Lucy she will meet him, even though she cannot come back to Narnia. He is in their world too, but there he has another name. "You must learn to know me by that name. This was the very reason why you were brought to Narnia, that by knowing me here for a little, you may know me better there."

When one little girl wrote to Lewis asking Aslan's other name, he told her he wanted her to guess. "Has there never been anyone in this world who (1) Arrived at the same time as Father Christmas (2) Said he was the Son of the Great Emperor (3) Gave himself up for someone else's fault to be jeered at and killed by wicked people (4) Came to life again (5) Is sometimes spoken of as a Lamb.... Don't you really know His name in this world?"[9] Because there has been considerable discussion over whether or not the Narnian chronicles are a Christian allegory, Peter Schakel suggests that while the stories contain some elements of allegory, like the death and resurrection of Aslan, they are not themselves allegorical: "The Christian meaning is deeper and more subtle than the term allegory permits.... When the Chronicles are at their best, they do not just convey Christian meanings intellectually ... but ... communicate directly to the imagination and the emotions a sizable share of the central elements of the Christian faith."[10]

The death and resurrection of Aslan parallels the death and resurrection of Christ—parallels, not repeats or allegorizes. For Aslan is a lion, not a man; he dies only for Edmund's sin, not to redeem the world. The creation of Narnia parallels the Genesis account—but there are significant differences. The land already exists when the children arrive, so that the order of creation is significantly altered. The animals are shown climbing out of the earth in vivid detail. There is no creation of mankind, for people already exist on earth; the nearest parallel to the account in 2 Genesis is the calling of certain animals by Aslan, who breathes upon them, making them the talking animals. There is no temptation and fall as such in Narnia. Evil is brought in by the children in the person of the Witch, but her presence is only the indirect result of their sin (when Digory strikes the bell, awakening

Jadis in Charn). Jadis does attempt to get Digory to take an apple for himself, but he does not succumb; the garden itself is more like the Hesperides than like Eden.

The end of the world in *The Last Battle* obviously draws on elements from the Apocalypse of Saint John, such as the sounding of a trumpet and the falling stars, but some reverse evolution creeps in, with the giant lizards devouring the vegetation before they themselves die, and after the sun goes out, utter cold descends on Narnia. Instead of ending the world with fire, like the Apocalypse, Lewis ends the world with ice, like Norse mythology. After the door is shut, we do see a new Narnia, but it is a world of gardens, not the new Jerusalem of the Apocalypse; the garden always had a greater appeal to Lewis than the city as image of perfection. Lewis was perturbed by the simpering, wishy-washy way goodness was portrayed in most religious teaching, making children inevitably feel that it was much more glamorous to be bad. He agrees with the aesthetic tradition that art should teach by delighting, by making the reader enchanted with an ideal. Emotions should be evoked in order to develop the imagination, so that the person can conceive of a higher level of existence. "Imagination exists for the sake of wisdom or spiritual health—the rightness and richness of a man's total response to the world."[11] The correct responses to life, although they may now be mocked as "bourgeois" and "conventional," are not innate; they must be carefully taught. Therefore, the older poetry, like that of Milton and Spenser, constantly insisted on certain themes—"Love is sweet, death bitter, virtue lovely, and children or gardens delightful." These writers were setting up models for each new generation to follow.[12]

And this is what Lewis himself is doing. When he presents the heroism of Peter and the treachery of Edmund, what child would not rather be Peter than Edmund? When we see Lucy giving up her water ration for Eustace, after he has attempted to steal water from the crew, what child would not rather follow Lucy than Eustace? Again and again the children are confronted with situations when doing the right will be painful and difficult. Lucy is told she should have followed Aslan alone, even if the others were not willing to come; she must climb up to the magician's study to help the Dufflepuds no matter how frightened she is. Shasta must run to warn King Lune of Archenland, even though he is exhausted by his trip across the desert. Jill, Eustace, King Tirian, and Jewel must fight bravely, although all Narnia is being destroyed around them. And there are smaller decisions, too, which change the course of events. For example, Puddleglum stamps out the fire of the Emerald Witch, burning his feet, and so dissolves her enchantment.

These fairy tales react on the readers, making us understand and long for the Good. Most writers make the bad characters more interesting, lively, and far more attractive than the good ones; Lewis does not, for he has a stern and splendid vision of goodness. We have been deceived, he says, by "that prosaic moralism which confines goodness to the region of Law and Duty, which never lets us feel in our face the sweet air blowing from 'the land of righteousness,' never reveals that elusive Form which if once seen must inevitably be desired with all but sensuous desire—the thing (in Sappho's phrase) 'more gold than gold.'"[13]

There is terror and joy in the goodness portrayed in Narnia. Aslan, we are constantly reminded, "is not a tame lion." We would do well to be frightened of him, as Mrs. Beaver tells the children when they first hear his name. "If there's anyone who can appear before Aslan without their knees knocking, they're either braver than most or else just silly."

"Then he isn't safe?" said Lucy.

"Safe?" said Mr. Beaver. "Who said anything about safe? 'Course he isn't safe. But he's good. He's the King, I tell you."

Jill has a similar reaction when she first meets Aslan, who is lying by a stream. The lion speaks to her in a "heavy, golden voice," a voice that is "deeper, wilder and stronger" than a man's, inviting her to drink. When Jill asks if he would go away first, he only growls.

> "Will you promise not to—do anything to me, if I do come? said Jill.
> "I make no promise," said the Lion....
> "*Do* you eat girls?" she said.
> "I have swallowed up girls and boys, women and men, kings and emperors, cities and realms," said the Lion....
> "I daren't come and drink," said Jill.
> "Then you will die of thirst," said the Lion.
> "Oh dear!" said Jill, coming another step nearer. "I suppose I must go and look for another stream then."
> "There is no other stream," said the Lion.

This lion, who has swallowed kingdoms, who will not promise safety, is far from the "meek and mild" Jesus many children meet (and despise) in Sunday school. He is *not* a tame lion, and his ways are unpredictable. Aslan quietly disappears during the celebration of the crowning of the four kings and queens of Narnia; Mr. Beaver warns them that "He doesn't like being tied down—and of course he has other countries to attend to. It's quite all right. He'll often drop in. Only you mustn't press him. He's wild, you know."

What this means, in practice, is that the children are very often left in extremely dangerous situations without Aslan's help. In *Prince Caspian* Aslan stays with the girls, sending Peter and Edmund alone to the Mound to overcome the hag and the werewolf and then to plan the military campaign. It seems hopeless; their forces are besieged by a far greater army. Peter tells them that Aslan is close. "We don't know when he will act. In his time, no doubt, not ours. In the meantime he would like us to do what we can on our own." So Peter bravely challenges King Miraz to single combat with no assurance that he will survive the fight. As it turns out, of course, Aslan comes in time to save him, but Peter does not know that when he decides to fight.

Often the children are placed in tight places with no assurance that they will be delivered—sold to slavers, imprisoned by giants, tossed in a dreadful storm at sea—and always they are delivered, but only after they have shown considerable cleverness and bravery of their own. Always they are delivered, that is, except for *The Last Battle*. Aslan does not appear in that book when the centaur is slain; when the holy trees are chopped down, killing the dryads; when the talking animals are made slaves of the Calormenes; or when Ginger cleverly forestalls their attempt to prove that the Narnians were in bondage to a fake Aslan. Aslan does not appear even at the battle itself, when Jill, Eustace, Tirian, and Jewel die bravely in combat. Indeed, they do not see Aslan at all until they go through the stable door, into Aslan's own land; they must go by faith, not sight.

This combination of Aslan's apparent unpredictability and the children's absolute responsibility for their own actions disturbs some people, for there is no cheap grace in Narnia. Eustace becomes a dragon for his greed and nastiness; he can be cured only by letting Aslan tear off the dragon skin with his claws, piercing him to the heart. Aravis is clawed by a lion as she flees to warn Archenland of the coming attack, punished for allowing her slave girl to be beaten for her. Sometimes it is difficult to follow Aslan's commands. As he himself warns Jill, the signs that seem clear and easy to remember on his mountain will not be as she expects them to look when she goes down to Narnia. She is at fault in forgetting to repeat her signs each day as commanded, but the reader is apt to have some sympathy with Eustace for not recognizing Caspian as an old man and with Jill for not recognizing the trench as a letter of her sign. That is what life is like, Lewis would reply. We are required to be obedient, to be alert, to be courageous in the face of adversity, with no assurance that we will succeed or that we will be saved from suffering and death.

But death is not the worst of all fates in Narnia. Prince Rilian, as they attempt to escape the rising flood in the Underworld, exhorts Jill and Eustace to courage: "Whether we live or die Aslan will be our good lord."

(To which Puddleglum adds a typical comment: "And you must always remember there's one good thing about being trapped down here; it'll save funeral expenses.") Earlier Puddleglum had defeated the enchantment of the witch, who had almost convinced them that there was no such thing as Aslan: "I'm on Aslan's side even if there isn't any Aslan to lead it. I'm going to live as like a Narnian as I can even if there isn't any Narnia." In *The Last Battle* Roonwit the centaur sends a message to his lord with his dying breath "to remember that all worlds draw to an end and that noble death is a treasure which no one is too poor to buy."

Death is *not* the worst evil, for death in Aslan's service, as we learn in *The Last Battle*, leads to glory. The worst evil is to reject goodness and joy, to choose to separate oneself from Aslan. In *The Horse and His Boy* the results of such a choice are given a comic touch. When Rabadash rejects the forgiveness of the Narnian kings, he is turned into an ass, becoming a figure of mockery to his own people. Uncle Andrew has a similar humiliation in *The Magician's Nephew*, when the animals plant and water him. But such a choice can have terrifying consequences too. The ape and Rishda Tarkaan, who call on Tash, are given to him; Ginger is punished by ceasing to be a talking beast. And most poignant of all, Susan is no longer a friend of Narnia. For such is Lewis's power to stir our emotions that we suspend the usual judgment of our age, finding in Susan, the only one *not* killed in a train crash, the only tragedy.

There is no arbitrary justice in Narnia. Each one is punished only by being what he or she is. When the children ask about the apple the witch ate, Aslan tells them, "Things always work according to their nature.... All get what they want; they do not always like it." The apple she has stolen will give her endless days, but they will be only misery to her. On the other side we have Emeth in *The Last Battle*, who has truly sought goodness all his life. Although he thought he was serving Tash, he was serving Aslan, "for all find what they truly seek."

As Clyde Kilby, founder and curator of the Wade Collection, observes, in Narnia we are presented not so much with characters who are good or bad as with characters who are progressing toward one state or the other by their choices.[14] And a person can alter direction, as Eustace and Edmund did— and as Susan, more tragically, did. Lewis firmly believes in free will, that we each must daily make the choices which will lead us to one destiny or another. In *The Last Battle* each animal and person looks into the face of Aslan, then either departs into his shadow, or enters into Joy. In an essay called "The Weight of Glory" Lewis explains the New Testament warning that we must appear before God to meet our judgment: "In some sense ... we can be both banished from the presence of Him who is present everywhere and erased from the knowledge of Him who knows all. We can be left utterly and absolutely *outside*.... On the other hand, we can be called in, welcomed, received, acknowledged. We walk every day on the razor edge between these two incredible possibilities." Each person we meet, even the "dullest and most uninteresting ... may one day be a creature which, if you saw it now, you would be strongly tempted to worship, or else a horror and a corruption such as you now meet, if at all, only in a nightmare." We each become one or the other by our choices, as the children choose in Narnia.

As is fitting in a book for children, Lewis does not dwell on the fate of those who disappear into Aslan's shadow. Instead, he makes each reader feel what it is like to choose rightly, to be welcomed into Joy, and this vision is perhaps his greatest appeal as an author. "Eucatastrophe" is the word invented by Lewis's friend J. R. R. Tolkien to cover this kind of joy, which grows out of the acknowledgment of sorrow and death: "the good catastrophe, the sudden joyous 'turn' (for there is no true end to any fairy tale)" does not deny the possibility of failure. "It denies ... universal final defeat and in so far is *evangelium*, giving a fleeting glimpse of Joy, Joy beyond the walls of the world, poignant as grief."[15] Nihilists would call this escapism; Lewis and Tolkien call it realism. They knew that for the Christian there can be—ultimately—no tragedy, although events may now appear tragic from our perspective. The most obvious example of eucatastrophe in Narnia is the death and resurrection of Aslan, but in each of the stories a similar turn occurs, bringing deliverance or redemption in unanticipated ways. The structure of the plots themselves thus reflects both the genre, the fairy tale, and the theological position of the author, Christianity.

Joy is often evoked in Narnia through dance, celebration, and feasting. After Aslan's resurrection he takes the girls for a romp, round and round the hilltop, "now diving between them, now tossing them in the air with his huge and beautifully velveted paws and catching them again, and now stopping unexpectedly so that all three of them rolled over together in a happy laughing heap of fur and arms and legs." Lucy could never decide "whether it was more like playing with a thunderstorm or playing with a kitten." In Prince Caspian even the wild dances of Bacchus and his Maenads have their place. As the dancers circle Aslan and the girls, laughing and shouting out "Euan, euan, eu-oi-oi-oi," grape vines spring up everywhere, even in Lucy's hair. Later Susan whispers, "I wouldn't have felt very safe with Bacchus and all his wild girls if we'd met them without Aslan." Lucy sensibly replies, "I should think not." After the defeat of the Telmarines, comes the "magic dance of plenty" and the feast itself: "sides of roasted meat that filled the grove with delicious smell, and wheaten cakes and oaten cakes ... peaches, nectarines, pomegranates ... pyramids and cataracts of fruit." In *The Silver Chair* Jill watches the great snow dance of the dwarfs, as they throw snowballs through the patterns made by the dancers in the moonlight. The dance is so wild and splendid that "I wish you could see it for yourselves," the narrator tells us.

But the evocation of Joy reaches a higher level, a mythic level, in three of the books. In *The Magician's Nephew* things are created "out of the lion's head…. When you listened to his song you heard the things he was making up: when you looked round, you saw them." His song is so beautiful, Digory "could hardly bear it," an evocation of the beauty that stabs like pain. Later Polly and Digory journey to that most mythic of places, the enclosed garden, with its echoes of Eden and the garden of the Hesperides. Their first hint of Paradise is the smell, "warm and golden," the air so sweet, it "almost brought the tears to your eyes." The sense of awe is increased by the placement of the garden on top of a very steep, smooth hill; it has a high wall around it, and a golden gate that magically swings open for those who should enter. The great silver apples, with a light of their own, are watched by a wonderful bird instead of the traditional dragon, but they are watched. The punishment for stealing is to find the heart's desire and have it bring despair.

The end of *The Voyage of the Dawn Treader* is a more powerful evocation of Joy. After they leave Ramandu and his daughter, there are no more adventures per se, just a growing sense of wonder, one of the most difficult effects to achieve in writing. Nothing much happens, except for seeing the Sea People; they just sail on toward the end of the world. Then Reepicheep falls overboard, tastes the water, and repeats the prophecy: "Where the waves grow sweet ... There is the utter East." They all drink the water. Caspian says "I'm not sure that it isn't going to kill me. But it is the death I would have chosen—if I'd known about it till now." The water is like light, making them able to look directly at the sun glowing on the white fields of water lilies. Everyone is filled with the kind of excitement that brings a hush as they are surrounded by the smell of the lilies, a smell Lucy said was a "fresh, wild, lonely smell that seemed to get into your brain and make you feel that you could go up mountains at a run." Their joy is so intense that they feel they cannot stand much more, yet they do not want it to stop. When the *Dawn Treader* must turn back, the children and Reepicheep continue east toward the light, toward a range of mountains rising beyond the world (no doubt the same unimaginably high peaks where Jill and Eustace meet Aslan, his own country). A breeze from the east brings them a smell and a musical sound. Afterwards Lucy could only say, "'It would break your heart.' 'Why', said I, 'was it so sad?' 'Sad! No,' said Lucy." There they meet a lamb who feeds them a breakfast of fish, as the disciples had been fed by the risen Christ who was called the Lamb of God. Then the lamb turns a tawny gold, becoming Aslan himself. It is a fitting climax to the silence and the piercing sweetness.

The Last Battle intensifies this feeling of Joy. When the kings and queens are mourning Narnia, they turn—and recognize the new Narnia, the same but more splendid than the old. Lord Digory explains that the Narnia they had known was only a shadow or a copy of the true Narnia, which has always existed in Aslan's real world. It is different, but only "as a real thing is from a shadow or as waking life is from a dream." Jewel the unicorn understands: "I have come home at last! This is my real country! ... This is the land I have been looking for all my life, though I never knew it till now. The reason why we loved the old Narnia is that it sometimes looked a little like this." He leads the cry of "Come further up, come further in" as the children run up mountains and swim up waterfalls, exulting in their new bodies in this fresh new (and yet eternal) land. They find magical fruit—and know that this time it is for them. At the golden gates of the Garden, Reepicheep welcomes them. They meet all those they have loved who had died, but this is not the end; it is the beginning "of the Great Story, which no one on earth has read: which goes on for ever: in which every chapter is better than the one before."

The vision, presented in the guise of a fairy tale, is all but prophetic. No one who experiences it fully will ever again assume that goodness must be dull, for to experience it fully is to experience Joy. In creating this effect, Lewis is drawing on the major symbols of Western tradition—the quest, the garden, the worlds of Greek, Norse, and Celtic mythology, in addition to the Bible. Of these traditions, the Arthurian is probably the most important to our appreciation of Narnia.

The court of Cair Paravel is apparently derived from the Arthurian court, perhaps as described at the beginning of *Sir Gawain and the Green Knight*, an English romance of the fourteenth century which Lewis loved. He said that he borrowed two of Aslan's characteristics, his brightness and sweet odor, from the Grail itself; the mystic table and stone knife also come from the Grail legends, which are part of the Arthurian myth.[16] The clothes, the armor, the weapons, and the pavilions are medieval; medieval, too, is the ideal of chivalry which the children and the Narnia kings seek to fulfill.

In an essay called the "Importance of an Ideal," Lewis quotes a description of Sir Lancelot, the noblest knight of Arthur's court: "Thou wert the meekest man that ever ate in hall among ladies; and thou west the sternest knight to thy mortal foe that ever put spear in the rest."[17] The importance of this ideal is the contrary demands it makes; the knight "is not a compromise or happy mean between ferocity and meekness; he is fierce to the nth and meek to the nth." The naturally meek person is not naturally fierce in battle; the naturally fierce person is not naturally gentle in peace. What is needed to preserve civilization (Lewis is writing during the darkest days of World War II) is someone who values learning and courtesy, and yet is courageous enough to defend them against attack. Otherwise, he says, history becomes a series of raids on civilization by hardy barbarians; when the barbarians become civilized, they become soft, and then the cycle is repeated. He admits that the ideal exemplified by Lancelot may be unattainable, may be escapism. "But it is 'escapism' in a sense never dreamed of by those who use that word; it offers the only possible escape from a world divided between wolves who do not understand, and sheep who cannot defend, the things which make life desirable."[18] The kings and queens of Narnia strive for that ideal balance, a balance that can be attained only by the most strenuous efforts. They endanger their lives to save their subjects from the Calormenes, or from the White Witch; they are compassionate to those who are weaker and forgiving to those who repent; they are strong in battle when it cannot be avoided, yet delight in music, in dance, and in listening to the stories of the bards. They seek peace, yet do not shrink from wars brought against them. And they never turn down an adventure, with the one exception of the Island of Dreams, a place no human can face.

Reepicheep the mouse, a noble warrior who goes into battle with his slender rapier and is aghast when his king turns back from the Island of Dreams, is given specifically Arthurian attributes. He challenges Eustace to a duel after Eustace has swung him around by his tail, a challenge the boy must take seriously. When Reepicheep plays chess, he loses because he sends his knight into incredible danger: "This happened because he had momentarily forgotten it was a game of chess and was thinking of a real battle and making the knight do what he would certainly have done in its place. For his mind was full of forlorn hope, death or glory charges, and last stands." As the Arthurian knights sought the Grail, so Reepicheep sought Aslan's country; the fulfillment of his quest was prophesied in his infancy. When the water is too shallow for the *Dawn Treader* as it draws near Aslan's country, Reepicheep takes off his sword, flinging it across the lilied sea; it lands upright, the hilt above the water in a clear allusion to Arthur's sword held up by the Lady of the Lake. Then he disappears over the wave; later he appears in the garden of the New Narnia, even as Arthur is said to have disappeared, and, according to *That Hideous Strength*, lives now in "the cup-shaped land of Aphallin, beyond the seas of Lur in Perelandra," where Ransom will join him at the end of that story.

All this chivalry, involving as it does sword fights and other violent combat, has caused some to say the books are not suitable for children, but Lewis answered this charge in his defense of the fairy tale. It would be false to pretend to children that they are not born into a world of death and violence. "Since it is so likely that they will meet cruel enemies, let them at least have heard of brave knights and heroic courage.... Let there be wicked kings and beheadings, battles and dungeons, giants and dragons, and let villains be soundly killed at the end of the book." Do not attempt to banish the terrors. "For in the fairy tales, side by side with the terrible figures, we find the immemorial comforters and protectors, the radiant ones."[19] Narnia is full of wicked kings, dragons, giants, and violence, but it is difficult to imagine more valiant heroes than the children who become its kings and queens, or a more radiant protector than Aslan.

Lewis is able to make us believe in this world made of pieces of Christian doctrine, Arthurian legend, Norse mythology, and English boarding schools because it is a real world, full of homey detail. We believe in it because we have walked through it. We know just how Mr. Tumnus has arranged the furniture in his cave, how he lights a lamp with a flaming piece of wood from the fire that he holds in tongs, how the tears run down his cheeks and trickle off the end of his nose. When Susan helps Mrs. Beaver with the potatoes, she drains them, then puts them back in the empty pot to dry on the side of the range. We so easily picture her fixing the potatoes in just that way that we suspend our disbelief that she is visiting beavers.

When Jill, Eustace, and Tirian spend the night in the tower, Puzzle and Jewel decide they would be more comfortable outside. "This perhaps was just as well, for a Unicorn and a fat, full-grown donkey indoors always make a room feel rather crowded." Well, yes, of course they would. But the use of the word "always" makes us feel that this is a normal social situation. We know what a centaur has for breakfast, filling its man-stomach with porridge, fish, kidney, bacon, omelette, cold ham, toast, marmalade, coffee, and beer, then its horse-stomach with grazing, hot mash, oats, and a bag of sugar. We know that no one would dare suggest putting saddles on centaurs, but when they courteously offer to carry Jill and Eustace, they speak to the children in a very grave and polite way, telling them herbs and roots, the influences of the planets, and the nine names of Aslan. These details are not explicit in Greek mythology, but they do fit in with what we know about centaurs from Homer.

We always know what the characters have to eat, whether it is boiled potatoes, marmalade rolls, or the delicate earths favored by the trees; we are told where the children wash (usually in a stream), and what kind of bed they have, whether it is a stone floor, heather, or a giant's nursery. We know whether the path is slippery shale, soft grass, or steep rocks, so of course we feel that we have walked it.

We know Narnia as Lewis says we know the world of Spenser's *Faerie Queene* or Robinson Crusoe's island; we have trudged from one end to the other on our own feet. If dropped suddenly into Narnia, careful readers could find the way from Cair Paravel to the Fords of Beruna. And these readers would have a clear understanding of what Aslan would expect of them if they were offered enchanted candy by a wicked witch, or were attacked by Calormenes, or were faced with a water shortage at sea. One critic complained to Lewis that fairy tales were not practical, they could not teach a child to build a boat. No, Lewis replied, but they would teach him how to act if he ever found himself on a sinking ship.

NOTES

1. Walter Hooper, *Past Watchful Dragons* (New York: Macmillan Publishing Company, 1979), p. 30. This is an expanded version of the essay "Past Watchful Dragons" included in *Imagination and the Spirit*, ed., Charles Huttar (Grand Rapids, Michigan: William B. Eerdmans Publishing Company, 1971).

2. Hooper, *Dragons*, p. 63. That fragment was apparently set aside, somehow surviving Lewis's habit of discarding manuscripts; the only other Narnia manuscript extant is a five-page fragment of Eustace's diary, an earlier draft of the version published in *The Voyage of the Dawn Treader*.

3. Green and Hooper, pp. 242–248.

4. Hooper, *Dragons*, p. 32.

5. Hooper, *Dragons*, pp. 41–44, reproduces Lewis's "Outline of Narnian History so far as it is known."

6. C.S. Lewis, *Of Other Worlds: Essays and Stories*, ed., Walter Hooper (London: Geoffrey Bles, 1966), p. 36.

7. Ibid., p. 37.

8. Walter Hooper, Preface to *The Lion of Judah in Never-Never Land* by Kathryn Lindskoog (Grand Rapids, Michigan: William B. Eerdmans Publishing Company, 1973), p. 13 (italics his).

9. C.S. Lewis, letter to an American girl, printed in Lindskoog, p. 16.

10. Peter Schakel, *Reading with the Heart: The Way into Narnia* (Grand Rapids, Michigan: William B. Eerdmans, 1979), p. 17. Schakel's perceptive study includes an archetypal analysis of the narratives stressing such patterns as initiation of the hero, descent and ascent, voyage, creation and dissolution, and the four phases of Northrup Frye's monomyth.

11. C.S. Lewis, *A Preface to Paradise Lost* (London: Oxford University Press, 1942), p. 54.

12. Ibid., p. 57.

13. C.S. Lewis, Preface to *George MacDonald: An Anthology* (London: Geoffrey Bles, 1946), p. xxxiv.

14. Clyde S. Kilby, *The Christian World of C.S. Lewis* (Grand Rapids, Michigan: William B. Eerdmans Publishing Company, 1964), p. 141.

15. J.R.R. Tolkien, "On Fairy Stories," in *Essays Presented to Charles Williams* (London: Oxford University Press, 1947), p. 81.

16. Hooper, *Dragons*, p. 90.

17. C.S. Lewis, "Notes on the Way," *Time and Tide* 21 (17 August 1940), p. 109.

18. Ibid., p. 111.

19. Lewis, *Of Other Worlds*, pp. 31–32.

DONALD E. GLOVER

The Chronicles of Narnia, *1950–1956:*
An Introduction

The history of the composition of these seven "children's" stories has been drawn in considerable detail by Walter Hooper in "Past Watchful Dragons" and more recently in *A Biography*, so that I will not rehearse these facts in detail, being satisfied merely to point to significant aspects which relate to this study.[1]

John Haigh, one of Lewis's critics, has suggested that Lewis moved into the new form of children's fantasy because he wanted to avoid repetition.[2] Lewis was, he felt, saying the same things but simply using another vehicle. Lewis himself commented that his children's stories were side chapels off the nave of his basic work, which suggests an acknowledged consistency running through all the fiction.[3] Even Robson grudgingly admits that these stories did embody "things" which Lewis was profoundly sincere about though the form was inadequate to what Lewis tries so hard to make it accomplish.[4]

There can be little question of Lewis's sincerity and seriousness in writing these books. Numerous letters attest to his interest in catching his readers, of all ages, off guard. "If I am now good for anything it is for catching the reader unawares—thro' fiction and symbol."[5] "The fairy-tale version of the Passion in *The Lion* etc. works in the way you describe because—tho' this sounds odd—it by-passes one's reverence and piety.... Make it a fairy-tale and the reader is taken off his guard (Unless ye become as little children....)."[6] His credo, stated in the letter to the Milton Society, makes clear that the imaginative man was "he who brought me, in the last few years to write the series of Narnian stories for children; not asking what children want and then endeavoring to adapt myself (this was not needed) but because the fairy tale was the genre best fitted for what I wanted to say...."[7]

The Lion, the Witch and the Wardrobe began, we know, with a picture of a Faun carrying an umbrella and standing in a snowy wood. The picture had been in Lewis's mind since he was about sixteen.[8] An early draft was begun in 1939 and put aside until the mid-1940s. Stimulated by reading Roger Lancelyn Green's *The Wood That Time Forgot*, Lewis had more mental pictures of a queen on a sledge and a magnificent lion and nightmares about lions.[9] He read his developing story to Green, who liked it although Tolkien did not, and Lewis records that with the entry of the lion, all the rest of the story came together as the Lion soon pulled the other six Narnian stories in after Him.[10] He began to fill in the events before the action of *The Lion, the Witch and the Wardrobe* but produced only the Lefay fragment.[11] The Lefay fragment, unpublished, is Lewis's first attempt at what later became in completely revised form, *The Magician's Nephew. Prince Caspian* (other titles: *Drawn into Narnia, A Horn in Narnia*) was finished by December 1949, and by February 1950, *The Voyage of the 'Dawn Treader'* was ready in manuscript. July 1950 saw the completion of the manuscript of *The Horse and His Boy* (other titles: *Narnia and the North, The Horse and the Boy*); November brought *The Silver Chair*. By October 1951, a version of *The Magician's Nephew* was shown to Green, but Lewis finished *The Last Battle* in March 1953 before making the revisions suggested by Green to *The Magician's Nephew*.[12]

There is little else that can be drawn from firsthand sources concerning the genesis of these stories. We may speculate on why Lewis came to write them when he did: the wartime evacuee children in his home in 1939, his lifelong admiration for Kenneth Grahame, George MacDonald, and E. Nesbit, the resurgence of his interest during the late forties after the success of *The Screwtape Letters* and the space trilogy in a form he last used in 1939, and his growing conviction that fantasy could act as a spiritual preparation for young minds. Retrospectively, in a series of essays on the subject of stories and fairy tales, Lewis made his intentions in using the genre quite clear. Moving from the general "On Stories," through "On Three Ways of Writing for Children," to the specific "Sometimes Fairy Stories May Say Best What's to be Said," we arrive at the following rationale for the writing and reading of stories. One might be tempted to say "use" of stories had Lewis not forbidden that as a possibility.

Stories move us by casting actuality into another perspective, catching us off guard, challenging our deeper imagination and sending us back with a renewed pleasure to the actual world from our sojourn in what Lewis calls plausible and imaginatively moving other worlds.[13] Stories, unlike realistic novels, do not set themselves up as actuality, fact or information, but they do intend to give us an exciting glimpse of the "as if," a sense of the unexpected, an adventure into possibilities, an image of what reality might be like at a more central region.[14] Art, the art of the story specifically in this case, is an invitation to come further in and higher up. We are not, as F. R. Leavis suggests, attracted to the thing in itself, its plot, characters, symbols, irony, or structure. Through the artistry, the "net" of plot or adventure and excitement, we are drawn out of ourselves and into meaning which we had not dreamed of before. Here it is tempting to suggest that the whole process of transcendence which is central to the *Chronicles of Narnia* is a metaphor for Lewis's mature view of the art of fiction, and that these stories were written to exemplify this theory, further in and higher up symbolizing the author's method and the reader's road as well as the evolution within each book and across the *Chronicles* as a whole. But an honest look at the facts forbids such neat theorizing, and the second essay on how one writes for children indicates that Lewis was observing what had happened in his own case and that of other writers, not giving us the outline of how he went about writing fairy tales. It is this delight in organic creativity which throughout acts as a balance to Lewis's otherwise overpowering rationality. He makes no attempt to explain the mechanics of writing stories or how an author succeeds in moving his readers. We are given no practical advice.

Having firmly established children as legitimate readers, not a group to be written at or down to, Lewis defends his use of the fairy tale on the basis of its appropriateness to his subject. His defense rests on the premise that life and art are organic and evolutionary. The creative acts of writing and reading are also evolutionary, a progression from meaning to meaning. Lewis's statements on his own writing and the evidence of his work show that writing is as much a journey of discovery for Lewis as reading his work is for us. He discounted, especially in the *Chronicles*, any preconceived program which Narnia would flesh out, and the facts of composition recently revealed in the Hooper and Green *Biography* bear him out.

The form attracted Lewis, he said, because of its restrictiveness, on the one hand, and on the other, the opportunity which fantasy and the fairy tale offered him to convey meaning in a way which is generally unavailable to the novelist. He particularly appreciated the enforced condensation, the check on his expository demon, the curtailment of length and scope, the exclusion of erotic love, the equally balanced chapter lengths, the restraint on description, and the virtual exclusion as he said of analysis, digression, reflection, and "gas."[15] Fantasy offered the chance, when presented in fairy tales, for using as Lewis said "giants and dwarfs and talking beasts.... an admirable hieroglyphic which conveys psychology, types of character, more briefly than novelistic presentation and to readers whom novelistic presentation could not yet reach."[16]

It seems fair to suggest, having seen in some detail what Lewis's fiction had developed into by this point, that he had come back, in a sense, to write the sort of fiction which had intrigued and delighted him as a child. But that was not his only motive. He had much to say about the achievement of Joy and to an audience whom from his own experience he knew to be turning away both from the literature which could suggest the sources of Joy and from the Church which should teach it. His motives for writing may have been multiple. First he wanted to convey the pictures he saw. Next came the expression of longing, the *askesis*, the spiritual exercise now identified with the creative act of fiction writing; third was the challenge of whether he could keep in control, not letting either description or argument overbalance each other. Finally he wanted to steal past the ever watchful dragons, the stereotyped responses to religion. Perhaps there were other reasons hidden even from himself: a desire to rival the *Hobbit*, a wish to emulate MacDonald, the psychological insistence of his pictures, dreams, and nightmares. We cannot know with certainty what all his motives were. The result, however, was Narnia, which expresses thematically and artistically all that is central to Lewis's art and theory of literature and which many critics feel will be that part of his fiction which gains him permanent literary recognition.[17]

Since I wish to trace the evolution of Lewis's technique as he wrote the stories without losing the overall pattern which emerges from reading the seven in the order he recommended, I will begin where he began, with *The Lion, the Witch and the Wardrobe* and deal with *The Magician's Nephew* just before *The Last Battle*, putting the framing books side by side in their compositional order. In the final analysis, I think this will do less damage than might be supposed since the greatest affinity is between *The Magician's Nephew* and *The Last Battle*, with the other five books falling into an order with an inner consistency. I do not propose separate chapters on each book since I have found them exemplary of Lewis's organic creativity, and thus I think they would profit by examination in one long chapter with subsections devoted to individual works. Critics have already cited many sources and parallels to other works admired or read by Lewis, so I shall confine myself to a study of his technique and themes in the light of the earlier chapters on his work to this point. Much has been written about the Christian allegory and symbolism to be found in Narnia; again, I leave the reader to other readily available sources since my attention will be directed toward the integration of meaning in the form Lewis chose rather than an exclusive selection of meanings.

THE LION, THE WITCH AND THE WARDROBE, 1950

As Lewis paused on the verge of a new creative adventure in the use of the imagination, the form he had chosen for what he had to say must have presented certain problems. In his earlier fiction, we have noted his use of traditional forms and the growing skill he displayed in adapting them to his particular purposes. Lewis was not a technical innovator, the creator of new forms. In fact, his belief in God's unique role as creator rather denied that possibility to him.[1] Authors never originate anything in the sense of creating it; they rearrange the pieces in new kaleidoscopic combinations. Bunyan stands behind *The Pilgrim's Regress*, Wells and Lindsay behind the space trilogy, and Milton lurks behind *Perelandra*. There are sources, if we want them, for everything Lewis wrote. So with fairy tales, there were daunting examples before Lewis as he began, tales he had admired as child and man; and his challenge was to offer something distinctly new, something imaginatively fresh. There were the problems of keeping the story simple without juvenilizing it; of treating his readers with respect without giving them analysis, digression, reflection, and "gas."

The form he chose was conventional: four children, an adventure in an old and mysterious house, and an unexpected journey to another world. There are echoes, as critics have noted, of E. Nesbit and others, but once the adventure begins, we start to see Lewis's distinctive quality.

One striking feature of his prose throughout the *Chronicles* is its consistent simpleness and evenness. There is a reasonableness and steadiness about the measured and balanced sentences which reassure us of the reality of whatever Lewis narrates or describes, whether it is the cold white arm of Jadis revealed to Edmund or the whiskery face of a beaver which greets Lucy upon her waking. Lewis evidently enjoyed the discipline which helped to maintain this basic tone because he repeatedly mentions it as a positive feature of writing these books. The calm, measured movement of the story, eminently readable by children and adults, moves the narrative along at a steady pace and provides that solid basis, the created reality, from which Lewis can depart on occasion without shaking our belief in his manufactured fantasy. The sentences are simple and short, the language carefully chosen to be expressive but not showy or eccentric. It never draws attention to itself, which is a great credit in a genre where some authors depend for the effect of their tale on the uniqueness of their descriptive language.

The descriptive technique used by Lewis here and throughout the *Chronicles* is worth studying at the outset since it carries the burden of convincing us of the reality of these adventures and is the heart of Lewis's technique for touching our deeper imagination. To say that the whole thing "began with a picture" may seem trite and repetitious, but it is the key to Lewis's method. We know that the whole process of creation of these stories was the accretion of pictures and their coalescence into thematic unity—a moving and evolving picture. This is much more an organic method than most critics are willing to allow Lewis, but we must, I think, accept his honest statement that he began not with a full-blown chronicle of Christian themes for children in mind but with pictures which formed a pattern and were fitted to a theme which had run through all of his earlier fiction. The technique depends on appealing to the reader's feelings through descriptions and thus moving him to thought by use of sublimity, as described by Longinus rather than by dialogue, as used by Socrates. The dialogue in all the stories is less effective generally than the descriptive sections, especially where the children are first introduced in *The Lion, the Witch and the Wardrobe*, and we sense that Lewis had never listened closely to how children say things though he caught what they would talk about. Later when they become kings and queens, their courtly language strikes a strange note, but by then we are so deep in the fantasy, the "as if," that we are hardly bothered by that incongruity. When the Witch, Aslan, and all the created world of Narnia appear, Lewis is on new ground and makes the speech of his creatures believable and appropriate.

John Haigh has pointed out the fact that images of sound and color predominate in Lewis's descriptions of Narnia; the aural and visual are used to present us, especially young readers, with the series of sensations which Haigh feels are characteristic of Lewis's method here.[2] He suggests that children respond to the narrative and descriptive interest; whereas, adults prefer the moral and spiritual vision.[3] On the contrary, it seems clear that you cannot have one without the other, and that in fact the strength of the method lies in the embodiment of meaning in imaginative description that is clear, moving, and credible.

Lewis's method parallels the already discussed organic creative process of the novels in a now more condensed and organized fashion. We are presented with pictures which create the most memorable and effective impression of Narnia; Edmund meeting Jadis, the children confronted by Aslan, Aslan being comforted by Lucy and Susan, and his death on the stone table. The pictures are drawn together by a slowly evolving theme which only at the climax reveals its central significance. The organic process works to draw us into Lewis's vision naturally, and it is the aptness of the pictures and the appropriateness of their prose description that does what Lewis wants, drawing us further in and higher up.

The plot structure follow that of Lewis's earlier fiction: a straight line, single thread development of tensions centering on a journey into the unknown, on tasks and choices which determine the outcome and establish turning points thematically, and on the lives of certain characters. A simple paralleling of two characters develops through reciprocating scenes where analogous actions serve as ironic commentary on the choices of these characters. The climax is a battle setting to rights the near catastrophe which precedes it, and the story ends in Tolkien's words, "eucatastrophically" or happily, sliding gradually off the tension of epic acts to the low normalcy of real childhood games in an old house, and thus coming full circle. This pattern is used with slight variations—the journey to Narnia is always managed in a different fashion each time—in each novel as it had been in *The Pilgrim's Regress* and the space trilogy and to an extent in *The Great Divorce*. *The Screwtape Letters* is the only work which lacks it. The plot pattern is hardly unique and shares such diverse probable sources as epic, and Arthurian legend, and medieval romance, as well as the romantic novel. The basic pattern of journey, perilous choice, battle, and victory are not new, but Lewis molds them to his purpose with great skill. Balance is one key feature of his method. Chapters are carefully balanced for length and ease in reading. Scenes are given equivalent scope so that there is little lingering over particular scenes of the sort that retard the movement of *Perelandra*. The movement is consistently forward with few episodic interruptions, the only serious one being the appearance of Father Christmas, who nearly jolts us back to London and whose intrusion may or may not improve with additional readings.

Turning to the book, Lewis shows us his considerable skill in opening the story. From the altogether understated beginning, "once there were four children whose names were ..." through their stilted initial dialogue, he quickly and expertly draws us into Narnia with Lucy, the sweetest and most susceptible, youngest of the Pevensie children with whom we identify and through whose eyes we judge what we see.[4] Her innocence and trust are the spectacles through which we see the unfolding action. Lewis could hardly have been more clever in disarming an adult's skepticism and disbelief. The wardrobe is a master stroke though it was to cause Lewis some worry resulting in the humorously overstated warning that it is very silly to shut yourself in a wardrobe, even if it is not a magic one. The genius of Lewis's choice of event and description lies in their appropriateness. Perhaps because he knew the archetypal state of childhood so well, though he knew little about children from firsthand experience such as one has as a parent, he invariably chose the appropriate image, action, or response for his children. Lucy's response to finding Narnia rather than the back of the wardrobe is the most natural thing in the book, and though she is surprised by Tumnus, she is not frightened but rather intrigued, and so she goes further in. The progress of the story and of the *Chronicles* as a whole is "further in," a phrase repeated in "She took a step further in" (p. 6), "Further in, come further in. Right in here" (p. 62), and symbolized in many ways by Edmund's descent into misery and Lucy's ascent to Aslan, and by the physical movement into Narnia and to Cair Paravel on the eastern shore from the western wilds; and finally by the spiritual penetration into the mystery of the incarnation and crucifixion.

Lucy, after a meeting with the faun reminiscent of that of Alice with the White Rabbit, returns to the "real" world, and Lewis cleverly plays off our budding allegiance to Lucy and Narnia, of which we have had just the taste to whet our appetite, against the disbelief of the other children, especially Edmund. Her adventure sets up theirs, and the questioning of her honesty firmly establishes us on her side and certifies Narnia's reality. The parallel scene done with such effect is Edmund's antithetical meeting with Jadis. Lewis uses the children's reaction to climate and food as a barometer of their spiritual condition, most obviously seen later in Eustace who is seasick and then dragonish. Lucy, without a coat, does not react to the cold and is treated to a lovely English tea and chat by the fire. Edmund, who went wrong by going to a "horrid school," finds himself in a strange, cold, quiet place, and throughout his adventures in Narnia he suffers from the cold. His alienation from his brother and sisters is reflected in his lonely rationalizing while awaiting the Witch. Their interview, ironically and almost humorously in contrast to Lucy's with Tumnus, sets up the basic antithesis between greed and pity, egotism and self-sacrifice, which governs the thematic development of the book. Food becomes the principal symbol of the difference between Edmund and Lucy.

The Turkish Delight is another master stroke. Whatever it was in Lewis's childhood, it is in fact now a highly overrated sweet, in my opinion. The name, with its Oriental and romantic overtones, suggests more than the product gives, and Lewis uses this idea simply but with great force in making the Witch appeal first to Edmund's greed and then to his desire for power. "I want a nice boy whom I could bring up as a Prince and who would be King of Narnia when I am gone.... I think I would like to make you the Prince— some day.... You are to be the Prince and—later on—the King; ..." (p. 34). The meeting which parallels Lucy's first encounter with Tumnus where he admits his temptation to do her harm and is forgiven, discloses Edmund's ready acceptance of betrayal in order to gain self-satisfaction and power. And with the advent of the Witch, we have Lewis's first maleficent fairy tale creation, caught in the phrase, "You shall know us better hereafter" (p. 28).

In the chapter, "Back on This Side of the Door," Lewis gives us further preparation for the final plunge of all four into the other world and allows Edmund to clinch his horridness and the Professor to prove logically that Narnia is a possibility. The third return is to a landscape now familiar to the reader, and Lewis cleverly shifts the basis of suspense to a larger arena: the Witch versus Aslan, Winter versus Spring, Old Law versus New Law. The children are immediately caught up in a momentous action, an epic struggle beyond their small sphere. Though they have roles to play: Edmund the betrayer, a Judas; Peter the Knight, a St. George against the Dragon; Lucy and Susan as the two Marys; the action has swept them up into great events, the significance of which they can hardly realize. Lewis had used the same technique in all three of the planetary novels, perhaps with greatest success in *Perelandra*. Here he gains the advantage of deepening and heightening the meaning of the adventure by suiting the tasks more judiciously to the capacities of those on whom they fall. Unlike our reaction to Ransom, who must be canonized and Weston who is dehumanized, with these children, we can place ourselves in the Beavers' paws and see if we can "get through."

The devastation of Tumnus's cave puts the homeliness of the Beavers' den in the delicious peril of the Witch's wrath; and the dinner, a classic in Lewis's fiction and children's fiction at large, is too long to quote but stands as an example of the effective reinforcement of meaning by description. The simple, domestic, homey fare echoes the mood and emphasizes the trust Lewis places at the center of his fellowship of animals and men. Edmund significantly trusts the Witch who appears human but is clearly unnatural ("Her face was white—not merely pale, but white like snow or paper or icing sugar, except for her very red mouth" p. 27). The Beavers reveal that she is nonhuman, suggesting that there isn't a drop of real human blood in her (p. 77). Beaver advises "when you meet anything that's going to be Human and isn't yet, or used to be Human once and isn't now, or ought to be Human and isn't, you keep your eyes on it and feel for your hatchet" (p. 78). The robin which Edmund suggests is a false guide, is true to nature and leads the children to safety. Nature is to be trusted, and it is the unnatural distortion of seasons which symbolizes the Witch's desire to destroy humanity. Freezing represents death and cold represents the inhibition of natural joy.

The choice on Edmund's part to defect initiates his journey to the Witch, paralleled by the children's journey into spring, and the ironic reversal of his expectations of a reward. He gets dry, stale bread instead of Turkish Delight, and his "reward" is played off against the Beavers' true meal. Edmund's policy and guile are appropriately rewarded as is the trust the children place in the Beavers.

The mention of Aslan's name, which has such a pronounced effect on all children, initiates the suspense with which Lewis prepares for his later appearance. By using this device, the mysterious effect of a "sacred" name, Lewis produces an aura of meaning around Aslan which is reinforced by the Beavers' explanation of what he is: "'Course he isn't safe. But he's good. He's the King, I tell you" (p. 76). As the antagonist of the Witch, the savior of Narnia, son of the Emperor beyond the sea, the King of the Beasts, he becomes the focus of our anticipation, as he is for the children, and ultimately the ruling symbol of the *Chronicles of Narnia*.

It is not for me to try to explain why Aslan works. An individual reader's reaction to an animal figure endowed with human and symbolic qualities is a very personal thing. Who would try to explain why we feel so drawn to Pooh, Tigger, Piglet, Toad, Mole, or even Badger? The essence of their ultimate appeal very probably springs from that personal response lying beyond the reach of analysis or critical dissection and examination. By the time the children hear Aslan's name, we are comfortably settled in a world of talking animals and a maleficent witch. We simply take it on faith that Aslan's very name has the power to affect the children, and even though we may not feel it, Lewis invites us to associate that feeling with one he knows we have all had.

> Perhaps it has sometimes happened to you in a dream that someone says something which you don't understand but in the dream it feels as if it had some enormous meaning—either a terrifying one which turns the whole dream into a nightmare or else a lovely meaning too lovely to put into words, which makes the dream so beautiful that you remember it all your life and are always wishing you could get into the dream again. It was like that now. (p. 64)

Thus Aslan becomes the embodiment of longing. He is the satisfaction of all longing, the source of all longing. He is good and terrible, huge, solemn, playful, golden, king, son, sun, beast, god, and father. He is nothing other than Lewis's Joy incarnate in a concrete form. And although Lucy and Susan can clutch at and romp with him on his reappearance, he disappears at the end before the festivities at Cair Paravel.

It is Lewis's craftsmanship in molding Aslan to his purpose more than any sources he may have drawn upon, like the Lion of Judah, which produces this astonishing and compelling centerpiece for the *Chronicles*. We are two thirds of the way through the book before we come face to face, and the extended preparation is justified by the effect of that meeting. Unlike the Witch who appears unannounced and is then described, we find Lewis first describing Aslan's effect and then showing him in fact. This preparation, perhaps symbolizing the *praeparatio evangelicum* which the book witnesses, is carefully keyed to the shifting balance of power reflected in climatic change. Edmund's cold and lonely journey to the Witch's house, his disfiguring of the stone lion, and his "reward" are placed in contrast to the coming of Father Christmas with rewards for trust in the particular form of utilitarian implements such as, sewing machine and sluice gate for the Beavers and sword, dagger, horn, and potion for the children's use in the coming battle.

Frankly, Father Christmas, for all Lewis's attempts at his rehabilitation as a Christian figure, strikes the wrong note, reminding us all too forcefully of childish pleasures and frivolous fantasies. In the freshly created newness of Narnia, he brings us with a shock back to reality, breaking the spell, if only momentarily.[5] It may be our fault as modern readers who associate St. Nicholas with the commercial Santa, but the fact remains that there is a momentary bump even though Lewis makes the occasion rather solemn and the gifts useful.

Lewis's descriptive power is at its height in the noises and sights of spring. Symbolically the turning point, the thematic shift of power from the Witch to Aslan, it is the heart of the book's beauty, and significantly it is Edmund who, tied to the dwarf and driven along, first sees it.

> In the wide glades there were primroses. A light breeze sprang up which scattered drops of moisture from the swaying branches and carried cool, delicious scents against the faces of the travellers. The trees began to come fully alive. (p. 118)

Then the others feel it, too.

> They walked on in silence drinking it all in, passing through patches of warm sunlight into cool, green thickets and out again into wide mossy glades where tall elms raised the leafy roof far overhead, and then into dense masses of flowering currant and among hawthorn bushes where the sweet smell was almost overpowering. (pp. 119–120)

Edmund, having experienced the silence of the stone courtyard with its immobilized creatures, is first to hear the change.

> A strange, sweet, rustling, chattering noise—and yet not so strange, for he knew he'd heard it before—if only he could

remember where! Then all at once he did remember. It was the
noise of running water. All round them, though out of sight,
there were streams chattering, murmuring, bubbling, splashing
and even (in the distance) roaring. And his heart gave a great leap
(though he hardly knew why) when he realized that the frost was
over. (p. 114)

Edmund's rebirth, kindled on the spark of his pity for the stone figures who
had recently been celebrating Christmas, moves through the rebirth ritual to
his near death and rescue, twice repeated. Aslan saves his soul, Lucy heals his
body.

The other children reach Aslan, portrayed as a medieval king in his
cloth of gold pavilion and surrounded by his courtiers, in this instance,
centaurs, dryads, unicorns, and the like. Battle is joined, Peter winning his
knighthood by killing the wolf Maugrim. As we move further in, the conflict
takes on deeper and more clearly spiritual significance. This point is a crucial
one, for here the message is closest to the surface and most nearly at the
center of focus. Often before when Lewis reached his point as in *Out of the
Silent Planet* at Meldilorn or the debate of Weston with the Lady and
Ransom in *Perelandra* and later the apocalyptic conclusion of *That Hideous
Strength*, the message eluded his control and declaiming itself, seized the
lead, and the delicate balance of the creative structure wavered. Here, by
keeping the theme firmly grounded in the children, who are our link with
deeper meaning and our window on inner truth, he keeps the significance of
Aslan's action in perspective. It is for Edmund's sake that Aslan suffers, and
Edmund, barely deserving such sacrifice, makes Lewis's point absolutely
clear. It is Susan's and Lucy's grief we feel, and their joy when Aslan appears
transformed. It is the understatement which Lewis achieves here in his
picture of sacrifice and redemption which affects us so keenly. The Deeper
Magic of mercy triumphs over the Deep Magic of the law of justice. But
solemn as the outcome is, it follows explanation with a celestial romp. Lewis
thus preserves the special quality of Aslan: playful but solemn.

There are only a few passages in Lewis's fiction such as the creation of
Narnia in *The Magician's Nephew* and the apocalypse of *The Last Battle*, which
equal the organic sanctity of meaning of the chapter titled "Deeper Magic
from before the Dawn of Time." By organic sanctity of meaning, I refer to
the fusion of meaning with structure which makes the implicit deeper
significance an inescapable reality in the experience of reading such passages.
The form and meaning are so organically fused that our inhibitions are
dispelled and the clamor for rational proof by the intellect totally quieted.
The meaning sanctifies the form and the form the meaning, lifting the whole

experience beyond pleasing instruction to belief. It is here that Lewis achieves the enviable result of making the reader feel the Joy, the sublimely indefinable exaltation of the spirit, which he sought throughout his life.

From Aslan's transformation to the end, the tension is released, and we move back gradually to the bare room with the wardrobe. The Witch's death, now a foregone expectation, is followed by the release of the captives, containing one of Lewis's finest descriptive touches, the description of the stone lion's release. "Then a tiny streak of gold began to run along his white marble back—then it spread—then the colour seemed to lick all over him as the flame licks all over a bit of paper—then, while his hindquarters were still obviously stone the lion shook his mane and all the heavy, stony folds rippled into living hair" (p. 165). We meet the giant Rumblebuffin, one of Lewis's more original creations, a giant with character, and we see the children safely enthroned. The anticlimax lets us gently back to earth and leaves us with the expectation of further adventures.

PRINCE CASPIAN: *THE RETURN TO NARNIA*, 1951

After the abortive attempt to give Lancelyn Green the origin of the lamp-post and the history of events preceding *The Lion, the Witch and the Wardrobe* which produced the Lefay fragment, Lewis turned back to the Pevensies and sent them back to Narnia, called by Susan's horn. It was the idea of the horn summoning the children back which started Lewis on the sequel and gave the book its early titles *Drawn into Narnia* and *A Horn in Narnia*.

Though we are dealing with the same four children and a journey to the same world of Narnia, hundreds of years after the first adventure, only a year in our time, the structure of the book and the thematic interests are quite different from those of *The Lion, the Witch and the Wardrobe*. There are no preliminaries before we are dragged bodily into Narnia along with the Pevensies, yanked into the other world off the railway platform. The first half of the book is much slower in pace than *The Lion, the Witch and the Wardrobe*. There is a certain ingenuity in Lewis's presentation of the slow realization by the children that they have returned, and that aids in acclimatizing both the children and the reader, who may be unfamiliar with the early story. The focus of attention is not, however, on the world they reenter but on what they are to do, which remains a mystery for the first seven chapters.

There is, in fact, little suspense while we listen to the recounting of the history of Prince Caspian, his wicked uncle Miraz, who acts as a representative of grown-up rationality and tyrannical policy, and Caspian's tutor Cornelius, who plays Merlin to Caspian's Arthur. This section of the book suggests a medieval romance framework with emphasis placed upon dynastic palace intrigue, usurpation, the flight of the rightful heir, the magic horn to be winded only in greatest need, and the wild ride into a kingdom where loyal followers await the true prince's call to arms. We have already been prepared for high and noble exploits by the children's discovery of the treasure room, the recovery of their "gifts," and the returning sense of obligation which kingship has laid upon them. Peter advises Susan to cheer up and grow up because in Narnia, she is a Queen (p. 21). At this point Lewis introduces us to the Old Narnians: Truffle-hunter, "I'm a beast, I am, and a Badger what's more. We don't change. We hold on"; Trumpkin, "Whistles and whirligigs!"; Nikabrik, who is the Black Devil and counterpart of Miraz in Old Narnia; and the three Bulgy Bears, Pattertwig the squirrel, Glenstorm the Centaur, Giant Wimbleweather, and Reepicheep, who will show both the gravity and humor of courtly life and be a more significant character in the next novel.

Though there are amusing moments and some lively description of characters and a few arresting depictions of scene, such as the dance of the fauns at the end of Chapter 6, the movement is slow and sometimes tedious. Lewis presents us with two worlds. The first is the Narnia we know through the children's recollection and our knowledge of *The Lion, the Witch and the Wardrobe*. This idyllic world, freed from the tyranny of the Witch, was one where the principle of *hnau*, drawn from *Out of the Silent Planet*, operates. Men and beasts are unified in a rational fellowship, all subjects of Aslan, guided under the headship of King Peter, the High King. There is a hierarchy, a Great Chain of Being, reflecting the order of the celestial Great Dance, and we see a fantasy world which is a microcosm of the great world of paradisal reality, or at least a reflection of it. Pagan and Christian elements mingle, as do men and beasts, in a world where mercy has triumphed over the claims of Mosaic justice and pagan blood-sacrifice. We see a fantasy Golden Age.

The other world, symbolized by Miraz and Nikabrik, is the modern, corrupted descendant of the Golden Narnia; it is a world of rationality, apostasy, tyranny, pessimism, and fear. The Telmarines we find are pirates who have unwittingly stumbled into and corrupted Narnia. But they are not alone in their destructive effect. The power of the Witch (you can always call a witch back, says the hag [p. 165]) abets the apparently natural pessimism and cynicism of the Black Dwarfs, whose disbelief we see again in *The Last Battle*, and brings degradation even within the remnant of Old Narnia to which Caspian flees. Lewis seems to see in Miraz all the adult, no-nonsense, unimaginative rationality which his fairy tales, at least on one level, represent a protest against. Miraz's disbelief in magic, in history, and his fear of water and woods, the two aspects of nature endowed with almost magical significance by Lewis, reveal him as the titular villain: Captain Hook, the authority figure who would spoil all daydreams and who is underneath the bluster rather comic, as Miraz is when he accepts Peter's challenge. A more serious and less comic menace is Nikabrik, cold and hard, a hater of humans and half dwarfs, a pragmatic rationalist, a racist and a traitor to the Tao; he is in fact immoral where Miraz is not; Nikabrik betrays his better instincts.

The story centers on the theme of belief. Each major character either accepts the truth, tests and accepts it, or rejects it without test. The Pevensies are not convinced they are in Cair Paravel until they find their "gifts." Trumpkin, a skeptic but not an apostate like Nikabrik, must be shown that Edmund and Susan are King and Queen by competitive feats of arms, an amusing trial which clearly reveals Lewis's theme—"we're awfully fond of children and all that, but just at the moment, in the middle of a war—but I'm sure you understand" (p. 97). Miraz and Nikabrik learn through death where reality lies. The recalcitrant lords of Telmarine are left on this side of the door, like *The Last Battle* dwarfs huddled in the stable, unwilling to test the truth.

It is the test of faith in Aslan which forms the basic and central theme of the book since it is Aslan who comes across the sea to put all things right. Once more, Lucy is the focal point of this test of belief. It is Lucy who senses the movement of the tree spirits and who calls them to life, and later it is to Lucy that Aslan appears. In scenes parallel to those on the same theme early in *The Lion, the Witch and the Wardrobe*, Lucy attempts to bring the others to her faith. She is supported by Edmund and democratically vetoed by the others for various reasons: Trumpkin out of ignorance, Susan from sloth, Peter from pride or expedience. Here Lewis reveals his disgust with the application of political principles to personal belief. You cannot legislate either faith or obedience. All the characters fail the test and are led on a pointless and symbolically exhausting rocky descent and ascent. Lucy, chastised by Aslan, realizes that belief must be seconded by obedience and thus the corollary theme appears, as it did in *The Lion, the Witch and the Wardrobe*. The emphasis here is on individual belief and obedience. As the four follow Lucy and Aslan through the night, they see him gradually materialize as their growing belief permits his revelation.

This relatively brief section of the book (pp. 121–150) is the thematic and structural center, the only portion of the book containing that organic sanctity of meaning which we see pervades *The Lion, the Witch and the Wardrobe*. Here rather than history or chivalric battles or rites of celebration, we have the children again acting as our window on the world of eternal truths. If you believe unquestioningly—"'Oh, don't be so stupid,' said Lucy. 'Do you think I don't know Aslan when I see him?'" (p. 122), then you obey unquestioningly. The result of blind obedience to false gods for Miraz, pride; for Nikabrik, self-interest is death.

Lewis's descriptions in this central section shine with some of the same luminous quality we find in *The Lion, the Witch and the Wardrobe*. Whether this should be attributed to the numinous quality of his subject matter or to the elevation of the theme remains a question of individual response, but undeniably they have the same quality and effect felt in Aslan's appearance in the earlier book. Lucy's first taste of the Old Narnia comes with associations of light, odor, and sound.

> It was cool and fresh; delicious smells were floating everywhere. Somewhere close by she heard the twitter of a nightingale beginning to sing, then stopping, then beginning again. It was a little lighter ahead. She went towards the light and came to a place where there were fewer trees, and whole patches or pools of moonlight ... (p. 111)

Later she joins the dancing trees and enters the charmed circle to meet Aslan. Then, accepting their obedience, Aslan roars, commanding the reawakening of nature, and a great romp begins.

> Pale birch-girls were tossing their heads, willow-women pushed back their hair from their brooding faces to gaze on Aslan, the queenly beeches stood still and adored him, shaggy oakmen, lean and melancholy elms, shock-headed hollies (dark themselves, but their wives all bright with berries) and gay rowans, all bowed and rose again, shouting, "Aslan, Aslan!" in their various husky or creaking or wave-like voices. (pp. 151–152)

With the arrival of Bacchus and Silenus, the ecstatic moments drop back into a pageantry which will characterize the conclusion of the book. In quick succession comes the victory over Nikabrik and his Hag and Were Wolf, symbolizing hatred, hunger, and thirst, the "practical" powers he prefers to Aslan. The challenge and single combat bring victory to Old Narnia, and the trees take a vengeance not unlike that of Fangorn in *The Lord of the Rings* though not so vicious. The story ends with a prolonged romp highlighted by the liberation of the young school mistress and the old nurse and the proper punishment of Miss Prizzle and the dumpy and prim little girls with fat legs. Reepicheep steals the show with his deathbed revival and his demand for a tail, and the book ends happily if a bit frivolously. Susan and Peter, grown too old, pass beyond Narnia; Edmund and Lucy will return to help Caspian find the seven lost lords in *The Voyage of the 'Dawn Treader.'*

In theme and structure this work follows the pattern which appears in the first story. The children give us our viewpoint on events, and Aslan's appearance is the focus of anticipation and the high point of our imaginative response. The journey, trial of faith, and test of obedience all reappear, and faith justifies the happy outcome, won by strength founded on trust in Aslan. We are introduced to a host of interesting characters, some highly imaginative creations like Reepicheep and Trumpkin, but on the whole the book fails to measure up to the pleasure we feel in reading *The Lion, the Witch and the Wardrobe.*

In addition to the pervasive theme of faith and obedience, we are given related but less pertinent and universal ideas to contemplate. Lewis seems to have been deflected from the theme of the incarnation of Joy which controls our response in *The Lion, the Witch and the Wardrobe*, to a host of lesser themes which are neither as engrossing nor as stimulating. Though Lewis brings medieval chivalry and high romance to Narnia with court intrigues and knightly combat, the struggle of adult skepticism and pessimism, the lost faith that leads to false idols simply do not stir us in the way Aslan's epic encounter with the Witch does. Neither the risks nor the triumphs are as great, and we leave the work feeling a bit let down, rather like Lucy, having called the trees into life and then feeling "that she had just missed something: as if she had spoken to the trees a split second too soon or a split second too late, or used all the right words except one; or put in one word that was just wrong" (p. 113).

Structurally the book suffers from the apparent division of purpose which the themes reflect. Though the children are drawn to Narnia to assist Caspian in gaining his throne, the first third of the book laboriously recounts past history. The adventure theme of the book, the surface plots, suggest that our interest will rest in Caspian's attempts to overthrow the power of Miraz, returning Narnia to its true nature, dethroning pragmatic rationalism and replacing simple faith in natural reason, the *hnau* quality Ransom admired on Malacandra. But Caspian is a pawn in Aslan's paws, and the plot descends from the promise of a deeply imaged midsection to the anticipated battles and celebrations which alternate with disturbing regularity throughout the last anticlimactic third of the book. The emphasis is unevenly divided between the children's reunion with Aslan and their trial by faith, and the adventures which they have been called in to Narnia to pursue. Our loyalties as readers are thus divided between, the expectation of another numinous book like *The Lion, the Witch and the Wardrobe*, and a children's chivalric romance. Tolkien faces a similar problem in *The Two Towers*, and only by the organic incorporation of Rohan and Gondor within the larger scope of the action does he succeed in keeping the chivalry in check under the master theme. Of Lewis's achievement here, we can say that the book is an interesting episode in the *Chronicles*, just as the orientalism of *The Horse and His Boy* is a curious highlight showing another side of Narnia and a new approach by Lewis. But we are not left feeling that either book gives us the essential Narnia found in *The Lion, the Witch and the Wardrobe*, *The Magician's Nephew*, and *The Last Battle*.

Having noted how the book fails to meet my demanding expectation, it is only fair to point to the very fine features which it does offer. Lewis has many reasons for limiting the number of characters when he introduces Narnia; and as it is, there are a great many who appear in *The Lion, the Witch and the Wardrobe*, but few are drawn with the care he lavishes on Trumpkin and Reepicheep. They reappear later, but their basic qualities are developed here. Reepicheep is his masterpiece in this book. A more unlikely figure would be hard to imagine as the representative of dauntless courage. Were he anything larger than an overgrown mouse, he would be insufferably pompous, and were he portrayed less skillfully, he would be ludicrous or insipid. As it is, Lewis hits that happy balance between humor and awe which is reflected even in Aslan's capitulation over the renewal of the tail.

It is around Reepicheep and Trumpkin that the humor, which is more strongly felt in this book than in *The Lion, the Witch and the Wardrobe*, circles to puncture the solemnity of the various ceremonial occasions which we witness. Trumpkin, the unbeliever, is shaken till his teeth rattle, the final proof of Aslan's reality. Reepicheep does not quail even before his hereditary adversary and overlord; his name hints of mouse "squeeks" as well as "cheek."

Humor and good feeling take many other forms in a book where evil hardly has a foothold. Miraz and Nikabrik talk an evil line, but they are essentially empty and easily toppled. Lewis must have loved bears. His brother wrote after a trip to Whipsnade Zoo that Lewis intended to introduce a bear into the family menagerie at the Kilns and name him Bultitude. The Bulgy Bears remind us of Bultitude and the old hross at Meldilorn. They represent all the sleepy, comfortable virtue of an uncomplicated existence, hibernating and sucking honey from their paws even as marshals in the list. The romps which counteract the heat of Peter's battle, though somewhat stagey with the appearance of Bacchus and Silenus, have the effect they were evidently intended to have, signaling the new reign of the Old Narnia—a Narnia that would belong to the Talking Beasts and the

Dwarfs and Dryads and Fauns and other creatures quite as much as to men. The imagination and fancy are re-enthroned as the Pevensies end another adventure.

NOTES

THE CHRONICLES OF NARNIA

1. *See also*: Walter Hooper, "Narnia: The Author, The Critics, and the Tale," *Children's Literature*, 111 (1974), pp. 12–22.

2. Haigh, p. 109.

3. Bod., c/220/1, #181, March 28, 1953, to W. L. Kinter.

4. Robson, p. 68.

5. MSFAC, c/48, #113, September 28, 1955, to Mr. Henry.

6. MSFAC, c/48, #123, August 18, 1953, to Allen C. Emery, Jr.

7. *Letters*, p. 260.

8. *Worlds*, p. 42.

9. *Biography*, p. 239 and Bod., c/220/4, #188, November 16, 1956, to C. A. Brady. "It might amuse you that the whole thing took its rise from nightmares about lions which I suddenly started having."

10. *Biography*, p. 240.

11. Walter Hooper, "Past Watchful Dragons," in *Imagination and Spirit* (Grand Rapids: Eerdmans, 1971), pp. 306–307.

12. *Biography*, p. 248.

13. *Worlds*, pp. 12,15.

14. *Worlds*, p. 15. *See also*: Letters, p. 283, to Mrs. Hook. Also: MSFAC, c/4, #145, December 29, 1958. This letter indicates that the "as if" in Aslan as Christ is not allegory. The point Lewis makes in the letter and in the essays is that we are, in fact, in another world, not just this world with a few changes. This is a crucial point because it is the "otherworldiness" which attracts us, seduces us, and gets us past the dragons. Narnia is not England anymore than the Shire is. One of Lewis's greatest achievements, parallel to Tolkien's in *The Lord of the Rings*, is his creation of a world. Certainly the only other fiction in which he approaches this success is *Perelandra*, and there I have pointed to the dichotomy and opposition between the world and what takes place in it. In Narnia there is no disunity of description and meaning.

15. *Worlds*, pp. 28, 36. *See also*: Letters, p. 307, December 2, 1962, to an Enquirer, on the restrictions imposed by this form of fiction.

16. *Worlds*, p. 27.

17. Father Walter Hooper suggested that Lewis may be known for these stories because they are classics in children's fiction.

THE LION, THE WITCH AND THE WARDROBE

1. *Letters*, p. 203, February 20, 1943, to Sister Penelope.

2. Haigh, pp. 250, 255.

3. Haigh, Chapter IV, "The Children's Fantasy."

4. C.S. Lewis, *The Lion, the Witch and the Wardrobe* (New York: Macmillan, 1974). All references to the *Chronicles* in the text are to Macmillan editions.

5. *Letters*, p. 279, September 2, 1957, to Jane Gaskell. Lewis counsels her to do nothing which would wake the reader or bring him back with a 'bump' to the common reality.

LEE D. ROSSI

C.S. Lewis:
The Later Fantasies

Turning from *That Hideous Strength* to *The Lion, the Witch, and the Wardrobe*, the first in the series of Lewis's children's stories, one is struck by the tremendous change in tone. Lewis's great burst of polemical activity, which had begun in the 1930s and become so frenzied in the 1940s (twelve books in nine years), stopped somewhat abruptly in 1947. He did not return to deliberately apologetic writing until 1958 with *Reflections on the Psalms*. The tone of this work and of his last volumes of apologetics, *The Four Loves* (1960) and *A Grief Observed* (1961), an autobiographical account of the death of his wife and its shattering effect upon his religious faith, is much more subdued and tentative. It would probably be too much to say that Lewis completely lost interest in polemic after 1947. He was very busy after the war with the sudden influx of students into English studies. Clyde Kilby asserts that Lewis was probably the most popular tutor and lecturer at Oxford at that time. Perhaps, however, this sudden and dramatic display of interest in himself and his work took the edge off Lewis's sense of isolation. John Lawlor recounts that in the 1930s there were very few students at Oxford in Lewis's subject, English. As a result he often had to double as a tutor in a subject he absolutely hated, Political Science. Moreover, the few students he did get in English were "of very uneven quality." Most of them were simply unable to satisfy Lewis's demands for breadth of knowledge and intellectual

From *The Politics of Fantasy: C.S. Lewis and J.R.R. Tolkien.* © 1984 by Lee D. Rossi.

rigor. But after the war, all that changed, and this seems to have had a pronounced effect on his writing.

The science-fiction trilogy is the work of a man battling with the world and with his imaginative materials. *The Lion, the Witch, and the Wardrobe*, on the other hand, is the work of a man completely at ease with himself and his materials. The violent and bloody fiasco of the banquet at Belbury, in which all the evil people are dispatched with considerable gore, and the pompous fertility ritual of the book's finale are left behind. Even the half-curious but still half-fearful encounter that Ransom has with the Martian, Hyoi, in *Out of the Silent Planet*, is too problematical for this new world. When little girls meet strange creatures in the wood here, they are not frightened:

> He was only a little taller than Lucy herself and he carried over his head an umbrella, white with snow. From the waist upwards he was like a man, but his legs were shaped like a goat's (the hair on them was glossy black), and instead of feet he had goat's hoofs. He also had a tail, but Lucy did not notice this at first because it was neatly caught up over the arm that held the umbrella so as to keep it from trailing in the snow. He had a red woolen muffler round his neck and his skin was rather reddish too. He had a strange, but pleasant little face with a short pointed beard and curly hair, and out of the hair there stuck two horns, one on each side of his forehead. One of his two hands, as I have said, held the umbrella: in the other arm he carried several brown paper parcels. What with the parcels and the snow it looked just as if he had been doing his Christmas shopping. (*LWW*, 7–8)

What might have been signs of moral or sexual depravity for Ransom—the horns, the hooves, the tail—are here simply charming oddities. We are in a world very like Kenneth Grahame's, where people are odd, indeed, but oh so very interesting and friendly on the whole.

Nevertheless, there is a good deal of similarity between the two series of novels. First of all, the science fiction and the fairy tales both present visions of a glorified or beneficent "Nature." Both Malacandra and Narnia have talking animals, and there is a definite similarity in conception between the baptized mythological deities of Narnia (e.g., the fauns, satyrs, the tree and water spirits) and the guiding spirits of Malacandra and Perelandra, who besides being angels are identified as the classical Ares and Aphrodite. A second important similarity between the two works is the formation of a small society which believes in the other world. Finally, in both works Lewis is engaging in the translation of Christian mythology into a slightly different language, not so that it becomes unrecognizable but so that it gains freshness. As in the science fiction, this procedure sometimes works and sometimes doesn't. In Narnia, Christ is figured as a powerful golden-maned lion. Via what Kenneth Burke calls "perspective by incongruity," Lewis gains a new concreteness for Christ's power and his difference from ordinary humanity while at the same time reinforcing Lewis's reverence for nonhuman nature. A second example is the way Lewis tries to transform death. Just as Ransom joins Arthur on Perelandra, so the children do not lose Narnia by dying but rather gain access to the real, perfect Narnia.

It is this instance and this procedure which reveal Lewis's deep affinity with an earlier Christian writer of children's stories—a writer who had an important influence on Lewis's own spiritual development—George Macdonald. In Macdonald's *At the Back of the North Wind*, a little boy named Diamond meets a beautiful sad-faced lady named North Wind, who leads him to a country beyond the end of the known world. He discovers that it is a very pleasant place, if a little dull, and he stays there for a very long time. Eventually, he returns home, like Dorothy in Oz, by waking from a serious illness, and discovers that he has been away only a little while. He has more interviews and adventures with North Wind until she reveals her other name, the name most people know her by, Death. But by then Diamond is not at all afraid of her and consequently not afraid of dying. When he does die, he goes with her joyfully and finds a place even better than the first place, which was only a picture or reflection of the Real Thing, a place so good that the author simply can't describe it for us. Here he hints not only of the time displacement, important to the relationship between Narnia and Earth, but also of the many Narnias, each more beautiful than the next, which become important to Lewis's teleology.

So much for the similarities. The differences are crucial in establishing the greater consistency and sureness of tone which assure Narnia's being an artistically more successful work. First and foremost is the difference in genre. Whereas the science fiction trilogy contains many elements of the realistic and psychological traditions of novel writing, e.g., love interest and close psychology, the fairy stories do not. This characteristic is no doubt due to the basic materials from which they sprang. The fairy stories began as a group of images, e.g., a faun carrying an umbrella, a queen on a sledge, a wonderful lion, which eventually arranged themselves into a series of events. These images seemed to demand the kind of treatment one finds in a fairy tale, a kind of treatment which precluded many of the ailments which Lewis's earlier fiction fell victim to: "analysis, digression, reflections, and 'gas'" (*OOW*, 37). Thus, Lewis seems to have learned that an ordinary novel such as *That Hideous Strength* was capable of getting out of control in his hands. Sexual and social relations drop out of the picture; what remains is a picture of the democracy of childhood, after the model of E. Nesbit's stories. What also drops out are the epistemological difficulties Ransom experienced in *Out of the Silent Planet*. In Narnia good and evil are readily apparent. Those who do not see evil are evil themselves and know it deep down. It is a situation very much like that of *The Wind in the Willows* where all right-thinking animals know that weasels and stoats are a bad lot. Ransom's philological enthusiasms are left out as well, and we are left with heroes and heroines whose major concerns are mundane ones of food, play, affection, adventure, and beauty.

Lewis wants to draw people to Christ by creating a world in which the gratification of natural desires leads to a desire for the "Ultimate Good." His confidence that men's natural desires will eventually lead them to Christ allows him to eschew the dogmatism which had previously weighed his work down. He no longer has to tell us that human affection if rightly ordered will lead us to Christ; he shows us Lucy and Susan fussing over, rubbing, and playing with Aslan. There is less doctrine and more morality; fewer imitations of medieval religion (and those better assimilated) and more day-to-day interaction between ordinary children.

All these factors contribute to the greater simplicity and cheerfulness of Narnia. There are other factors which, though they look at first as if they're going to complicate things, actually enhance the simplicity. The first of these changes is the addition of the narrator as a permanent fact of the fiction. This actually simplifies the emotional response of reading because it gives the reader "authoritative" cues as to what's going on in the scene and as to the proper mode of response. How are we to respond to the evil Queen's gift of "Turkish Delight" for which Edmund develops such a craving? We are suitably dismayed when the narrator tells us that "this was enchanted Turkish Delight and that anyone who had once tasted it would want more and more of it, and would even, if they were allowed, go on eating it till they killed themselves" (*LWW*, 33). The narrator, safe, sane, and friendly person that he is, is the author's guarantee that nothing irrational or violent is going to frighten us more than we can bear.

The second factor, which though complicating the fiction, enhances the effect of simplicity, is the time differential between Earth and Narnia. Time goes by much more quickly in Narnia than on Earth. The whole cycle from creation to apocalypse—many thousands of years—takes place in two or three generations on Earth. Thus when once the children leave Narnia they never know what to expect when they return. In one instance, a young Narnian friend has grown old in the interval and is about to die. But feelings of loss are mitigated quite simply by the continued existence of the characters from Earth. They, like the reader, survive quite nicely the various shocks the flesh is heir to. Moreover, the Wellsian vision of death and detritus is rebutted; Narnia does not simply end—it becomes the gateway to a new glorified Narnia. With this particular dramatic device, Lewis has captured quite nicely a sense of the soul's desire for transcendence in the face of the passing of material things, and assured his readers of the friendliness of Narnia and the attractiveness of his world view.

The one complicating factor in this cunningly simple world is the presence of evil, both physical and moral. In the science-fiction trilogy the glorified planets of Mars and Venus are proposed mainly as contrasts to the evil condition of Earth. The presence of evil on either one is an "intolerable obscenity." Evil has been present in Narnia, however, ever since the hour of its creation. Like Earth it is a fallen world. But it still has magic. It is like Lewis's vision of Earth before the death of Merlin, "an era in which the general relations of mind and matter on this planet had been other than those we know" (*THS*, 201). It was a world in which the fields, the forests, the rivers, the wild animals still spoke to and obeyed man.

So much for the relation of the stories to the science-fiction trilogy. As to the general drift of the stories themselves, the first four concern the founding of the relationship between Earth and Narnia and the building of the company of Narnia. The next two involve mainly the extension of the Narnian world in space and time. We remember Lewis's enthusiasm for fictional works which create whole worlds of wonders. In the final volume, we have the end of both Narnia and the company of Narnia—or, as Lewis would have it, their beginning. The fallen Narnia of their earlier experience is replaced by the glorified Narnia of their desire.

The Lion, the Witch, and the Wardrobe, the first of the stories, is one of the most charming of the group. It is the story of four children, Peter, Susan, Edmund, and Lucy Pevensie, staying at an old professor's house in the country during the London blitz. It is a very large house and on rainy days the children play exciting games of hide and seek. Once during such a game, Lucy, the youngest of the children, hides in a wardrobe full of fur coats and as she moves toward the back finds she is in a snow-covered forest. She meets the Faun, Tumnus, who invites her to his cave for a gorgeous snack. The light and cheerful tone of these first moments in Narnia is suddenly undercut, however, for Tumnus shamefacedly explains that he has been a villain and that he had intended to kidnap Lucy for the White Witch. He repents though and leads her back to the forest. When she gets out of the wardrobe not two minutes after she had gotten in, she runs to tell the others of her adventure. But they don't believe her.

Another time both Lucy and Edmund, the second youngest, get into Narnia through the wardrobe. Edmund meets the White Witch and, enchanted by her magic candy, promises to bring the others to her. (The witch fears that these are the four human children who are prophesied to end her rule.) Finally all four children enter Narnia and meet some friendly animals who warn them against the witch. While eating dinner with beavers, Edmund, hungry for the candy and the power which the witch has promised him over the other children, slips away to tell her that the others are in Narnia. They soon discover his treachery and set off for the hill of the Stone Table, where they hope to meet Aslan, son of "The Emperor Across the Sea," who is the best chance for defeating the witch. As they rush to meet him, the winter that had settled over the land for a hundred years suddenly dissolves into a magical spring. They meet Aslan and rescue Edmund. But the witch demands her right as stated in "the deep Magic from the Dawn of Time"— the traitor must die. Aslan takes Edmund's place and the witch kills him. Lucy and her sister Susan come to mourn their dead friend, but at dawn he comes alive again. He frees the witch's victims from their marble state and leads them to where Peter and Edmund and the Talking Beasts under their command are fighting the witch's army. With the arrival of Aslan and reinforcements, the battle is soon over, the witch is killed, and the children are installed as kings and queens of Narnia. Their reign is the Golden Age.

The marvelous quality of this particular story—and of other of the Narnia books—is its lightness and cheerfulness of tone. We have already met with sprightly figure Tumnus. Equally engaging is the wonderful tea he prepares for himself and Lucy:

> And really it was a wonderful tea. There was a nice brown egg, lightly boiled, for each of them, and then sardines on toast, and then buttered toast, and then toast with honey, and then a sugar-topped cake. And when Lucy was tired of eating the Faun began to talk. He had wonderful tales to tell of life in the forest. He told about the midnight dances and how the Nymphs who lived in the wells and the Dryads who lived in the trees came out to dance with the Fauns: about long hunting parties after the milk-white Stag who could give you wishes if you caught him; about feasting and treasure-seeking with the wild Red Dwarfs in deep mines and caverns far beneath the forest floor; and then about summer when the woods were green and old Silenus on his fat donkey would come to visit them, and sometimes Bacchus himself, and then the streams would run with wine instead of water and the whole forest would give itself up to jollification for weeks on end. (*LWW*, 13)

Good stories and good food, Lewis tells us in an essay called "Three Ways of Writing for Children," have always been things which he enjoyed, not only as a child, but as an adult, and his own zest for these things enters his writing. You cannot write down to children and please them, he says; you must write about experiences and joys you have in common with them. Lewis's enjoyment of the simple pleasures of childhood is found throughout the novel. For example, when Aslan frees the animals, who had been turned into statues by the witch, the result is a riot of color and sound:

> Instead of all that deadly white the courtyard was now a blaze of colours; glossy chestnut side of centaurs, indigo horns of unicorns, dazzling plumage of birds, reddy-brown of foxes, dogs, and satyrs, yellow stockings and crimson hoods of dwarfs; and the birch-girls in silver, and the beech-girls in fresh, transparent green, and the larch-girls in green so bright that it was almost yellow. And instead of the deadly silence the whole place rang with the sound of happy roarings, brayings, yelpings, barkings, squealings, cooings, neighings, stampings, shouts, hurrahs, songs and laughter. (*LWW*, 166)

There is enthusiasm for nature in this passage, but also a joy in the language too. This is very good writing. Though the syntax is simple, there is a fullness of presentation and a subtle strangeness in the vocabulary (centaur, indigo, unicorn, satyr) which makes it memorable.

As we move into Narnia with Lucy we feel that we have moved into something strange and exciting but not unfriendly. "Lucy felt frightened, but she felt very inquisitive and excited as well. She looked back over her shoulder and there, between the dark tree-trunks, she could still see the open door way of the wardrobe and even catch a glimpse of the empty room from which she had set out" (*LWW*, 7). There is something very cozy about moving from a closet of furs into a forest of firs. There is little of the fear that haunts John (in *Pilgrim's Regress*) or Weston (in *Perelandra*) or Orual (in *Till We Have Faces*), that we will disappear down a black hole never to return. Likewise, Lewis seems to have made peace with his imagination and accepted its fantasies. These stories betray no fear of the moral evil of subjectivism or the psychological danger of solipsism. The imaginary world, though a limited good, is accepted and enjoyed as such.

This is much the same attitude as that of E. Nesbit, whose children's stories Lewis admired very much. In fact, the original situation of *The Lion, the Witch, and the Wardrobe* is similar to that of many of her stories—ordinary children on vacation look for adventure and find it. Also like Nesbit, Lewis concentrates on the ethical qualities of the children's life together.

Some of the other really good touches also take us back into the best of English children's books. The beavers' nest reminds us of the coziness of Mole's home in *Wind in the Willows*: "There were no books or pictures and instead of beds there were bunks, like on board ship, built into the wall. And there were hams and strings of onions hanging from the roof and against the walls were gum boots and oilskins and hatchets and pairs of shears and spades and trowels and things for carrying mortar in and fishing rods and fishing nets and sacks. And the cloth on the table tho' very clean was very rough" (*LWW*, 69).

Other touches are Lewis's own. We remember his fondness for classical and Christian images in the science-fiction trilogy (where the pagan gods Ares and Aphrodite become the angels who guide Mars and Venus in their spheres), and we notice that the White Witch is a gorgon. She turns her unruly subjects into statues. But she is also a devil, and one of Lewis's most evil creations. Even more characteristic and effective is the incident in which the witch changes into a boulder to escape Edmund's rescuers. When the narrator remarks that "she could make things look like what they weren't," we are reminded of Lewis's concern with metaphors of blindness. We feel we are looking at the real witch, something cold, hard, and desolate. But also the irony of the gorgon's changing herself into stone is delicious.

Another touch equally characteristic of Lewis is his description of the Stone Table. "It was a great grim slab of grey stone supported on four upright stones. It looked very old; and it was cut all over with strange lines and figures that might be the letters of an unknown language. They gave you a curious feeling when you looked at them" (*LWW*, 121–22). This is deliberately vague, filled with suggestions of weird rites, of unimaginable cruelty, of immemorial and iniquitous antiquity.

A final touch that signs the book as Lewis's own is the contrast of spring and winter. The witch is queen of winter. With her dead white face, she reminds us of Wither in *That Hideous Strength*. But the Lion brings spring, not only in the spiritual sense but also to remind us that he is the author of all the good we receive from nature. We experience something of Lewis's own joy in nature in the description of that sudden spring. It is an exact parallel of Lewis's description of his own re-admittance to the company of "Joy" when an adolescent.

Lewis's description of the Golden Age in Narnia reminds us of the deep strain of anarchism that resides on English children's literature. "They made good laws and kept the peace and saved good trees from being unnecessarily cut down, and liberated young dwarfs and young satyrs from being sent to school, and generally stopped busybodies and interferers and encouraged ordinary people who wanted to live and let live" (*LWW*, 180). Nesbit's *Five*

Children and It and Barrie's *Peter Pan* are other stories in which the attempt of children to escape a world run by adults is seen as wholesome and healthy. But it is even more of an achievement for a man like Lewis, who has spent his whole working life in school, and is able to suddenly "liberate young dwarfs and young satyrs from being sent to school."

One of the few elements of the story which remind us of the more unfortunate aspects of Lewis's opinions are his insistence that while it is unnatural for girls to fight, it is wholly fitting and heroic for boys.

Moreover, the murder of Aslan and the subsequent events are almost too close a parallel with the crucifixion and resurrection of Christ. We even get the rending of the temple veil and the women at the Tomb. In fact, the last section of the book, from the meeting with Aslan on, doesn't have the same quality of imagination as the first half. The parallels with Christian myth take over the story and pin down the meaning too specifically (something for which there is much precedent in Lewis's career). For example, as soon as the Stone Table becomes more than a symbol of a rich, wild, and barbaric past and becomes the Old Covenant, the magic of the story fades. The pathos of Aslan's death is forced, for what we are viewing is a ritual reenactment, the Mass, and not an imagined event. During her debate with the Lion, the witch says, "You know that every traitor belongs to me as my lawful prey and that for every treachery I have a right to a kill" (*LWW*, 139). This is "the Deep Magic from the Dawn of Time." But it is also a translation of the terms of the Old Testament, "an eye for an eye." To supersede it we have the "Deeper Magic from before the Dawn of Time," in which the innocent Aslan substitutes for the traitor Edmund. Aslan says, "If the witch could have looked into the stillness and darkness before Time dawned, she would have known that when a willing victim who had committed no treachery was killed in a traitor's stead, the Table would crack and Death itself would start working backwards" (*LWW*, 160). This is also a simple translation of the New Covenant inaugurated by the death of Christ. Not only is the sequence lacking in imaginative power, it is almost an ad hoc addition to the story of the little girl and the faun. As Lewis had once said, "Once you get your characters to the other world, they have to do something," and all Lewis could think to do with them was to let them observe a reenactment of the central Christian dogma. In fact, this concept of the "Deep Magic" does not appear in the later stories and is not mentioned at all in the story in which we learn of the origins of the White Witch, *The Magician's Nephew*.

The central event of the first book is Aslan's sacrifice, the central virtue, self-sacrifice. The second book, *Prince Caspian*, a straightforward adventure story, is equally clear. The key event is the restoration of Prince Caspian to his throne and the central virtue is reverence for nature and tradition. The story is this: Caspian's throne is usurped by his uncle Miraz, who is a cruel and tyrannical ruler. Not only does he line his pockets with his people's hard-earned money, he is also engaged in a vicious campaign to eradicate all memory and trace of Old Narnia, the dwarfs, talking beasts and trees. But he is not the first to pursue this impious policy. He belongs to a race, the Telmarines, who settled Narnia after the Golden Age and sought to exterminate the natives. Caspian, however, because of the wonderful stories his nurse and tutor tell him of Old Narnia, longs to meet these strange creatures. When his uncle has a son, Caspian, the true heir, is in danger of his life. He flees to the forest where he is befriended by Old Narnia. The Telmarines attack the Narnians and Caspian, in desperate straits, blows the magic horn of Queen Susan. Help arrives in the form of Aslan and the four children from Earth. While Aslan gathers reinforcements, Peter challenges Miraz to single combat; but there is treachery in the enemy ranks. Miraz is killed by one of his own men. The Telmarines set upon the embattled Narnians but Aslan arrives in time with an army of trees and the day is saved. Aslan makes a door in the air and those Telmarines unhappy with Narnia return to Earth, their original home. Others, mostly young ones, stay. Old Narnia once more takes its rightful place in society and at the councils of the king, and the children return home.

The basic theme reminds us, of course, of certain elements of *That Hideous Strength*, where the holy hush of Bracton Wood was destroyed by the bulldozers of NICE and where vast armies of unfeeling technicians performed experiments on animals and criminals. In this book, however, where the tone isn't quite so shrill, Lewis is much more successful in persuading us of the value and the integrity of nature. In the first place, tradition is living, and it is a group of creatures with a peculiarly charming and quaint way of life. Moreover, we can respect the integrity of nature because nature, in the persons of the various Talking Beasts, is so obviously stamped with character. Reepicheep, the mouse with the heart—and mouth—of a lion, is the foremost example. He is a splendid and dashing fellow. "He was of course bigger than a common mouse, well over a foot high when he stood on his hind legs, and with ears nearly as long as (though broader than) a rabbit's.... He wore a tiny little rapier at his side and twirled his long whiskers as if they were a moustache. 'There are twelve of us, Sir,' he said with a dashing and graceful bow, 'and I place all the resources of my people unreservedly at your Majesty's disposal'" (*PC*, 75). Or consider the courtesy of the three "bulgy" bears:

> There was a noise like a small earthquake from inside and a sort
> of door opened and out came three brown bears, very bulgy

indeed and blinking their little eyes. And when everything had been explained to them, (which took a long time because they were so sleepy) they said that a Son of Adam ought to be King of Narnia and all kissed Caspian—very wet, snuffly kisses they were—and offered him some honey. Caspian did not really want honey, without bread, at that time in the morning, but he thought it polite to accept. It took him a long time afterwards to get unsticky. (*PC*, 69)

As we have already seen in *The Lion, the Witch, and the Wardrobe*, Narnia is a much happier place than fairy worlds of the science-fiction trilogy. The tunes in *Perelandra* are so solemn. But listen to the pipe music of this passage. We meet

a youth, dressed only in a fawn-skin, with vine leaves wreathed in his curly hair. His face would have been almost too pretty for a boy's, if it had not looked so extremely wild. You felt, as Edmund said when he saw him a few days later, "There's a chap who might do anything—absolutely anything." He seemed to have a great many names—Bromios, Bassareus, and the Ram, were three of them. There were a lot of girls with him, as wild as he. There was even, unexpectedly, someone on a donkey. And everybody was laughing: and everybody was shouting out, "Euan, euan, eu-oi-oi-oi."

"Is it a Romp, Aslan?" cried the youth. And apparently it was. But nearly everyone seemed to have a different idea as to what they were playing. It may have been Tig, but Lucy never discovered who was It. It was rather like Blind Man's Bluff, only everyone behaved as if he was blindfolded. It was not unlike Hunt the Slipper, but the slipper was never found. What made it more complicated was that the man on the donkey, who was old and enormously fat, began calling out at once, "Refreshments! Time for refreshments," and falling off his donkey and being bundled on to it again by the others, while the donkey was under the impression that the whole thing was a circus, and tried to give a display of walking on its hind legs. And all the time there were more and more vineleaves everywhere! And soon not only leaves but vines. They were climbing up everything. They were running up the legs of the tree people and circling round their necks. Lucy put up her hands to push back her hair and found she was pushing back vine branches. The donkey was a mass of them. His tail was completely entangled and something dark was nodding between his ears. Lucy looked again and saw it was a bunch of grapes. After that it was mostly grapes—overhead and underfoot and all around. (*PC*, 152–53)

I hope I may be forgiven for quoting such a lengthy passage, but this is one of the best passages in all of Lewis's writing and deserves attention. Obviously he leaves a lot of the classical conception of Bacchus— drunkenness and violence—out of this description, but a lot of bacchic spirit has been infused into Lewis's Christianity. I don't think that anywhere else has Lewis so deftly mobilized classical myth on behalf of his own feeling for nature and for physical enjoyment. His Ares and Aphrodite are wooden puppets by comparison. Only his unbaptized Venus in *That Hideous Strength* displays a similar energy and strength of conception.

There is an unwonted joy in this world and a new attitude to physical indulgence. Drinking in *That Hideous Strength* is quite simply a sign of moral depravity, as when Mark repeatedly blinds himself to the evil of his situation and actions with alcohol. In other places, the drinking of wine is almost a sacramental action, as when Ransom (and later the magician in *Voyage of the Dawn Treader*) lives on a diet of bread and wine. Here it is one of the good things of life.

Even his villains are better. Consider, for instance, the "dull, grey voice" of the werewolf. "I'm hunger. I'm thirst, Where I bite, I hold till I die, and even after death they must cut out my mouthful from my enemy's body and bury it with me. I can fast a hundred years and not die. I can lie a hundred nights on the ice and not freeze. I can drink a river of blood and not burst. Show me your enemies" (*PC*, 160). That will scare almost anybody. But we notice also the care in the writing, the careful grouping of sibilants and long 'i' sounds that give the passage a spooky feeling. Lewis is very successful at giving this villain a distinctive voice.

The joy of the Bacchus passage carries over into the rest of the book. At the restoration of Old Narnia, the company interrupts a Telmarine schoolroom, and one of the children decides to come with them. "Instantly she joined hands with two of the Maenads who whirled her round in a merry dance and helped her take off some of the unnecessary and uncomfortable clothes that she was wearing" (*PC*, 195).

We remember that during the Golden Age the High King Peter had let young dwarfs and fauns out of school. In fact, Lewis's attitude throughout this book seems to be generally opposed to school. The book begins with the four children glumly waiting to go back to school and ends with the observation that "It was odd, and not very nice, to take off their royal clothes and to put on their school things" (*PC*, 215). Obviously, we should feel here

Lewis's animus against the schools of his own youth. Here, as everywhere else in the Narnia books, the fantasy world, the world of childhood, is superior to the world run by adults.

With *The Voyage of the Dawn Treader* we begin to feel that the impetus that first created Narnia is dying out. There is a good deal of satire—nice but irrelevant to the purposes of a fairy tale—at the expense of an Eustace Scrubb, a new member of the company, and his up-to-date parents and school. More importantly there is the absence of a central action as well as a central theme to guide the progress of the book. King Caspian has sworn to go in search of the seven nobles—the last of those loyal to himself and his father—sent by Miraz on a journey in the Eastern Sea to find the end of the world. Obviously the image of voyaging among islands is very significant for Lewis—it is the one he uses to describe his life after his mother's death. It is also a very odd image for a spiritual quest. In Donne's "Easter Morning—Travelling Westward" the movement away from the rising sun is a sign of alienation from God, just as Lewis's movement toward the orient sun is a movement toward God. It is not irrelevant in this context that George Macdonald's hero in *The Phantastes* travels in a generally easterly direction. But we are never sure whether the central action of the novel is the search for the lost nobles or one of the adventures on the way or the very act of voyaging toward the end of the world.

No controlling value is clearly emphasized. Is it Caspian's faithfulness to his promise to seek out the seven lords? Is it Reepicheep's noble daring as he sails over the edge of the world? Is it Caspian's devotion to duty and his country as he turns back from following Reepicheep? We just can't tell. There are too many loose ends.

Nor are the episodes equally good. Eustace's stint as a dragon is good, especially his discovery of his plight. He finds a dead dragon and its hoard of gold, and he falls asleep on top of the hoard. When he awakes, he notices an ominous presence in the cave with him.

> He moved his right arm in order to feel his left, but stopped before he had moved it an inch and bit his lip in terror. For just in front of him, and a little on his right, where the moonlight fell clear on the floor of the cave, he saw a hideous shape moving. He knew the shape: it was a dragon's claw. It had moved as he moved his hand and became still when he stopped moving his hand. (*VDT*, 73)

At first he thinks it is the dead dragon's mate, but then he realizes the truth. "Sleeping on a dragon's hoard with greedy, dragonish thoughts in his heart, he had become a dragon himself" (*VDT*, 75). The discovery that what had seemed an objective menace was really only his own foul subjectivity is a worthy invention of Lewis's ethical imagination. Good also is the fact that Eustace makes the best of his condition—he fells timber for the repair of the ship and scavenges food for the crew.

Then there is the moment of imaginative clarity when the fantasy world develops according to its own demands—as Lewis in his essay "Of Science Fiction" had seen that it must. Lucy spies an undersea kingdom, with its own fields, flocks, and castles. What puzzles her, however, is why they build their castles on mountaintops instead of in the valleys like sensible folk. The reason is astoundingly simple:

> In the sea, the deeper you go, the darker and colder it gets, and it is down there, in the dark and cold, that dangerous things live— the squid and the Sea Serpent and the Kraken. The valleys are the wild, unfriendly places. The sea-people feel about their valleys as we do about mountains, and feel about their mountains as we feel about valleys. It is on the heights (or, as we would say, "in the shallows") that there is warmth and peace. The reckless hunters and brave knights of the sea go down into the depths on quests and adventures, but return home to the heights for rest and peace, courtesy and council, the sports, the dances and the songs. (*VDT*, 193)

This is exactly what Lewis meant when he talked of "the intellect, almost completely free from emotion, at play." His interest in fully developed imaginary worlds, constructed on an impossible hypothesis, is caught here in microcosm.

By contrast with these two episodes, the episode of the Dark Island is not nearly so effective. But Lewis tries to make it harrowing. The voyagers discover a cloud of darkness on the sea, which they enter and which completely blots out the rays of the sun.

> How long this voyage into the darkness lasted, nobody knew. Except for the creak of the rowlocks and the splash of the oars there was nothing to show that they were moving at all. Edmund, peering from the bows, could see nothing except the reflection of the lantern in the water before him. It looked a greasy sort of reflection, and the ripple made by their advancing prow appeared to be heavy, small and lifeless. As time went on

everyone except the rowers began to shiver with cold. (*VDT*, 154)

Eventually they are discovered by a castaway who tells them, "This is the island where dreams come true." And of course this is just the pretext for Lewis, the Christian polemicist, to plumb the depths of human depravity. "It had taken everyone just that half-minute to remember certain dreams they had had—dreams that make you afraid of going to sleep again—and to realize what it would mean to land on a country where dreams come true" (*VDT*, 157). Immediately the rowers row backwards, hoping against hope that they will escape the Dark Island. Finally they pull out of the darkness and away from the island. Who isn't afraid of the dark, when asked to remember his nightmares? But, as can be detected from the abstractness and generality of the quotation, the incident as a whole remains a sketch for an episode rather than a fully developed creation.

The incident with the Duffers is in many ways very picturesque. They have only one foot and must hop around. (They are derived from the medieval tradition of Unipeds, who live near the equator and use their giant foot as a shield against the fierce noonday sun.) Also the Duffers are invisible. Dinner with the Duffers is a very interesting experience indeed.

> It was very funny to see the plates and dishes coming to the table and not to see anyone carrying them. It would have been funny even if they had moved along level with the floor, as you would expect things to do in invisible hands. But they didn't. They progressed up the long dining-hall in a series of bounds and jumps. At the highest point of each jump a dish would be about fifteen feet up in the air; then it would come down and stop quite suddenly about three feet from the floor. When the dish contained anything like soup or stew the result was rather disastrous. (*VDT*, 123)

Also they have the most curious conversational style:

> Indeed most of their remarks were the sort it would not be easy to disagree with: "What I always say is, when a chap's hungry, he likes some victuals," or "Getting dark now; always does at night;" or even "Ah, you've come over the water. Powerful wet stuff, ain't it?" (*VDT*, 124)

The problem is that Lucy and the other crew members who have been captured by the Duffers are threatened with a type of violence unheard of so far in Narnia, not the heroic violence of war but the cowardly violence of brigands and slaves. It is not a struggle between equals but an unfeeling victimization of the innocent. The Duffers explain that they have been changed into monopods by the evil magician who rules their island. Disgusted with their appearance, they send their Chief's daughter into the magician's room to find the right spell which will make them invisible. Eventually they get tired of being invisible and want to change back, but now they are afraid to send one of their own children to do the deed. The magician also has been made invisible by their spell and only waits, they fear, for another such attempt to unleash his magic against them. Consequently they wait until they can kidnap a stranger like Lucy, whom they can terrorize into doing their will. Fortunately Lucy discovers that the magician is really a servant of Aslan and that he has been set over the Duffers for their own good. They are not evil in themselves, but their opportunism leads them into cruel and treacherous actions. In this regard, they are the forerunners of the evil dwarfs of Book 7.

The episode of Deathwater Island is a morality play that is neither fully developed nor motivated. Caspian, Edmund and Lucy come upon a lake where everything that touched the water turns to gold. Caspian is suddenly seized with the impulse to claim it for Narnia and threatens the others if they reveal its location. The boys draw their swords against one another, but suddenly Aslan appears. The curse is lifted and they row away chastened. What's disturbing is that it is completely out of character for the noble Caspian and the ennobled Edmund.

Similarly, the stars whom the travelers meet at "the beginning of the end of the world" are conceptual cousins of the Ares and Aphrodite of *Perelandra* but without their redeeming ineptness. "It was like an old man. His silver beard came down to his bare feet in front and his silver hair hung down to his heels behind and his robe appeared to be made from the fleece of silver sheep. He looked so mild and grave that once more all the travelers rose to their feet and stood in silence" (*VDT*, 176).

In many ways, *The Voyage of the Dawn Treader* is the weakest of the Narnia stories. The next book, *The Silver Chair*, although not up to the excellence of *Prince Caspian*, nevertheless represents a definite recovery of narrative control. The central event is the rescue of Caspian's son Prince Rilian from the enchantment of an evil witch. There is a strong secondary plot in which Eustace and his schoolmate Jill Pole, after effecting Rilian's rescue, return to their school with Aslan and chasten the school bullies who had made their life so miserable. It is interesting to note that this is the same pattern as in the trilogy where Ransom travels to a strange world and returns with powers who will chastise the enemies of God. The central moral event of this novel is Jill's faithfulness to Aslan's commands.

The first thing one notices is that the tone of the book has changed from the earlier works. Life is getting much harder, much more strenuous in Narnia. This has something to do, of course, with the fact that for the first time in the series, Aslan is little more than a minor character. He appears at the beginning to give Jill her instructions and at the end to lead her back to school, but the adventure is almost entirely her own responsibility. Only once does he show up to help her and that in a dream. Also Lewis seems now to distrust what had earlier been one of his major tools for attracting his audience, the excitement of adventure. Lucy is able to indulge her love of adventure quite licitly in *Prince Caspian*. But a similar taste is completely out of place for Jill. She is criticized for being a callow little schoolgirl and not realizing that duty is duty regardless of whether the adventure is exciting or just plain difficult. The four Pevensies ride to adventure in complete comfort, or at most slight discomfort. Eustace and Jill set out in the midst of winter on a journey that takes many days of walking in endless cold, sleeping on rocky ground, catching their meals as they can. Self-indulgence of the most innocent kind—hot food and a warm bed—almost spells disaster when, seeking food and lodging at a giant's castle, they are instead put on the menu. Obviously Lewis wants to wean his audience from a taste for mere adventure and in this book his morality is becoming more rigorous and adult.

The prospect, however, is by no means completely grim. Despite their mistakes and their lapses in duty, they finally accomplish their task and return home to round out their triumph over evil. Even the journey itself is not so bad. The tedium and the danger are relieved by the presence of their guide, one of Lewis's most original and loveable characters, Puddleglum, the Marshwiggle. Now the Marshwiggles are serious folk and given to the most pessimistic observations. After comfortably settling the children in his wigwam, he says, "There you are. Best we can do. You'll lie cold and hard. Damp too, I shouldn't wonder. Won't sleep a wink, most likely; even if there isn't a thunderstorm or a flood or the wigwam doesn't fall down on top of us all, as I've known them to do. Must make the best of it—" (*SC*, 56). But balancing this pessimistic bias in his character is an unexampled kindness, generosity, resourcefulness, and bravery. Puddleglum leads them through the dangerous land of the giants, feeds them, and saves them from the witch's enchantment by thrusting his foot in a fire. Nor is he a complete wet blanket. When things seem blackest to Pole, when they're prisoners of the witch's gnomes, he reminds her, "Now don't you let your spirits down, Pole.... There's one thing you've got to remember. We're back on the right lines. We were to go under the Ruined City, and we *are* under it. We're following the instructions again" (*SC*, 128). Yet his seriousness is more than something to laugh at. Beside it, the laughter of the enchanted prince is shallow and foolish. The prince's description of the invasion of the uplands which the witch is preparing is what tips Jill off that something is wrong with him.

> But fie on gravity! Is it not the most comical and ridiculous thing in the world to think of them all going about their business and never dreaming that under their peaceful fields and floors, only a fathom down, there is a great army ready to break out upon them like a fountain! And they never to have suspected! Why, they themselves, when once the first smart of their defeat is over, can hardly choose but laugh at the thought! (*SC*, 138)

Nor is the book without real adventure. (As Lewis would say, if you keep secondary things in their proper place, you get to keep them.) After they escape from the giants' castle, they are captured by the witch's army. The journey in the Underworld in the kingdom of the witch, however, succeeds where the episode of the Dark Island does not. The darkness becomes smothering and suffocating in a very convincing way. Jill knows what it is all about.

> She hated dark, underground places. And when, as they went on, the cave got lower and narrower, and when, at last, the light-bearer stood aside, and the gnomes, one by one, stooped down (all except the very smallest ones) and stepped into a little dark crack and disappeared, she felt she could bear it no longer. "I can't go in there, I can't! I can't! I won't," she panted. (*SC*, 124)

Lewis is evoking our animal fear of death and yoking it with his own hatred of evil. Particularly effective in recreating this deadening of the spirit is their journey on the underground sea.

> When they woke, everything was just the same; the gnomes still rowing, the ship still gliding on, still dead blackness ahead. How often they woke and slept and ate and slept again, none of them could ever remember. And the worst thing about it was that you began to feel as if you had always lived on that ship, in that darkness, and to wonder whether sun and blue skies and wind and birds had not been only a dream. (*SC*, 128)

This is obviously an expansion of the Dark Island episode in Book 3. But here it works much better and we can believe the final sentence. Here it is prepared for, becomes part of a major structure of images and thought. There it was just a blot out of the blue. Further enhancing the effect is the description of the Dark City:

> It was a queer city. The lights were so few and far apart that they would hardly have done for scattered cottages in our world. But the little bits of the place which you could see by the lights were like glimpses of a great sea-port. You could make out in one place a whole crowd of ships loading or unloading; in another, bales of stuff and warehouses; in a third, walls and pillars that suggested great palaces or temples; and always, wherever the light fell, endless crowds— ... but there was not a song or a shout or a bell or the rattle of a wheel anywhere. The City was as quiet, and nearly as dark, as the inside of an ant-hill. (SC, 129)

This might be London in a fog or one of the industrial cities.

It seems to owe something to Baudelaire and Eliot. But this city has an important economic dimension. The gnomes are enchanted too and work for the witch only because they are forced. It is only when they return to their own place, the fiery land of Bism, that they are happy again.

We here get a view of Lewis's deeply pastoral instincts. He was raised in the suburbs of Belfast at a point, he says, where the country met the town, and he conceived there a deep affection for the peace and privacy of unsullied nature. We remember that St. Anne's is a country estate beyond the last spur of the railroad, while the NICE want to turn sleepy little Edgestow into a noisy chaotic city like Birmingham. The Calormene capital of Tashbaan in Book 5 is seen as the seat of a vast tyranny and corruption. In comparison, Cair Paravel, the Narnian capital, is more of a country estate than a thriving administrative and mercantile center. We notice also, in Book 6, that the first king of Narnia, a London cabby originally from the country, loses his city-bred aggressiveness and flatness of speech once he is in the healthful air of Narnia for a few minutes. Lewis is obviously a person for whom the joys of nature and of solitude ring truest.

The adventure underground, then, is structured on contrasting images of joy and sadness. The gnomes' sadness is played against the prince's laughter. Both are signs of the witch's domination. At the end, however, after the witch is killed, the gnomes jump gleefully into Bism, while Rilian, like his father, remembers his duty and starts with new-found soberness toward his home in Narnia.

This pattern is repeated in the subsidiary action in which Jill, Eustace, and Aslan rout the bullies at school. The bullies are routed and the weak are gladdened. Yet we detect in the latter action a covert polemical intent not readily apparent in the former. The school is the embodiment of irreverent progressivism. It is called Experiment House; it is co-educational and secular and its evils result directly from the lack of traditional discipline. But we wonder why Lewis should want to lay these evils at the feet of educational innovation. Despite its secularism, despite the fact that it is a school for both boys and girls, we recognize behind his portrait the looming presence of Lewis's own public school. Despite its pretense to religiosity and reverence for tradition, Wyvern is the very model for the evils he criticizes in Experiment House. This, of course, is from the man who in *The Abolition of Man* had thrown down the gauntlet not just to positivism or secularism but to "the Innovator" (*AM*, 36) himself. Lewis's insecurity is getting in the way of a faithful and truthful rendering of modern society. The place is worse than it has to be and the joy of chastising the bullies a little too pure. "With the strength of Aslan in them, Jill plied her crop on the girls and Caspian and Eustace plied the flats of their swords on the boys so well that in two minutes all the bullies were running like mad, crying out, 'Murder! Fascists! Lion! It isn't *fair*'" (*SC*, 215). Fortunately, it's not quite the bloodbath at Belbury but it's close enough. W.H. Lewis remarks that his brother was probably too harsh on his public school and suggests that he found so much evil precisely because he was looking for it (*L*, 4–5). We might suppose that his distaste for it was to some extent the cause and not the result of his bad treatment there, and that a young boy with Lewis's habits of privacy would not mix well to begin with. Lewis, who emphatically distinguishes his own fantasy from more typical children's fare, the "school story" in particular, because he feels that such stories pander to a child's basest desires for social eminence and constitute the rankest wish fulfillment, might have taken his own advice. An impulse, very strong, very narrow, and very evil, is coursing through this whole episode. Not only for the reader, but for the author as well, does this story constitute a sorry form of self-indulgence.

The fifth book of the series, *The Horse and His Boy*, is the story of Shasta, a boy living in Calormen, who is in reality the kidnapped son of the king of Archenland, Narnia's good neighbor. He leaves his home rather than be sold to a cruel Calormene noble, and flees to freedom in Narnia with the nobleman's horse, a free Talking Beast of Narnia, who has been a dumb slave for many years. On the way they join up with a girl of the Calormene nobility who is fleeing north rather than enter into an arranged marriage. They have many narrow escapes and while in Tashbaan, the capital, they learn of a plot by the Emperor's son Rabadash to conquer Archenland and from there to invade Narnia. Rushing across the desert, Shasta warns the king of Archenland and gathers reinforcements for the king in Narnia. The

Calormenes are all killed or captured. Aslan changes Rabadash into a donkey and threatens that if he ever sets foot out of Tashbaan again he will change into a donkey forever. Consequently his reign is peaceful; he can't go to war himself and he can't send his generals off to win glory in war and return to overthrow him (his own father's route to power). Shasta is recognized as the king's lost son and raised as the heir apparent to the throne. Eventually he marries the girl.

The central virtue of the book is humility, which is carefully discriminated from its defect, pride, and its excess, that false humility which keeps one from daring all he should. On the political level this virtue is associated with the orderly reign of the High King Peter and contrasted with the autocracy of Calormen.

At first this seems like a complete break from the previous pattern where English children are brought to Narnia to be strengthened in virtue. About halfway through the book we meet Susan and Tumnus and much later on Lucy and Edmund, but this time they are adults, the kings and queens of the Golden Age, as well as very minor characters. But this may very well be a needed break. The first time reading the series one has the feeling that the pattern is getting a little too stiff: first the Pevensies; then when Peter and Susan get too old, Eustace; then when Lucy and Edmund get too old, Jill Pole. The progression in these earlier stories, moreover, is strictly forward in time; this one goes back to the time when the adventures first began and forces us to recover all the ground we have covered already.

Yet in a more basic sense the pattern is not broken at all. The four major characters, Shasta, the girl Aravis, and the two horses Bree and Hwin, act much like the Pevensies. The relationship starts out unbalanced, the noblewoman Aravis lording it over the humble fisher's lad, Shasta, the noble warhorse trying to think for demure Hwin. As the story progresses and Shasta shows great bravery and perseverance, Aravis comes to respect him more and herself less; Bree is chastised by Aslan, and Hwin, who had been closest to a normative character, shows forth in the eyes of the others with her true dignity. Similar also to earlier stories is Aslan's constant intervention on behalf of the travelers.

Moreover, *The Horse and His Boy* gives Lewis a chance to reiterate the importance of story in bringing souls to Christianity and in inculcating proper social virtues. For the novel is merely the retelling of a story popular at the court of Caspian. Like the New Testament in our own culture, *The Horse and His Boy* is important in keeping alive in latter-day Narnia the ideal of humility and the love of freedom. In fact, with the mention of the story fresh in our memory from *The Silver Chair*, it is almost like being at Caspian's court, sitting at a feast and listening to the bard calling to mind the virtues and heroism of the Golden Age. The importance of a cultural tradition for Lewis cannot be stressed too often.

The telling of a story is almost a good in itself. (The inability of the chief Duffer, in *Voyage of the Dawn Treader*, for instance, to tell his story well is just one more sign of his people's general culture and moral decadence.) Almost the only thing Lewis sees to admire in Calormen is its tradition of storytelling. We get a bit of the grand manner when Bree asks Aravis to tell them her story. That story is full of images, such as "the sun appeared dark in her eyes," and phrases, "Now it came to pass," that mark out a highly developed tradition of oral storytelling. The language is elevated and artificial, as when Aravis relates how Hwin kept her from suicide by saying, "'O my mistress, do not by any means destroy yourself, for if you live you may yet have good fortune but all the dead are dead alike.'" But Hwin remarks, "I didn't say it half so well as that" (*HB*, 35). It is very artificial but very effective:

> Aravis immediately began, sitting quite still and using a rather different tone and style from her usual one. For in Calormen, storytelling (whether the stories are true or made up) is a thing you're taught, just as English boys and girls are taught essay-writing. The difference is that people want to hear the stories, whereas I never heard of anyone who wanted to read the essays. (*HB*, 32)

This is not realism but it is perfectly in keeping with Lewis's own notions about stories. Stories are not there simply to be taken literally. In fact, he doesn't believe that there is a child alive stupid enough to believe in the wonders and marvels of his fairy tales. It is quite enough that a sense of wonder be stirred and the desire for "joy" be kindled.

Another important aspect of *The Horse and His Boy* is the way it extends the geographical boundaries of the world around Narnia. *The Voyage of the Dawn Treader* and *The Silver Chair* had both done this to a limited extent. But it is even more important in Book 5 because the book fulfills recurring hints about that other kingdom, Calormen, which also inhabits Narnia's world. Here in the south we find a dry treeless land whose basic feature is the glare of sun on sand. Matching the forbidding terrain is the character of the people and their works. Where Narnians are carefree and laughing, Calormenes are grave and mysterious; where one is open-handed, the other is "practical," tight-fisted, and miserly; where one is kind and gentle, the other is cruel and harsh.

We should probably, at this point, notice the British prejudice, which Lewis shares, against "wogs." But we should also recognize that Lewis makes a very un-British use of the stereotype. For Narnia is not Britain (but a fantasy refuge from Britain); it is a small, vulnerable country threatened with destruction by a large, warlike neighbor. The situation is much more like that of Greece and Persia, than Britain and Egypt (or India). In fact, we might even see in Calormen some of the evils which Lewis recognizes in Britain and in the modern world in general.

Tashbaan itself is a place of squalor, bad smells, and poverty-stricken crowds.

> It was much more crowded than Shasta had expected: crowded partly by the peasants (on their way to market) who had come in with them, but also with water-sellers, sweetmeat sellers, porters, soldiers, beggars, ragged children, hens, stray dogs, and barefooted slaves. What you would chiefly have noticed if you had been there was the smells, which came from unwashed people, unwashed dogs, scent, garlic, onions, and the piles of refuse which lay everywhere. (*HB*, 52)

It is a place rife with the evils of class distinctions. There is only one traffic regulation in Tashbaan: "Everyone who is less important has to get out of the way for everyone who is more important; unless you want a cut from a whip or a punch from the butt end of a spear" (*HB*, 53). The scene where the powerful Grand Vizier, Aravis's intended, grovels like a dog before the Tisroc, the emperor, and sustains the kicks of the emperor's son is equally telling. The worst of it is that no one sees how bad it is. Having just seen from concealment the Vizier's miserable treatment, Lasaraleen, a flighty acquaintance of Aravis who is hiding her from her father, tries to persuade her to stay and marry the man. "Won't you change your mind? Now that you've seen what a great man Ahoshta is!" But Aravis is incensed. It takes a country girl like her to see through the pretenses of the great capital.

All in all, *The Horse and His Boy* is a very accomplished and workmanlike production from a writer who was feeling quite sure about what he wanted to say and how he wanted to say it. All the threads of the story fit quite nicely into the whole scheme. If there is not much of the magic that distinguishes earlier and later volumes in the series, it is not missed very much. The one bit of magic, the hermit's pool in which the final battle pitting Archenland and Narnia against the horde of Rabadash is viewed by Aravis and the horses, is mainly a bit of storytelling magic, i.e., it demonstrates the value of objective narration by an omnipresent observer over the subjective viewpoint of large events.

The Magician's Nephew, the next volume, is magical with a vengeance. We can appreciate Lewis's canniness in sticking to a straight adventure for the preceding book. If he had continued to simply feed us one magical tale after another, we would have probably become bored with the device. Coming as it does on the heels of an adventure completely without magic, this story of magic rings, strange places, and evil magicians, is exceedingly marvelous and delightful.

Within the scheme of the whole sequence, this particular novel has two important functions. First of all it extends our knowledge of Narnia back to its very beginning and prepares us for the sudden eruption of evil into this benign world which we experience in Book 1. Moreover, it returns us to the centrality of the company of Narnia. Here we learn of its foundation. *The Magician's Nephew* is the story of how two Victorian children, Digory Kirke (Professor Kirke of *The Lion, the Witch, and the Wardrobe*) and Polly Plummer, are the occasion for bringing evil into Narnia on the very morn of its birth. Digory's uncle, a dabbler in the black arts and a thoroughly nasty man, induces Polly to put a strange shimmering yellow ring on her finger, whereupon she immediately disappears. He then explains to Digory that he must go search for her and give her a green ring so she can return. The children however are only guinea pigs. Uncle Andrew is not at all sure that the green rings will work. Digory finds Polly in an enchanted wood full of pools that lead to different worlds, and after making sure they can return to London, they decide to explore the various worlds their rings give them access to. They discover first the dead world of Charn where Digory, against Polly's wishes, awakens an evil queen. They are forced to take her back to London. She threatens to destroy earth but the children succeed in getting her back to the wood and into another world. This world is Narnia at the moment of its creation. After some of the beasts are given the power of speech, a London cabby, who had, with his horse, been drawn along by the magic of the rings into Narnia, is made the first king of Narnia. Digory and Polly are sent for a seed which keeps the witch away from Narnia for many years, and Digory is rewarded with an apple which will heal his sick mother. The promise is made that even though the witch will rule over Narnia for a hundred years of winter, the sons of Adam and the daughters of Eve will eventually crush her. Digory plants the seed from the magic apple in his backyard. It grows into a tree which is toppled in a storm. From the wood is made the wardrobe through which the Pevensies first entered Narnia.

This is a development of the moral world we have experienced already in *The Silver Chair*. The unifying theme of the novel is not an action but an intellectually complex moral contrast, and the central moral act is considerably more complex too, involving as it does the choice of a spiritual good instead of a physical good. In *The Magician's Nephew*, the desolation caused by lust for power, represented in Charn, is contrasted with the fecund world created by Aslan. With *The Magician's Nephew*, the Narnia chronicles can be said to have reached a new stage of intellectual maturity. The crux of Digory's problem is whether he will take the fruit of the tree in the garden back to Aslan as he was instructed or home to his mother, who is dying and whom the fruit can cure. He must choose between two goods and not simply good and evil. The only clues he has to help him in this decision are the character of Aslan and the world he has created and the character of the witch, her world, and her would-be lover, Digory's fatuous Uncle Andrew.

Uncle Andrew exemplifies that priggery which Lewis sees as the chief danger of the intellectual life. He is a comic version of those same attitudes which Lewis had earlier dealt with in the figure of Weston. When Digory objects to his telling lies and endangering Polly's life, he replies:

> But of course you must understand that rules of that sort, however excellent they may be for little boys—and servants—and women—and even people in general, can't possibly be expected to apply to profound students and great thinkers and sages. No, Digory. Men like me possess hidden wisdom, are freed from common rules just as we are cut off from common pleasures. Ours, my boy, is a high and lonely destiny.... You will keep looking at everything from the wrong point of view.... Can't you understand that the thing is a great experiment? The whole point of sending anyone into the Other Place is that I want to find out what it's like. (*MN*, 18–22)

But of course he is too cowardly to go himself. "It's like asking a general to fight as a common soldier," is how he puts it. But he is only a pantomime demon.

The Queen of Charn is the real bill of goods. The witch represents the ultimate in human depravity and selfishness. She has destroyed her whole planet, peoples, cities, animals, and forests rather than lose her rule to her sister. The power of Lewis's portrait of her rests in his combination of imaginative materials ready at hand. The first of these is the decaying universe of H. G. Wells:

> The wind that blew in their faces was cold, yet somehow stale. They were looking from a high terrace and there was a great

landscape spread out below them. Low down and near the horizon a great, red sun, far bigger than our sun. Digory felt at once that it was also older than ours: a sun near the end of its life, weary of looking down upon that world. To the left of the sun, and higher up, there was a single star, big and bright. Those were the only two things to be seen in the dark sky; they made a dismal group. And on the earth, in every direction, as far as the eye could reach, there spread a vast city in which there was no living thing to be seen. And all the temples, towers, palaces, pyramids and bridges cast long, disastrous-looking shadows in the light of that withered sun. Once a great river had flowed through the city, but the water had long since vanished, and it was now only a wide ditch of grey dust. (*MN*, 59)

As we have already seen, the city is one of Lewis's favorite images for spiritual desolation, but the stale wind and giant red sun are images borrowed directly from Wells. Nonetheless they are effective and fresh because they are given a new and illuminating context. This is the personality of the queen herself. She is, as Digory recalls, the most beautiful woman he has ever seen. She has extraordinary physical and mental powers. She is unimaginably old. Digory finds her asleep with the corpses of her ancestors and we see her plan to establish her rule over London. Finally, she offers Digory and his mother everlasting life. Now if we feel that we've seen this all somewhere before, it's because we have. In fact, all these details belong to the central character of H. Rider Haggard's famous adventure, *She*. As with Haggard, Lewis's witch represents a consummate development of human personality, but a development which has the most evil consequences for it is selfish.

Contrasted with this dead world, we have Narnia where we see

a stretch of grassy land bubbling like water in a pot.... In all directions it was swelling into humps. They were of very different sizes, some no bigger than mole-hills, some as big as wheel-barrows, two the size of cottages. And the humps moved and swelled till they burst, and the crumbled earth poured out of them, and from each hump there came out an animal ... the greatest moment of all was when the biggest hump broke like a small earthquake and out came the sloping back, the large, wise head, and the four baggy trousered legs of an Elephant. And now you could hardly hear the song of the Lion; there was so much cawing, cooing, crowing, braying, neighing, baying, barking, lowing, bleating, and trumpeting. (*MN*, 113–14)

Here we have the wonder of the creator (Lewis this time, as well as God) and his creation and that different relation of mind and matter spoken of in *That Hideous Strength*. It is a world full of growing things. Even the iron bar which the witch had thrown at the lion starts to grow into a lamppost. This gives Uncle Andrew ideas for a great industrial empire. "The commercial possibilities of this country are unbounded. Bring a few old bits of strab iron here, bury 'em, and up they come as brand new railway engines, battleships, anything you please. They'll cost nothing, and I can sell 'em at full prices in England. I shall be a millionaire" (*MN*, 111). But it gives Digory food for thought, so that when he encounters the witch and she tempts him to eat the fruit himself or else give it to his mother, he can resist. That the character of the witch at the moment of her ultimate defiance is particularly repulsive only helps to stiffen his resolve. "She was just throwing away the core of an apple which she had eaten. The juice was darker than you would expect and had made a horrid stain round her mouth. Digory guessed at once that she must have climbed in over the wall. And he began to see that there might be some sense in that last line about getting your heart's desire and getting despair along with it. For the witch looked stronger and prouder than ever, and even, in a way, triumphant: but her face was deadly white, white as salt" (*MN*, 159–60). All the metaphors of eating heretofore had been only trial runs for this fine passage.

It is interesting to note the intimate relation this novel has with Lewis's own biography. Professor Kirke could easily be Lewis himself, especially as he views his role as a Christian intellectual writing for children. As a child, Digory grows up at about the same time as Lewis. Like Lewis, he hates the city. And like Lewis, his mother is slowly dying. Like Lewis, Digory is tempted toward isolation and defiance, but he is able to see their true character even as Lewis is able to write a novel which mocks Uncle Andrew and underlines the profound evil represented by the witch.

Despite the book's general consistency of tone and incident, it does have small problems. As usual in the Narnia books, these problems are associated with the appearance of Aslan. Sometimes Lewis can't resist the opportunity to point to a moral, even though it doesn't happen to be the one his story makes—in this case about self-sacrifice. Aslan warns that the destruction on Charn is a pressing possibility for man in the 1950s. He tells Polly, "It is not certain that some wicked one of your race will not find out a secret as evil as the Deplorable Word and use it to destroy all living things. And soon, very soon, before you are an old man and an old woman, great nations in your world will be ruled by tyrants who care no more for joy and justice and mercy than the Empress Jadis" (*MN*, 178). Tyranny and atomic destruction are twin perils of the modern age. What is more interesting about this passage, however, is its tone of fatalism and political despair.

Although *The Magician's Nephew* ends on a note of conciliation and peace, this warning, which is seemingly adventitious, signals an important development in the plot and tone of the final book. Tyrants will rise, he says, and so Calormen, always jealous of the freedom of Narnia, makes another and successful attempt to subdue her neighbor. The door to the conquest is opened by Shift, an ape, who persuades his friend, the donkey, Puzzle, to wear a lion skin and parade himself as Aslan. As in the *Book of Revelations*, where the Antichrist is a sign of troubles and apocalyptic change, the arrival of this Anti-Aslan marks the beginning of a period of great evil for Narnia and the approach of its final moments. Shift, speaking for the Anti-Aslan, orders the Talking Beasts to work in the Tisroc's mines and to cut down the Living Trees. King Tirian, learning of these things, despairs. He fears that the good and kind Aslan he had worshipped is actually cruel and demanding. In his despair he rashly kills two Calormenes who are beating a Talking Horse. But quickly he repents his evil action and with equal rashness surrenders himself to the false Aslan to be punished. As soon as he sees Puzzle, however, he realizes the hoax. Before he can alarm the other creatures, he is bound and gagged. At this point, he prays to the real Aslan for help. The two youngest of the company of Narnia, Jill and Eustace, appear to help him. But the cause is lost. The Calormenes have taken Cair Paravel. Formerly dependable members of Old Narnia, such as the dwarfs, have deserted not only the king but Aslan as well. The worst happens when the Calormene god, Tash (Satan himself), enters Narnia to take Puzzle's place. Eventually, Tirian, Jill, Eustace, and their friends, are captured and thrown into the stable, where Tash abides, as offerings to be devoured by him. But when they all enter the stable, they discover in it a green and sunlit country. Aslan greets them and banishes the evil Tash. The two children surprisingly meet the rest of the company of Narnia, Dr. Kirke and Polly and the four Pevensies. Then begins a mad race to "the garden in the West," which reveals itself to be another bigger and better Narnia. There they meet old friends—Caspian, Rilian, Reepicheep, and the rest—whom they had thought dead. The older children ask why they have been allowed to return to Narnia. Aslan tells them that this is not the same Narnia they had first entered; it is the "real Narnia" that the other had only been pointing to. They have all been killed in a train crash and can now receive their reward. And so began "the real story."

The central organizing principle of this story is once again a contrast, this time between the historical Narnia and the "real" Narnia. The organizing virtue, however, is more militant than the corresponding virtue in earlier books. It is the courage to face a desperate situation well. Not as intellectually complex as the preceding book, it is much more strenuous. There are, for instance, repeated comments critical of the Narnians for forgetting how to defend their country and their belief in Aslan. This helps set in perspective the hopeless lament of King Tirian, who wishes that he had died before all this talk of a cruel Aslan had begun. It also provides the angle from which to criticize the false humility of Puzzle, who lets the ape lead him into actions he knows are wrong.

The striking thing about this particular volume in the series is its bleakness of tone. This is partly the result of the use of a more objective narrative technique. Even in Book 6, intellectually the most complex of the series, the narrator is always making his presence felt in order to let us know that things are going to turn out all right. In *The Last Battle*, however, he is almost totally absent, especially at the beginning. This tone is also the product of the characters' hopelessness in the face of an awful situation. The parallels with *Revelations* also intensify the portents of disaster. But most of all it is involved with Lewis's evocation of another famous fantasy novel, George Orwell's *Animal Farm*. It is a thoroughly nasty and brutish world we enter as we open the pages of *The Last Battle*. Puzzle is unmercifully exploited by Shift and thinks no worse of Shift or himself for it. Like Orwell's pigs, Shift takes to wearing human clothes and to calling himself a man. He even strikes up a pact with humans, the Calormenes, to exploit the other animals. But this isn't an historical parable about the failure of the Communist Party. It is about the inability of a moral project like Narnia to survive in a world of economic exploitation and power politics. Shift and Puzzle have curiously abstract names, corresponding to a general human condition which their relationship is supposed to epitomize. The only way this condition can be overcome is to leave Narnia, which is ultimately subject to the same pressures as Earth, for the "real" Narnia, the land of heart's desire, where permanence and stability are guaranteed by Aslan.

Narnia is a decaying society in Book 7. The animals and humans are not prepared to defend it. The black dwarfs are as hostile to the king as they are to the Calormenes.

Lewis reveals his debt to Orwell in another way. The much reiterated slogan of the conspirators, "Tash is Aslan; Aslan is Tash," reminds us of double think, as well as of Orwell's—and Lewis's—horror of the abuse of language. This is, of course, also a continuation of Lewis's concern with distinguishing Christianity from other systems which attempt to swallow it up, e.g., Westonism and various other humanisms.

Some of the lightness and magic of the earlier books is recovered as soon as Tirian exchanges hope for despair. Yet it is a particularly cheerless adventure. The centaur, who is sent for reinforcements, is shot to death. The palace is captured. The dwarfs turn against Aslan and then the king. They indiscriminately murder Tirian's vassals and the Calormenes. It is only after the company enters the door of the stable that the tone of the novel changes significantly. Suddenly it is radiant and peaceful. For once they enter the door they are in the green sunlit plains of Aslan's kingdom. There they meet the rest of the company as well as the brave young Calormene whom Aslan had claimed for his own. From there they witness the awesome spectacle of the planet's death, a spectacle which adds extra poignance and savor to their own joyful situation. They speed across the landscape, swimming up waterfalls, scaling sheer mountains effortlessly, until they come at last to the real Narnia. They discover that time is merely the dream of eternity and observe that "the reason why we love the old Narnia is that it sometimes looked a little like this." They learn that the spiritual is inconceivably more beautiful and wonderful than the material. "The further up and the further in you go, the bigger everything gets. The inside is larger than the outside" (*LB*, 180). This is the ultimate triumph of the subjective over the objective. Nothing good is ever lost. "But you are now looking at the England within England, the real England just as this is the real Narnia. And in that inner England no good thing is destroyed" (*LB*, 181).

The only element to disturb this harmony, the only trace of the sardonic and the bitter in this radiant universe is the fate of the black dwarfs who are thrown into the stable with Tirian and the children. They are blinded to the beauty around them; they see only darkness and smell only dung. Aslan offers them a glorious feast, but vulgar boors that they are, they horribly mistreat it.

> One said he was trying to eat hay and another said he had got a bit of old turnip and a third said he'd found a raw cabbage leaf. And they raised golden goblets of rich red wine to their lips and said "Ugh! Fancy drinking dirty water out of a trough that a donkey's been at! Never thought we'd come to this." But very soon every Dwarf began suspecting that every other Dwarf had found something nicer than he had, and they started grabbing and snatching, and went on to quarreling, till in a few minutes there was a free fight and all the good food was

smeared on the faces and clothes or trodden under foot. (*LB*, 147)

As Walter Hooper says in his introduction to Lewis's essays on fairy tales and science fiction, Lewis detests politics, but we can't conclude from this that he refrains from criticizing various political groups or tendencies. His linking of the city and commerce with death and decay also has political overtones of an anarchistic nature. What we have, then, in the incident of the black dwarfs is a highly critical picture of the self-conscious working class, "The Dwarfs are for the Dwarfs" is obviously a parody of the Marxist maxim of "the working class for itself." But in this way, however, it seems much more selfish than it does in the Marxist context, where the working class constitutes the vast majority of the population as well as represents the noblest aspirations of the human race. But Marxists see that these aspirations are necessarily in conflict with the established order, while Lewis maintains that all anyone can do is fill his station in life.

This does not mean that Lewis is a "reactionary" so much as that his real interest is in another world, where there is real freedom and an escape from the world of government and economics he so abhors. We see this most clearly in *The Last Battle*. Faced with the imminent threat of tyranny and the ultimate defeat imposed by the end of the physical universe, human aspiration is driven "inward," a very revealing word, to the land of heart's desire. Thus Lewis's striving against his own subjectivistic tendencies never take him beyond his own subjective moral life and his personal circle of friendships. We again find that the real England is constituted, like the Logres, by "a happy few." Only in such a group does Lewis discover a happy accord between individuality and community which he sought all his life.

Lewis's last novel, *Till We Have Faces*, is a retelling of the Cupid and Psyche myth. Published the year after *The Last Battle*, it employs much the same brooding tone. But it also marks a return to the psychological interest of the science fiction trilogy. It traces the growth of ethical awareness in its narrator, Orual. As in his trilogy, Lewis is once again concerned with the tension between self-assertion and self-denial, between pride and love. Orual embodies Lewis's own problem—will she be "her own woman" or will she admit her responsibilities to other people and to the gods. In the course of her development she realizes that her life of political activity as a queen has been meaningless and has distracted her from her ethical duties to others. On the whole, it is a much more complex and powerful work than Lewis has ever written before. Owen Barfield calls it "the most muscular product of his imagination."

Orual, the oldest daughter of a petty king on the border of the Hellenistic world, tells the story of her youngest sister, Istra, whom their Greek tutor calls Psyche, of how Psyche is separated from her adoring older sister, and how they are brought together again. When Orual's mother dies, the king, who has already had two daughters by his first wife and is desperate for a male heir, takes another wife who dies giving birth to another girl. The father ignores her, but the child, under the loving care of Orual and "the Fox," the tutor, grows into a prodigy of beauty. She is so beautiful, in fact, that the people worship her as a goddess. But plague and drought are on the land and the priest of Ungit (the barbarian Aphrodite whose shape is a huge rock upon which the blood of countless sacrifices is spilled) says that the curse will be lifted only with the death of the accursed. The villain, says the priest, is Psyche, who parades herself as a goddess. She is taken to the mountain to be offered to the Beast, Ungit's son. Orual is too sick to go with the procession, but goes as soon as she is able in order to bury her sister's remains. She finds no body and after some searching finds her sister alive and thriving in a beautiful valley. Psyche tells her that "Westwind" swept her out of her bonds and brought her to the valley, to a beautiful palace, the home of a god, where gentle voices beckoned her enter, fed her, and bathed her. In the night the god came to her and made her his wife. He made her promise, however, that she would never look or ask to look at him. "But where is the palace," asks Orual. "Can you not see it," says Psyche, "We are sitting on its steps. Touch it." Orual, whose only thought has been to get Psyche away from the Mountain, thinks her mad and tries to wrestle her into submission but fails. Orual recrosses the river and spends the night with her guide, the captain of the palace guard, Bardia. During the night she sees a splendid castle but in a second it is gone. Convinced that the gods are only playing tricks with her, she resolves that she will tear Psyche from her madness even if she has to kill Psyche or herself. When she returns to the mountain, she again tries to persuade Psyche to leave or else to look at the god, but her sister remains firm. Finally Orual stabs herself in the arm and threatens to do worse not only to herself but to Psyche as well. Knowing how dire the consequences of her disobedience will be, Psyche nevertheless agrees to look at the god. That night Orual watches from across the river as Psyche uncovers the lamp. The next moment a great voice rends the night, a storm rages, and the god appears to Orual, looks upon her with great disdain, and prophesies that "You also shall be Psyche." Orual hears her weeping sister moving away down the valley but is unable to reach her in the storm. In the morning the beautiful valley is a desolate wasteland. Orual returns home thwarted in her plans to regain her sister, and sets about burying the pain of her love by diligent application to swordcraft and affairs of state. The rest of part 1 recounts her successes as queen. Through it all, however, she apprehensively waits for the punishment meted out to her sister to overtake her. In the final pages of the section she recounts how she came to write the book. She discovered a temple to Psyche in which the story of the goddess—told by an ignorant old priest—tells how her trials resulted from the jealousy and treachery of her sisters. Orual accuses the gods of lying and of taking from her the only thing she ever loved.

Part 2, much shorter, involves a recantation of the original draft and an admission that most of it was distortion and lies. The first chink in the armour of her self-righteousness is caused by her meeting with the eunuch Tiran who had once very long before been her sister Redival's lover. He tells her how Redival, whom Orual had always despised as shallow and flighty, was so lonely when Orual abandoned her first for the Fox and then for Psyche that she threw herself at every man who came along. The second is when Orual learns how much she has used and used up her subordinates. Bardia's wife tells her that she is "gorged with other men's lives; women's too. Bardia's, mine, the Fox's; your sister's; both your sisters" (*TWHF*, 275). Then come her dreams and visions. First she dreams that she is Ungit devouring all that comes within her power. She tries to kill herself, but the god, who had appeared to her earlier, tells her she cannot escape Ungit by going to the land of the dead. She resolves to practice true philosophy, as her tutor had instructed her, but she finds herself lapsing into the same evils. She dreams that she is trampled by a herd of golden sheep, which she interprets in her despair as a sign that the divine wrath can in no way be swayed from exacting its toll of her. Another dream comes in which she is Ungit's slave and must dip her bowl in the river Styx. But when an eagle asks her what she wants, the bowl has changed into her book. She is borne suddenly underground by shadow people to a great chamber where she is instructed to read her complaint. But where before she had seen only justice and righteousness, she now sees her own selfishness echoed in every word. The shade of her tutor then leads her to a room in which the trials of Psyche are figured in murals on the walls. But the tasks that Orual had despaired of in her dreams, Psyche accomplished with lightness of heart and relative ease. Finally she meets the goddess Psyche who has become more beautiful but more like herself than ever before. But Orual has learned her lesson. She admits her selfishness. "Never again will I call you mine." And then the god comes, dreadful and beautiful, with the fulfillment of the prophecy. It is not the dread punishment she had expected for so long, but a gift of beauty. The manuscript breaks off shortly after this, at a point where Orual renounces her hatred and denunciation of the gods. In the postscript, Arnom, the new priest of Ungit and counsellor to Orual, asks that the manuscript be taken to Greece.

From this outline we can see that Lewis retains all the major features of the action of the myth as told by Apuleius: the goddess' wrath, the sacrifice, the love of Cupid for Psyche, the treachery of her sister and her trials. But the changes are even more significant. Cupid is no skulking adolescent who has a go-between instruct that the girl be sacrificed. Instead the charge comes directly from the priest of the goddess. The king is a much more unsavory character, a lecher, a drunkard, and a tyrant to his daughters. Psyche, on the other hand, is a much severer and loftier character than in the Latin novel. She disobeys her lord not by imbibing the fears of her sister; she is true to him and disobeys only lest her sister do further violence to herself. In the final trial, moreover, when she is sent on a journey to the Queen of the Dead to ask for beauty for her mistress Ungit, she is admonished to speak to no one, and she withstands the pleas not only of a shadow-Fox but also a mock-Orual to address them. In Apuleius, she not only receives no such injunction, but falls victim to her own pride and curiosity by opening the box to take some of the beauty for herself. Lewis's Psyche, finally, fulfills her tasks with a grave joy not hinted at by Apuleius.

The temptation, also, is much different. In *The Golden Ass*, Psyche's sisters, both beautiful and themselves married to kings, see her splendid home and envy her good fortune. They are simply jealous and wish to ruin her happiness. In Lewis's version, there is only one tempter and she is very ugly and unmarried. She ruins Psyche's idyll not out of envy, she says, but out of love and a desire for her sister's happiness. This is only to point, however, to the major difference between the two works and that is the difference in points of view. Apuleius' version is basically that given by the old priest at the shrine of Psyche. Good persons and evil persons are easily sorted out and all motives are patently clear. This is precisely what Orual is reacting against. What makes the story so interesting is that it is told from an antagonistic point of view. This is the first time Lewis has given a warped consciousness full control of one of his books, and the tension between the story as Orual imagines it and the real story produces art of a very high order. We must not confuse this technique with that used in *Screwtape*. There we could not mistake Screwtape's words for the truth; here we can almost believe Orual. Further complicating the effect is the fact that there is no simple dichotomy between belief and unbelief. At least at first, the alternative between belief in the bloody primordial earth-goddess Ungit and the shallow but sincere rationalism of the Greek tutor is not heavily weighted on the side of belief.

Moreover, the structure of the book is highly complex, consisting of a series of contrasts on different but complementary levels. On the cultural and economic level we have a contrast between the kingdom as it existed under King Trom, Orual's father, and the reformed kingdom under Queen Orual. In the first stage agriculture and war are its only products; plague, drought, and famine are common; and a mirror from the Greek lands or a slave with a Greek education are signs of a paramount culture. In the second:

> I had all the laws revised and cut in stone in the centre of the city. I narrowed and deepened the Shennity till barges could come up to our gates. I made a bridge where the old ford had been. I made cisterns so that we should not go thirsty whenever there was a dry year. I became wise about stock and bought in good bulls and rams and bettered our breeds. (*TWHF*, 245)

Drought and famine are put at abeyance. Wars are averted by skillful diplomacy, and commerce is encouraged.

On the religious level, the old goddess is a rude stone said to have been pushed from the bowels of the earth. Her house is a dark narrow egg-shaped pile of stone filled with the stench of blood. She is a jealous goddess demanding the wastage of the best of the people's cattle as well as their most beautiful daughters. The new goddess, a piece of wood shaped by the hand of man, by an artist somewhat trained in the Greek technique, is housed in the old temple which has been newly brightened and which is freshly washed after each sacrifice. Yet for all its rudeness and barbarism, the old religion is much more heartfelt, much closer to real worship than the abstract and arcane mutterings of the new priest. An old woman explains her sacrifice to the old Ungit, saying, "Ungit has given me great comfort. There's no goddess like Ungit.... That other, the Greek Ungit, she wouldn't understand my speech. She's only for nobles and learned men. There's no comfort in her" (*TWHF*, 283). The old Ungit is also capable of uniting the dissident elements of the kingdom. Finally, unlike the new priest, who doesn't really believe in the old religion but uses it to achieve power, the old priest through his belief generates real authority. As Orual herself admits:

> The Fox had taught me to think—at any rate to speak—of the Priest as of a mere schemer and a politic man who put into the mouth of Ungit whatever might most increase his own power and lands or most harm his enemies. I saw it was not so. He was sure of Ungit. Looking at him as he sat with the dagger pricking him and his blind eyes unwinking, fixed on the King, and his face like an eagle's face, I was sure too. Our real enemy was not a mortal.

> The room was full of spirits, and the horror of holiness. (*TWHF*, 62)

As is suggested by this quote, this contrast is repeated on the intellectual level in the contrast between the Fox, who taught the new priest as well as the daughters of the king, and the old priest. The epitome of the fox's wisdom is involved in the Stoic acceptance of the evils of life. "Today I shall meet cruel men, cowards and liars, the envious and the drunken. They will be like that because they do not know what is good from what is bad. This is an evil which has fallen upon them and not upon me. They are to be pitied"... (*TWHF*, 76). But when he meets true belief as in the person of the priest he is reduced to mere sophistries and scoffing. He is a victim of his own logic-chopping. As Psyche, facing the day of sacrifice, says:

> The Priest has been with me. I never knew him before. He is not what the Fox thinks. Do you know, Sister, I have come to feel more and more that the Fox isn't the whole truth. Oh, he has much of it. It'd be dark as a dungeon within me but for his teaching. And yet ... I can't say it properly. He calls the whole world a city. But what's a city built on? There's earth beneath. And outside the wall? Doesn't all the food come from there as well as all the dangers? ... things growing and rotting, strengthening and poisoning, things shining wet ... in one way (I don't know which way) more like, yes, even more like the House of [Ungit]. (*TWHF*, 78–79)

Orual is actually much more like the priest than like the fox in that she also believes passionately in the gods. Only she hates them. "It never entered the Fox's mind—he was too good to believe that the gods are real, and viler than the vilest man" (*TWHF*, 79). She is the believer manque and on the ethical level of the novel she is completely contrasted with Psyche, whose faith in the god is as deep as Orual's hate. As a relief from her failure with Psyche, Orual submerges herself in affairs of state. Yet this involves a kind of perversion and a kind of death. "I did and I did and I did—and what does it matter what I did." The mask that she wears throughout her reign is a sign of her alienation not only from her subjects but also from herself. The novel suggests that she becomes less a woman and more a man; the affective impulses, which are to Lewis woman's closest ties to nature, are stifled. It is an insight typical of Lewis. Her horrified distaste for the womblike oppressiveness of Ungit's house reminds us of Jane Studdock. Her reaction is comparable to Jane's horror at the unbaptized Venus.

Orual's love is no more than a kind of spiritual greed, thereby proving herself the direct descendant of Screwtape and the Mother in *The Great Divorce*.

> Orual is (not a symbol) but an instance, a "case" of human affection in its natural condition, true, tender, suffering, but in the long run tyrannically possessive and ready to turn to hatred when the beloved ceases to be its possession. What such love particularly cannot stand is to see the beloved passing into a sphere where it cannot follow. (*L*, 274)

At times her hate is directed as much at Psyche as at the god.

Psyche, on the other hand, does all she can to admit Orual to her happiness and then sacrifices her own happiness for her. Finally, however, her sacrifices make Orual realize the strength and unselfishness of true love. Psyche is, as Lewis calls her in one of his letters, "*anima naturaliter Christiana*."

> It was beauty that did not astonish you till afterwards when you had gone out of sight of her and reflected on it. While she was with you, you were not astonished. It seemed the most natural thing in the world. As the Fox delighted to say, she was "according to Nature;" what every woman, or even everything, ought to have been and meant to be, but had missed by some trip of chance. (*TWHF*, 30)

She is the epitome of glorified nature, "Nature" under divine direction and as such already almost a goddess. She embodies the obedience, faith, and loyalty, which Lewis desired in the education of Jane Studdock.

Yet if this contrast embodies ideas we have already seen about the nature of women and displays an attitude toward politics—that it is a distraction from the important issue of personal salvation—perfectly consonant with earlier writings, the relation of these two characters reveal on another level the spiritual autobiography of the author. We can see in Orual's ugliness some of Lewis's apprehension at his own physical unattractiveness, and in the king's choleric personality something of Lewis's father. Moreover, if we let Orual stand for Lewis's public self and Psyche for the real self capable of expressing "joy," we have just the major developments Lewis traces in his autobiography. From the unconscious and innocent love and enjoyment of one in the other during childhood, we come to Orual's attempt to win Psyche back from her other love, the love for whose sake she was so beautiful. This suggests Lewis's attempt to win the subjective experience for its own sake rather than seeking out "the object of his desire." We also have in both the two separate lives, the real self drawing one ever onward to a final confrontation with God, and the public self concerned with the bric-a-brac of social and political existence and with its own selfish demands and sense of worth. Finally, we have in both the confrontation with and adherence to the god.

It is easier to understand the richness of this novel if we have before us not only the framework of the myth but also the key developments of Lewis's own life. This core of biographical truth allows Lewis to develop his pairs of theses and antitheses with unusual assurance. All these levels revolve around the basic dilemma of Orual's choice, which is also Lewis's choice—will he give himself wholeheartedly to the god or will he reject him. Politics and rationalism, although important to a total picture of the world, are ways of avoiding the issue, and ultimately ways of fighting him. This is why the action of the novel becomes more and more interiorized—in dreams and visions—toward the end. We are approaching the arena of real importance.

It is a very fine novel. Lewis develops his ideas and characters with complexity and richness. An idea does not condemn a person in *Till We Have Faces*; the Fox is better than he says. His kindness and loving care for Orual speak of a deeper philosophy than he perhaps knows. Even the cultural and social setting seem well researched and well thought out, even despite the obvious parallel with the modern situation as well as Lewis's own ideological bias. The transition from a communal religion to a class religion is a particularly fine observation on the role of ideology in social revolutions. It is the kind of point Lewis in his other fantasies does not take care to attend to.

The only thing the novel does not really convince us of is the *total* worthlessness of Orual's political activity. She accomplishes real goods during her reign, whatever the character of her personal life. This incompatibility between story and theme reveals once again Lewis's own deep alienation from politics.

Lewis's productions after this are all extremely minor and can be described in a sentence or two. The story "Forms of Things Unknown" is about an astronaut who meets a gorgon on the moon and is turned to stone; it is meant to illustrate the observation in *Perelandra* "that what was myth in one world might always be fact in another" (*OOW*, 119). "Ministering Angels" is the closest, I think, Lewis ever gets to bedroom farce. A scientific study reveals that astronauts cannot go without sex for the long, long periods of space travel without becoming psychopathic. The only two women the government can get, however, to minister to their tensions are a fat aging madame and a thin-lipped, flat-chested spinster who believes in science and sexual therapy. Obviously, the astronauts do not take up the offer. "The Shoddy Lands" is slightly more interesting. It portrays Lewis's fall into the nightmare world of a modern woman's consciousness.

> Here and there in the shoddy grass there were patches of what looked, from a distance, like flowers. But each patch, when you came close to it, was as bad as the trees and the grass. You couldn't make out what species they were supposed to be. And they had no real stems or petals; they were mere blobs. As for the colors, I could do better myself with a shilling paintbox. (*OOW*, 101)

Eventually he comes upon a giant woman, better built and with better teeth than the real woman but obviously the same girl, admiring herself naked in a mirror. Nothing is real in this world except what contributes to her own monstrous egoism. We wouldn't do the author any disservice if we saw behind his diatribe his own failures with women. We might even accuse him of fashioning a woman worthy of his fear, a kind of self-congratulatory fantasy.

Lewis's final attempt at fantasy, an unfinished novel to be called *After Ten Years*, was another retelling of myth, this time the Trojan War. As in *Till We Have Faces*, the interest is more on personal psychology, personal relations, and ethical decision than the panorama and sweep of war. The novel opens with the final battle at Troy and the question posed is, after the war what are this aging warrior and this aging beauty queen, Menelaus and Helen, to make of each other? For Menelaus the problem is more acute. Will he live with the real Helen or with his memory of her? The problem is not resolved, but it remains an interesting fragment if only for Lewis's ability to unite his various interests, the moral and the mythical, into a fiction which makes the legendary concrete and which gives the familiar an archetypal status.

If Lewis's primary attitudes can be said to have developed at all after his mythical novels, it would have to be in the direction of increasing despair over modern social and political life. After the calm and relative unconcern of early Narnia and *Till We Have Faces*, statements in his letters about the "frightening monotony" of modern life become quite common. The conscientious man finds himself increasingly frustrated and overwhelmed by the tyranny of modern institutions. In a letter to I.O. Evans, he says:

> There is a grain of seriousness in my sally against the Civil Service. I don't think you have worse taste or worse hearts than

other men. But I do think the State is increasingly tyrannical and you, inevitably, are among the instruments of that tyranny.... This doesn't matter for you who did most of your service when the subject was still a free man. For the rising generation it will become a real problem at what point the policies you are ordered to carry out have become so iniquitous that a decent man must seek some other profession. (*L*, 259–60)

Capping this pessimism is an addition made to a 1962 edition of Screwtape entitled "Screwtape Proposes a Toast." On one level, it represents a return to the polemical stridency of some twenty years earlier. Worse than that, Lewis, for all his railing against it, once again reveals himself as a prig. Taken as a whole, the piece is a lament over the irremediable mediocrity of modern life.

For "democracy" or the "democratic spirit" (diabolical sense) leads to a nation without great men, a nation mainly of sub-literates full of cocksureness which flattery breeds on ignorance, and quick to snarl or whimper at the first hint of criticism. (*SL*, 169)

The moral consequence of the great progressive ideas of the nineteenth century—freedom and equality—is a spread of the spiritual disease of envy, the feeling "which prompts a man to say *I'm as good as you*" (*SL*, 162). The only reaction to the tyranny of the "Normal" and "Regular" has been the alienation of the intelligentsia, which "is very useful to the cause of Hell" (*SL*, 164). Lewis's own position is not, of course, very different from the secular and atheist intellectuals he criticizes. It is a matter of attitude. He won't have any of the half-baked correctives of the Marxists or the behaviorists. He wants his fantasy of the good old England where "children have been made to work in school, where talent is placed in high posts, and where the ignorant mass are allowed no say at all in public affairs" (*SL*, 169). But even this attitude isn't any less alienated than the intellectuals he criticizes. He doesn't have a politic or even a consistent social ideal. Both his Christianity and his fantasy are ways of escaping the problems of modern society.

The most damning thing that can be said about Lewis's lack of politics is that he fails—on his own terms, as an ethical thinker—to deal with problems of property, status, and social organization, which absorb so much of the attention of the adult in bourgeois society. This has generally been recognized even by those sympathetic to Lewis. Chad Walsh says, "His blueprints for personal morality are clear and usable, but we have seen that he offers little guidance to the Christian concerned with the large-scale application of religion to society."[1] Walsh concludes that Lewis did so much else well that it is wrong to criticize him for failing to deal with this one area. But is it? Lewis might more reasonably have been expected to avoid theorizing about sex. He was a bachelor, after all, till he was 58, and he displayed little or no interest in women before that time. Yet he devotes a great deal of time and energy, in *Perelandra* and *That Hideous Strength*, especially, to discussing the proper roles of the sexes. But this is not the case with politics. Except for scattered comments in which he is by turns an arch-conservative and an anarchist, he never in all his work seriously considers politics as a source of value. Lewis's attitude represents almost a complete bracketing of these concerns. Class and social position is always a matter of destiny—the three biologically distinct species of Mars pursue their different kinds of labor in complete harmony and satisfaction; the Pevensies become kings and queens of Narnia in fulfillment of a prophecy. This is strange because, given Lewis's penchant for alternative worlds, one would have thought that he had enough imaginative freedom to create an alternative social organization. But there is no rival organization—only a vague longing for freedom from worrying about such things.

From *Spirits in Bondage*, his first volume, to *Till We Have Faces*, his last completed novel, his heroes are confronted by the impoverishment of social and political life. As a result, the metaphor of flight and escape is a central one in his work. In *Spirits in Bondage*, he escapes "the scarlet city" for a "green Hidden Country." In *Dymer* the hero flees the authoritarian "Perfect City" for the forest. In *The Pilgrim's Regress*, John flees Puritania and its Landlord (God), who "was quite extraordinarily kind and good to his tenants, and would certainly torture most of them to death the moment he had the slightest pretext," for an island he had seen in a vision. In the science fiction trilogy, Ransom leaves war-ravaged England for the splendors of Venus. In *The Lion, the Witch, and the Wardrobe*, the Pevensies escape the boredom of their childish existence into the magical world of Narnia. It is no coincidence, either, that this story like the science fiction trilogy opens in time of war. In *The Last Battle*, at a time when Narnia has ceased to be benign and uncomplicated, when it succumbs to problems of politics and oppression, the imaginary world is destroyed, and the company retreats into "the real Narnia" where permanence and stability are guaranteed by God. In *Till We Have Faces*, Orual's political activity becomes meaningless to her and an escape, to reverse the image, from really important ethical concerns.

As we have seen, Lewis's unconcern with politics and his flight from political society into fantasy is a response to a situation in which all political and social realities assumed a threatening aspect. The first such reality, of course, was his father. After the death of his mother, but even before, his father, a well-to-do lawyer, was very remote and inaccessible to his sons. Lewis imitated his father's preoccupation with politics in his earliest stories as a child but this temporary enthusiasm failed to close the distance between father and son. Yet Lewis, for all his distrust of his father and what he stood for, still admired his father greatly. His ambivalence toward his father hardened into a pattern of withdrawal from politics and society only after his various disasters at school, especially his public school at Wyvern. Hereafter his interests were limited to imaginative literature and to a small circle of friends. So tough was this armor that even World War I failed to make much of a dent. It is this withdrawal from the competition, status-seeking, and materialism of bourgeois society—as experienced in the person of his father and later in his schools—which forms the basis of his various personal concerns, fantasy literature and Christianity being the two most prominent of them. But as we have seen, Christianity, with its guarantee of heaven, is a logical extension of the fantasy impulse. Thus if W.H. Auden is right in saying of Yeats that "mad Ireland hurt you into poetry," we might say with equal truth of Lewis that mad Ireland (and England) hurt him into fantasy.

NOTE

1. Chad Walsh, *C.S. Lewis: Apostle to Skeptics* (New York: Macmillan, 1949), p. 160.

JOE R. CHRISTOPHER

The Romancer (II):
The Chronicles of Narnia (1950–56)

W hy, after a decade and a half of prose for adults, did Lewis, in the 1950s, suddenly publish seven children's books and one poem—"Narnian Suite" (latter half, 1952; whole, in *Poems*, 1964)—laid in the magical kingdom of Narnia? Lewis's enjoyment of children's fiction was mentioned in the biographical chapter, but this does seem a sudden shift.

Perhaps the best way to describe the Chronicles, and to answer this question, is with an equine metaphor: Narnia, out of E. Nesbit by Tolkien. Lewis thought of the Chronicles as being similar to E. Nesbit's children's books that he enjoyed as a boy, mentioning in 1948 he had plans to complete a book in her tradition. Lewis probably was thinking of her three fantasy books about the children named Cyril, Robert, Anthea, and Jane—*Five Children and It* (1902), *The Phoenix and the Carpet* (1904), and *The Story of the Amulet* (1906)—for in the third book, by means of the Amulet, the children journey as far back in time as Atlantis and as far forward as a future Utopia à la H.G. Wells. Admittedly, Lewis's children move to another world, like Lewis Carroll's Alice or George MacDonald's Anodos in *Phantastes*, instead of to different ages; but the magical adventures of a group of siblings seem to have been Lewis's starting place. And perhaps his mention of E. Nesbitt came from his unconscious, for Roger Lancelyn Green convinced him that the journey through a wardrobe in *The Lion, the Witch and the Wardrobe* was

From *C.S. Lewis*. © 1987 by G.K. Hall & Co.

taken, down to some of the dialogue between Lucy Pevensie and Mr. Tumnus the Faun, from E. Nesbitt's "The Aunt and Anabel," which Lewis must have read on its magazine appearance in 1908 and, at the conscious level, forgotten.

If the starting point was E. Nesbitt, however many other influences come into individual books, then the overall pattern of the Chronicles, taken according to its internal chronology, probably is indebted to Tolkien's works on Middle-earth. This is a controversial assertion, since Tolkien disliked the Narnian books for their softening of mythology: if Lucy had really met a faun—that is, a satyr[1]—the result would have been a rape, not a tea party. But Lewis had listened to much of Tolkien's *Silmarillion* (1977) in 1929–30, had read *The Hobbit* (1937) before its publication, had listened to *The Lord of the Rings* (1954–55) as it was composed, had written two reviews of *The Hobbit*, and would write two of *The Lord of the Rings* as it appeared in the same period as the Narnian books. Admittedly, Lewis and Tolkien shared a general medieval orientation as a result of their professional interest, and shared a Christian faith, despite their denominational differences, which gave them a biblical pattern of Creation to Day of Judgment; but neither of these, in themselves, explains Lewis's impulse to produce a work that, in its overall pattern, is close to Tolkien's. Perhaps Nesbitt provided the impulse to children's fiction, at least to the first volume written, *The Lion, the Witch and the Wardrobe* (1950); and Tolkien, the form the series was to take.

The following survey covers mainly the Narnian material in the books, not emphasizing (yet mentioning) the children. The most obvious parallels to Middle-earth will be drawn.

First in the internal chronology of the books is *The Magician's Nephew* (1955).[2] Narnia begins in darkness, although the children—Polly Plummer and Digory Kirke—and some others who have arrived there via magic rings are able to stand on something—Narnian ground, it turns out to be (chaps. 8–9). A voice begins singing; soon the stars come into existence and sing with the original voice. (This echoes Job 38:7, in its account of creation "When the morning stars sang together.") The first voice sings into being the sun, the vegetation, and the animals. With the coming of the sun, the singer is revealed to be a lion. This is Aslan, who is the Narnian equivalent (with some differences) of Jesus. (His creation of Narnia is based on the statement in the Gospel of St. John 1:3, referring to Christ, the Divine Logos, that "All things were made by him; and without him was not any thing made that was made.") The general parallel with Tolkien is that Ilúvatar (God) and the Ainur (angels) at the first of *The Silmarillion* sing into existence the World, as Tolkien calls it in his old-fashioned diction, meaning the universe. Actually, they sing into existence a model of it, from which the Ainur construct the suns and planets. This creation to music in both Lewis and Tolkien is an ancient concept, best known in British literature for its appearance at the first of John Dryden's "A Song for St. Cecilia's Day" (1687).[3]

A minor echo of Tolkien in this creation account occurs in the episode in which Digory's uncle, Andrew Ketterley, who is also in Narnia, loses some gold and silver coins from his pocket. By the next morning, in the creatively charged soil of Narnia, they have produced a Golden Tree and a silver tree (chap. 14). In Middle-earth, Laurelin the Golden and Telperion the Silver are the two trees that give off light for the world before the sun's rising.[4] Lewis's version is almost a parody, particularly in the context of Ketterley's fears of the animals and other problems, of Tolkien's mythic concept; but Lewis's world is intended for children, unlike *The Silmarillion*, and its tone is correspondingly lighter.

An interesting aspect of this creation account, unrelated to Tolkien, is in the gift of speech to some of the animals who had been created: Aslan breathes on them and they can then talk (chaps. 9–10; cf. Ford, "Gift of Speech," "Holy Spirit"). Lewis's biblically oriented reader may think of the creation of Adam (Genesis 2:7), but the animals are here already alive. The passage parallels one of Lewis's letters (LCSL, 237) in which he imagines the first men being called out of the anthropoid stock to be humans, as Abraham was called from his family and city to be the ancestor of the Hebrews. The result of Aslan's breath in this case is to give the animals a rational soul, rather in St. Thomas Aquinas's sense. If this is a symbol of God-directed evolution, here the events, as is appropriate for a child's book, are condensed in time. Tolkien is more of a creationalist in *The Silmarillion*.

In *The Lion, the Witch and the Wardrobe* (1950), the four Pevensie children—Peter, Susan, Edmund, and Lucy—enter Narnia through a magic wardrobe, finding a later period of Narnian history. The main connection with the first book is that Queen Jadis of Charn, who entered Narnia with the two children at the creation, is now ruling Narnia and is usually called the White Witch. The generation of the plot is the desire to rescue Mr. Tumnus the Faun from Jadis, by whom he is being punished for not having turned Lucy in when she first came to Narnia by herself.

But the major parallel to Tolkien occurs in the latter portion of the book (chaps. 14–15) in which Aslan substitutes himself for Edmund, who has given himself to the White Witch in exchange (at first) for candy; Aslan is executed. The biblical parallels are obvious. Aslan's sadness on the afternoon before his death suggests Christ's prayer that the cup may pass from Him; the binding, shaving, and vilifying of Aslan, the arrest, beating, and mocking of Christ; the cracking of the Stone Table, the tearing of the curtain of the Temple as well as the earthquake at the rolling away of the stone from

Christ's tomb (the latter, Matthew 28:2 only); and Aslan's resurrection at sunrise and his appearance to Lucy and Susan at the Stone Table, the angel's appearance to the two Marys who came at sunrise to the empty tomb (Matthew 28:1–8 only). These are not all the parallels either in this account or in what follows: the freeing of the enchanted statues from the White Witch's castle (chap. 16), for example, seems much like a slightly displaced Harrowing of Hell.[5]

But it is the parallel of Aslan's and Christ's deaths and resurrections that has stuck in the craws of many critics. Lin Carter, in a popular work on fantasy fiction, for example, writes of "a blatantly symbolic Crucifixion-and-Resurrection scene" that "is very much out of place in these pages."[6]

Two things may be said to this. First, it is in a general way parallel to Gandalf's death and resurrection in *The Lord of the Rings*. Gandalf falls in a fight with a Balrog in underground caverns—falls literally, being pulled into the depths. He then chases the Balrog up ancient stairs to the mountain top, where they both die in battle. Gandalf's spirit (if his spirit and body can be separated) is, after a while, sent back to conclude his mission; he is now Gandalf the White, not Gandalf the Grey (bk. 3, chap. 5). With the help of "The Istari" in *Unfinished Tales* (1980) and "Valaquenta" in *The Silmarillion*, a reader can find out the Christian background of this. Gandalf and the Balrog are both Maiar—that is, lesser angels; Gandalf has been incarnated to help the peoples of Middle-earth to fight against Sauron, another Maia. Both the Balrog and Sauron are fallen angels, obviously, unlike Gandalf—that is, they are demons. There *are* theological differences between an incarnated good angel and the incarnated Son of God; but both die, in the fictional equivalents, and both are resurrected. A critic cannot even say the means of death are greatly dissimilar: Aslan is killed by the White Witch, who is an archetypal figure of evil much as the Balrog is. Both die protecting others: Aslan, Edmund; Gandalf, the Company of the Ring. The main difference is that Aslan is passive, a sacrifice, and Gandalf is active, a fighter. Although a reader may feel that Tolkien has hidden his Christian analogy more deeply than Lewis has—and, in doing so, has been more artistic—the difference may be one of audience. Tolkien is writing for adults (he thought) in *The Lord of the Rings* who probably would be irritated by obvious parallels to Christ (technically, foreshadowings of Christ, since Middle-earth is supposed to be laid in an ancient earthly setting); Lewis is writing for children, who may not find Aslan's similarity to Jesus as obvious as adults do.

Second, critics who object to the death and resurrection of Aslan may be reacting to what they believe is crude propaganda, written with a cynical use of child's story. It is well to remember that Lewis's conversion to Christianity hinged on an argument over pagan myths of dying and resurrected gods. On 19 September 1931, Lewis, H. V. D. Dyson, and Tolkien spent an evening arguing about Christianity: Dyson and Tolkien told Lewis that the account of Jesus' death and resurrection was a myth, like the pagan myths that he responded to emotionally, but one that was also historically true. Whatever one makes of this in terms of argumentation, it suggests that Lewis is not putting in the episode cynically. At the time he wrote this book, he was not planning the others; therefore, possibly in an attempt to say what he thought important, he included an episode that resonated with his own interests, pre-Christian as well as Christian.

The Horse and His Boy (1954) overlaps in Narnian time with the last chapter of *The Lion, the Witch and the Wardrobe*—the period when the four Pevensies, grown to adults in Narnia, are ruling that country. The plot is based on the attempts of a boy, a girl, and two talking horses to escape from Calormen, a country to the south of Narnia; they have various reasons for wanting freedom—the boy is in danger of being sold into slavery by his foster—father, the girl is being forced into an unwanted marriage, the horses are having to pretend to be dumb animals—and their adventures end with their helping to thwart a Calormene invasion of Narnia. The parallel to Tolkien is one based on the history and geography of Europe; as Peter J. Schakel has noted, the Calormenes "are Moors: they are identified by their dress, weapons, and manners as the traditional enemies in medieval romances" (*Reading with the Heart*, 13–14). Likewise, to the south of Gondor and Mordor in Middle-earth lies such places as Harad and Khand. The main fact known about Harad is that it is a home of Oliphaunts (elephants), which suggests an African basis; the men of Far Harad are black.[7] Lewis is working from medieval romances about the Saracen; Tolkien is probably more geographic, since he does not give details suggesting a Moslem culture in his prehistorical setting—but they are both generally parallel in their European/African imaginations.

Prince Caspian (1951) begins what may be called the three-volume Caspian cycle in the Chronicles. This first book tells of the rebellion by Prince Caspian and some Narnian followers against the usurping rule of King Miraz, many years after the action of the preceding volume; the Pevensie children are called into Narnia by the blowing of a magic trumpet by Prince Caspian's forces in their need. The war is concluded—or it is supposed to be—with the individual combat of Peter and King Miraz. Actually, the individual combat ends in a general battle, and what concludes the war is the Tolkienian parallel, the coming of the walking trees. This, of course, is an ancient folklore motif, and Shakespeare used it, in a rational way, in *Macbeth*. But it is striking that two fantasists who knew each other and one of whom had heard the other read his work as it was written should use it at approximately the same time. Tolkien is more Northern than Lewis: he adopts the Anglo-Saxon word for giants into his Ents. The Ents and Huorns do march—which is the parallel—on Saruman's Tower and win the battle of the Hornburg (*The Lord of the Rings*, bk. 3, chaps. 4, 7–9). Lewis, on the other hand, is semiclassical in his approach. Lucy Pevensie, as she and her siblings go in the company of a dwarf to Prince Caspian's aid, speaks one night to some trees, calling them "Dryads and Hamadryads" (chap. 9), and asks them to wake up. They stir but do not wake. The next night Lucy sees the trees dancing in a stately manner, one of them (in a sort of double vision) looking like "a huge man with a shaggy beard and great bushes of hair" (chap. 10)— rather like Tolkien's Fangorn. In this episode, they are called. "wood-gods and wood-goddesses." When the woods march, they are only called "birch-girls," "willow-women," "oak-men," and so forth (chap. 11); however, they are accompanied by Bacchus and Silenus, so the classical motif is continued. It is also notable that Lewis's trees simply chase and capture the Telmarines (chap. 14), unlike Tolkien's Huorns who quietly kill the Orcs—or at least make them vanish. Again, the juvenile emphasis rules Lewis's work—mass slaughters are not appropriate.

In *The Voyage of the "Dawn Treader"* (1952), Lucy and Edmund Pevensie and their cousin Eustace Scrubbs enter Narnia through a picture—in this case, the picture of a ship. They find themselves on shipboard with King Caspian, who has sailed to seek seven nobles sent by the dead King Miraz to the east. The sea-quest that follows is episodic, but by the end of it Caspian has fallen in love with the daughter of a star met on one island. Her father, the star, is presumably something like an Intelligence, as discussed in *The Discarded Image*, or an Oyarsa, as in the Ransom Trilogy; if so, he has here taken the form of a man while awaiting his rejuvenization and return to the skies. The questers also have sailed to the end of the world (Narnia is flat), in sight of Aslan's country beyond the sun's rising point. In this book, as in *The Horse and His Boy*, the main parallel to Tolkien is geographic, although here with the directions reversed. To the far west of Middle-earth, across the Sea of Belegaer, lies the land Aman, where dwells the Valar (a group of angels)—this is before the world is made round, when it is still flat. Between the two is not a series of islands, as in *The Voyage of the "Dawn Treader,"* but one large island, Númenor; there are also a number of small islands just off the coast of Aman. Whichever the direction, both writers imagined divine lands that can be reached by sea-voyages across flat worlds, rather like the Celtic Isle of the Dead to the west of Europe.

In the third of the Caspian trilogy, *The Silver Chair* (1953), Eustace Scrubb and Jill Pole enter Narnia through a door in their school wall—more precisely, they are on the Mountain of Aslan, not in Narnia, and they are blown by Aslan's breath to Narnia, "into the west of the world" (chap. 2), which suggests (but does not actually prove) the same geographic framework as *The Voyage of the "Dawn Treader."* If there is any Tolkienesque parallel here it is to Taniquetil, the highest mountain in Aman, from which Manwe (an angel) looks eastward at Middle-earth. (Lewis's mountain does not have ice or snow on top, as Tolkien's does.)

Jill and Eustace are sent into Narnia to search for Rilian, the son of Caspian, who is being held captive (it turns out) by the Queen of the Underland. They first head north into the land of giants; Tolkien mentions some stone-giants living in mountains in *The Hobbit* (chap. 4), but drops them from his adult books. Then Jill, Eustace, and a Narnian companion descend into the underworld—into large caves with a sea and with Earthmen serving the queen. Lewis calls the Earthmen gnomes (chap. 10); their role at first is that of the traditional dwarfs of folklore (one meaning of *gnome*), not that of the Paracelsian elementals of the earth (another meaning)—but, after the queen is killed and they and Prince Rilian are loosed from their enchantments, they turn out to be more like elementals, dropping down to the depths of the world where salamanders (another elemental) swim in a river of fire (chap. 14). Tolkien's material most like this is the two chapters in *The Fellowship of the Ring* recounting the journey of Gandalf, Frodo, and others through the Mines of Moria: a journey through partial darkness, past many passageways and chambers cut by dwarves earlier, and finally—in reverse of Lewis—a fiery danger from the depths, the Balrog, and a fall into the depths by only two characters, Gandalf and the Balrog, when Gandalf breaks a bridge to stop the Balrog (bk. 2, chaps. 4–5). The Orcs who are in the Mines are slightly like the gnomes who are prepared to fight before they learn that Prince Rilian and his companions are friendly (chap. 13).

The final Narnian book, *The Last Battle* (1956), tells of Narnia's final days and its Last Judgment, just as *The Magician's Nephew* told of its creation. Jill and Eustace return to Narnia—it is revealed only at the end of the story that they were killed on Earth in a train wreck (chap. 16)—to rescue King Tirian who appeared to them on earth in a vision (chap. 4); it is about two hundred years after their rescue of Rilian (chap. 5). The forces opposed to Tirian are several: Shift the Ape has dressed Puzzle the Donkey in a lion's skin and has proclaimed him Aslan returned (the Antichrist motif from Matthew 24:23–24), the Calormenes are in league with Shift, the Calormene god Tash (a demon in Narnian terms) comes north, and a number of dwarfs declare themselves on neither side. Eventually Tirian and his side lose, and Aslan ends Narnia with a number of events that echo the Book of Revelations and other apocalyptic New Testament passages. For example, Aslan sits at the door to the new Narnia (like the New Heavens and New Earth of Revelations 21:1; the archetypal Narnia in Platonic terms) while all the creatures come up to him—some turn aside into darkness, others enter in; this is a version of the parable of the sheep and the goats in Matthew 25:31–46 (chap. 14). Peter Pevensie closes the doors to Narnia and locks them with a golden key (chap. 14) in a reminiscence of St. Peter as the Gatekeeper to Heaven (cf. Matthew 16:19). The last two chapters are spent in a description of the characters' journey further into the new Narnia. This conclusion—the salvation of the protagonists and their meeting with earlier inhabitants of Narnia—is equivalent to what Tolkien calls the Eucatastrophe, the good turn at the end of the fairy tale, in his essay "On Fairy-Stories." Strictly speaking, Tolkien's Middle-earth has nothing like this—at least, if Tolkien wrote a version of it, it has not been published. But there are four references to Middle-earth's Day of Doom in *The Lord of the Rings* and eight references in *The Silmarillion* (Foster, "End"): then evil will be defeated in "the Last Battle" (Tolkien uses the phrase), Middle-earth will be cured of its wounds, and the Second Music will sound.

Literally, no number of parallels can prove an indebtedness, but here the use of common motifs is impressive and suggestive of influence. Further, this survey of parallels between Middle-earth and Narnia is not meant to indicate that Lewis is a simple copyist. Tolkien and Lewis shared biblical, medieval, and Nordic cultures; years of hearing Tolkien's works read had further impressed the images into Lewis's imagination. But everywhere Lewis transforms these common images with a new handling. Sometimes his handling is more obvious, as with the death and resurrection of Aslan; sometimes Lewis is more detailed, as with the Arabian-like culture to the South; sometimes he seems to be doing a simple reversal, as with the holy lands and a tall mountain to the east, not west, of Narnia.[8]

The general parallel between Tolkien and Lewis as creators has been suggested. Tolkien in "On Fairy-Stories" called for the writer as a subcreator to make a Secondary World with its own laws. This is not a completely original position: A. G. Baumgarten in 1735 argued that all literature (not just fairy stories) is made up of heterocosmoses;[9] Sir Philip Sidney, in the sixteenth century in *Defence of Poetry*, said the poet brought forth a golden world, in contrast to the real world of brass (sec. 3). Tolkien was bothered as an artist that Lewis's fauns did not obey their own nature, for (Tolkien thought) they were fixed myths that could be introduced into a Secondary World only as the myth had been established. It is true that Tolkien himself elevated the nature of his elves in *The Lord of the Rings*, but at least their beauty often had been there originally. Lewis elevated the nature of Mr. Tumnus more radically; also, no tea parties exist in Grecian legend; that is, he changed the nature of the myth. Other critics are upset over Aslan's death and resurrection; the Secondary World is not separate enough from the Primary World. This is also the argument of Roger Lancelyn Green over the appearance of Father Christmas in *The Lion, the Witch and the Wardrobe* (chap. 10): what is a symbol tied to a Christian celebration in the Primary World doing in the Secondary (cf. G&H, 241)? Whatever the flaws in Lewis's Narnia (and these three examples come from the first book written), the overall pattern of a world—a Secondary World— parallel in some details to the Bible and in others to Middle-earth, is apparent.

But these likenesses to Tolkien are not all the probable borrowings. Lewis also echoes Dante in the heptology. For an obvious example, there seem to be a number of Garden of Eden-topped hills in Narnia, where the image comes both from Dante's *Purgatorio* and from Milton's imitation of Dante in *Paradise Lost*. The closest to Dante and Milton is the green hill in the Western Wilds that has an earthen wall around an orchard (*The Magician's Nephew*, chap. 13); the version in new Narnia (*The Last Battle*, chap. 16) has the Narnian equivalent of Adam and Eve on the thrones, and, when Lucy and Mr. Tumnus look down from the garden, it turns out to be on the top of a high, stony mountain. The hill, topped with a garden and a central pool, seen in Eustace Scrubb's dream vision in *The Voyage of the "Dawn Treader"* (chap. 7), seems to be related—both to the other hills here and to the mountain-top valley with a pool at the end of *Perelandra*. Finally, the Mountain of Aslan that appears at the first and end of *The Silver Chair* seems to be another Dantean variation.

Among several other possibilities of Dantean influence, the most interesting suggestion has been made by Marsha A. Daigle: that the voyage of the *Dawn Treader* is suggestive of Dante's journey in the *Purgatorio* and the *Paradiso*. Certainly, the Silver Sea of white, water-lily-like flowers at the end of the voyage, before three of the voyagers meet Aslan at the edge of the world (chap. 16), and Dante's vision of Heaven as white rose (cantos 30–32), before his concluding vision of God (canto 33), suggest the imagistic likeness.[10]

In his essay "Sometimes Fairy Stories May Say Best What's to be Said," Lewis speaks of the attraction of the fairy-tale genre for him when he considered what to make of his mental images at the time he wrote the Narnian books: no emphasis on love or close psychology, brevity, restrained description, generic flexibility, and lack of digressions. With the decision to use the genre came also limits on vocabulary. These items sum up the artistry of the Narnian tales fairly well. Perhaps one should add that Lewis often uses complex, traditional images (the garden-topped hills are an example) that replace the richness that would come in adult works from vocabulary.

NOTES

1. Lewis lists both fauns and satyrs in *The Silver Chair* (London: Geoffrey Bles, 1953), chap. 3; Paul F. Ford, *Companion to Narnia* (San Francisco: Harper & Row, 1980; rev. ed., 1983), in his note under *satyr* says satyrs are more goatlike and sexual than fauns; perhaps so, but most reference books seem to believe them identical. One later reference to Ford's book in the text will be by section listing, so either edition can be consulted.

2. This discussion does not mean the Narnian books should be read in the order of their internal chronology; Peter J. Schakel, *Reading with the Heart* (Grand Rapids: Eerdmans, 1979), 143–45, n. 6, makes a good case for reading them in the order of their publication; so does Ford, near the end of his introduction to both editions of his book.

3. Cf. John Hollander, *The Untuning of the Sky* (1961; New York: Norton, 1970), 240–41 (Cowley's account of creation to music in bk. 1 of *Davideis*), etc.

4. J. R. R. Tolkien, *The Silmarillion* (Boston: Houghton Mifflin, 1977), "Quenta Silmarillion," chap. 1.

5. Hart, "C.S. Lewis's Defense of Poesie," 297.

6. Lin Carter, *Imaginary Worlds* (New York: Ballantine Books, 1973), 106.

7. The blackness is not noted in Robert Foster, *The Complete Guide to Middle-earth* (New York: Ballantine Books, 1978), "Far Harad."

8. For a longer and, at a number of points, different comparison of Narnia and Middle-earth, see this author's "The World of Narnia," *Niekas*, no. 32 (Winter 1983): 46–57. A number of similar comparisons have been published.

9. A. G. Baumgarten, *Meditationes philosophicae de nonnullis ad poema pertinentibus* (1733), cited in Graham Hough, *An Essay on Criticism* (New York: Norton, 1966), 12, 17, 77, 130.

10. Marsha A. Daigle, "Dante's *Divine Comedy* and the Fiction of C.S. Lewis" (Ph.D. diss., University of Michigan, 1984), 200–13. Daigle's dissertation was finished too late for it to be consulted generally for this book; the author thanks Dr. Daigle for sending him a copy of the chapter on the Chronicles of Narnia. (Her dissertation covers almost all of Lewis's fiction, including *The Pilgrim's Regress* and *The Screwtape Letters*, but excluding *Till We Have Faces*.)

KATH FILMER

Images of Good and Evil in
the Narnian Chronicles

In his essay 'On Three Ways of Writing for Children', Lewis wrote that fairy stories have a particular polemic value because of their power to 'liberate archetypes' (OTOW 62). The title of another of his essays in which this topic is discussed is declarative: 'Sometimes Fairy Stories May Say best What's to be Said' (OTOW 71–75). It is very clear that Lewis believed that 'something' had to be said. But the choice of the fairy story and the chivalric mode for the setting of his children's stories also betray much about the man himself. Here is clear evidence, sufficient even if he had not taken the time to admit that he was a 'dinosaur', a model of 'old Western man' ('De Descriptione Temporum' SLE 13–14), an admirer of 'the discarded image' of medievalism (DI 216), that Lewis's heart was anywhere but in the twentieth century, and that his ideals were far from those of the industrial and technological age.

But the Narnian Chronicles reveal much more than a distaste for things modern. Like the adult fictions, they also deal with evil manifested in ordinary things—in contemporary education, in Turkish Delight, in the love of fripperies (for women, of course), and in the misuse of power, particularly in the misuse of the natural world. But, also like his adult fictions, the Narnian Chronicles focus relentlessly upon the notion of evil arising from enslavement to the unredeemed, self-serving self.

From *The Fiction of C.S. Lewis: Mask and Mirror.* © 1993 by Kath Filmer.

That these themes appear in the Narnian Chronicles establishes a strong thematic link between them and the remainder of Lewis's fictional oeuvre; but of course the same themes recur throughout the range of his apologetics, and, interestingly enough, in his literary criticism as well. For example, in his 'A Note on Jane Austen' (1954), Lewis takes care to remark favourably on Austen's pattern of 'awakening' or 'undeception' by which characters 'discover that they have been making mistakes both about themselves and about the world in which they live. All their *data* have to be reinterpreted' (SLE 177, emphasis in original). This is, of course, precisely the 'pattern' of Lewis's own fiction. Nowhere is it more evident, however, than in the experiences of the children who find themselves in Narnia—a magical parallel universe in which the children's perceptions of themselves and their own world are challenged through encounters with the Lion Aslan, and with the various forms of evil which arise, either in Narnia itself, or in the hearts of the visiting children.

Evil emerges 'by little and little' in the first book of the Narnian series, from the foolishness of Edmund who forgets that children must never shut a wardrobe door behind them (LWW 30), and later, with Edmund's greed for Turkish Delight. He is seduced (in the sense of beguilement, but in Lewis's fiction there is always an underlying sense of a male fear of female sexuality) by a White Witch, whose evil nature is marked by several archetypal attributes. There is, for example, a marked similarity between this Witch and Hans Christian Andersen's Snow Queen, since both create a thraldom of winter, which is, according to Northrop Frye's table of Mythoi, itself an archetypal seasonal image for the rule of evil (Frye, *Anatomy of Criticism* 16). The Witch's face is 'white like paper or icing sugar' (LWW 33), suggesting at once the disguise of a paper mask and the notion of disease and nausea (from the ingestion of icing sugar—which, incidentally, coats some varieties of Turkish Delight). The whiteness is bloodless and deathly, barren and cruel; the White Witch has no love relationship and no progeny, and Medusa-like, turns living beings into stone. Readers are reminded of the bloodless, barren technology of the NICE in *That Hideous Strength* and the turnip and cabbage fields near the sinister hideout of Weston and Devine in *Out of the Silent Planet*. This association of evil with the lack of organic life further exemplifies the consistent use of images Lewis uses to depict elements of his moral lexicon.

Aslan, by contrast, not only is resurrected from death, but gives life back to the witch's statues; he represents the Good, and is quite clearly a figure of Christ, transposed to the new, animal/human world of Narnia. If upon earth, animals were placed under the dominion of humans (see Genesis 1:26), in Narnia humans are under the dominion of the Lion, and what rule they enjoy over the Narnian populace of human and non-human characters is only imputed to them by Aslan.

The White Witch is, readers learn later, another manifestation of Queen Jadis of Charn, and like Lewis's other evil characters, she betrays herself through her speech. In *The Magician's Nephew*, the book which flashes back to the creation and fall of Narnia, Jadis reduces the world of Charn to ruins through her use of 'the Deplorable Word' in order to gain ascendancy over her sister. The Deplorable Word destroys all living things, sparing only the person who speaks it, and Jadis thinks nothing of the fact that in using this power she has destroyed her own people: 'What else were they there for but to do *my* will?' she asks (MN 61). Jadis, seeking to dominate and destroy others, is another version of Pam from *The Great Divorce* and Orual from *Till We Have Faces*, the mother in *The Screwtape Letters*, and to some extent, Fairy Hardcastle from *That Hideous Strength*. But Jadis is also something of a comic character; in this instance as with Edmund in the earlier book, Lewis wants his juvenile readers to scorn evil for its clownish ineptitude.

Uncle Andrew, for whom Jadis is 'a dem fine woman' (MN 171), allies himself with her and for his trouble is also constantly seen as a figure of fun, a bungling magician, a clown himself in the farcical scene when he and Jadis take to the streets of London. Andrew is also whiningly self-serving; he is eager enough to send the children into the mysterious 'Other Place' accessible through the use of his magic rings, but he refuses to go himself, sprouting excuses: 'at my time of life ... in my state of health ... you might meet anything—anything' (MN 26).

In the Narnian Chronicles, Lewis draws not from a Christian but from a chivalric ethos to depict evil as cowardice. Uncle Andrew is cowardly, so too is Eustace in *The Voyage of the Dawn Treader*, a bully who really is 'a puny little person who couldn't have stood up even to Lucy, let alone Edmund, in a fight' (VDT 7). Eustace is made to reveal himself in a kind of confessional diary (the same device, essentially, that Lewis uses for Orual; the entire novel *Till We Have Faces* consists of Orual's *Confessions*). Eustace's diary is a farrago of complaints, self-pity, hypochondria and petty spite. The use of a diary in this way is a neat ironic device, since Eustace's complaints about the others on the voyage are turned against Eustace himself, but Lewis does not rely entirely on the device of irony, since the other characters whom Eustace despises are already well known to (and presumably well liked by) readers of the series. Further, there is the determinedly moral tone of the omniscient author, as in his adult fiction, Lewis insists on an authorial 'presence', either through a fictionalised version of himself or through his authorial voice.

Eustace is concerned only for himself; that is clear from his willingness to take more than his ration of water and so deprive others on the voyage.

He seeks to protect himself from reproof or punishment by lying, despite being caught with the cup in his hand, and he protests at the unfairness of the others when they accept a (true) version of the episode from Reepicheep the mouse. At every stage of the event and its consequences, Eustace is seen to be self-serving and greedy. This trait proves to be his undoing, since he is overwhelmed by greed at finding a dragon's treasure; as a result of his greed and selfishness, Eustace is transformed into a dragon.

The argument is, of course, that Eustace's behaviour has always been 'dragonish'—that is, in Lewis's moral lexicon, 'devilish'—and like Orual, Eustace must undergo the same process of self-knowledge and self-individuation. Eustace must see the dragon in himself and put it to 'death'. The persistence of this theme and its endless retellings in Lewis's fiction suggest a preoccupation with it which must have sprung from Lewis's perception of his own spiritual state. This is not surprising, since such preoccupations probably beset most who care about their spiritual pilgrimage and growth, what is surprising is that there should be so little change in the theme and its treatment, so little evidence that Lewis felt that he had achieved at least some measure of growth. It may be, of course, that Lewis felt that the process was necessarily ongoing and repetitive, a constant and unending struggle with the dark aspects of the self. If that was indeed his belief, it is a tragically narrow one.

Eustace is finally rescued from his shape-shifting when he allows Aslan to 'undress' him; that is, to remove the layers of dragon skin from him. This is an unmasking very similar to Orual's in *Till We Have Faces*; the redeemed Eustace emerges after much suffering and is bathed in 'perfectly delicious' water, and finally is given 'new clothes' (VDT 89). Clothes, like the face, express the character and nature of the person behind them. New clothes for Eustace parallel the new faces for Orual and Psyche. The similarity of images is perhaps understandable since *The Voyage of the Dawn Treader* was published only four years before *Till We Have Faces*, although the bathing echoes the episode in Lewis's first novel, *The Pilgrim's Regress*, when John and Vertue cross the brook at the end of their pilgrimage (PR 173, 198).

A more intriguing collection of characters appears in the same book on the island of the Magician and the Monopods. The Monopods with their one foot are obviously physically incomplete, while their incomplete spirituality is demonstrated by their conceit and self-centredness. They provide yet another example of Lewis's ability to adapt fantastic or mythological elements to his polemic purpose, since it is obvious that the Monopods owe something at least to 'such men that have but one foote' described by Sir John Mandeville in his *Travels* (118).[1]

The Magician is a servant of Aslan's and defers to him with the obedience and submission of a subject. He drinks only wine and eats only bread (VDT 126), which suggests a priestly role; he has power over the Monopods and indeed has been responsible for the removal of their second leg (129). This seems to be unnecessarily cruel, despite the disclaimer that this measure was for the Monopods' own good. The Monopods (or 'Dufflepuds' as they call themselves) are harmless and lovable, but as Lucy realises, they must learn to surrender their pride and self love. If, as the imagery suggests, this is a picture of the church with priest and laity, it is hard to be sympathetic to the Magician/priest. The removal of a leg—even by magic—seems an extreme way by which to effect obedience. It appears that Lewis had not quite lost his notion (expounded in *The Pilgrim's Regress*) of the clergy as stern landlords.

The forms of evil in *The Horse and His Boy* are those of enslavement, both physical and spiritual. Shasta is enslaved to the fisherman Arsheesh; when the fisherman decides to sell Shasta, the boy overhears the bargaining and learns that he is not the son of Arsheesh, and decides to run away. He is abetted by the Horse owned by the great lord who has offered to buy Shasta; this is a talking horse from Narnia, whose disobedience to his mother resulted in his capture by the Calormenes, among whom both he and Shasta now live. 'All these years I have been a slave to humans, hiding my true nature ...' the Horse confesses (HB 9).

Similarly, Aravis, the lord's daughter who joins Shasta in his flight to Narnia and freedom, is threatened with marriage to a man she heartily dislikes: she is also 'enslaved', having no control over her own destiny. Narnia symbolises, for Aravis and Shasta and their two horses (Aravis' horse is also a captured Narnian), freedom—from enslavement of various physical kinds, and also, as the quartet later learn, from enslavement to the fallen self as well.

Aravis's friend, Lasaraleen, is also enslaved, this time to fripperies and material possessions and high rank. Although she offers help of a kind, Lasaraleen chooses to remain enslaved to the riches and indulgences of the Calormene court. And Lewis makes sure that his young readers realise that the Calormenes represent evil; the Tisroc and his court are planning to invade Narnia and capture Susan, still reigning as one of the four Kings and Queens of Narnia enthroned in *The Lion, the Witch and the Wardrobe*.

In many ways, this story is a kind of 'pilgrim's progress', since the physical dangers parallel spiritual ones. Each of the four pilgrims is 'undeceived' in a confrontation with Aslan. Shasta learns that he must attend to his own story, not that of anyone else (HB 159); Aravis learns the same lesson, having been made to suffer the same punishments she has inflicted upon her stepmother's slave (HB 194); Hwin offers herself sacrificially to

Aslan to be 'eaten'; and Bree admits, 'I must be rather a fool' (HB 192–93). And in these lessons of humility and self-realisation, the four discover spiritual freedom.

In *The Silver Chair*, Prince Rilian allows himself to be imprisoned by a Green Witch. Like Edmund, he is 'seduced' and beguiled; like Weston on Perelandra, he becomes an un-man, released from his spell only for short periods each day. He begs the children, Jill and Eustace, to help him to escape so that he 'should be a man again' (SC 142). In the enchanted state, Rilian is unable to know his 'true self'.

This is by now a familiar theme, in which the evil magic of the Green Witch symbolises the thraldom of evil and the diminution of the real self which is its result. Evil and deception, whether by an outside agent such as the Green Witch, or self-deception, as in the case of Eustace and Weston, are always paired in Lewis's fiction; and deception is the major motif in *The Last Battle*. Narnians are deceived on several occasions: by the White Witch, by King Miraz in *Prince Caspian*, and by the Green Witch in *The Silver Chair*. They, like Lewis, do not seem to have learned much from earlier experiences; they continue being deceived. In every case, however, the earth-children are able to carry out the instructions of the Lion Aslan and rescue Narnia or individual Narnians from evil. Indeed, in each book there is some kind of rescue operation. Did Lewis long for his own *deus ex machina* to rescue him from the tribulations and anxieties of life? Or was Lewis suggesting that humans have very clear roles to play in the redemption and rescue of their fellows, in the style of the old revivalist hymn, 'Throw out the Lifeline'? But whether one must rely upon rescue or 'work out your own salvation with fear and trembling' (Phil. 2:12) is a matter of theological debate.

Whatever the theological implications, however, there seems to be little relief from the unrelenting pessimism of the beginning of the final Narnian Chronicle, *The Last Battle*, where the narrative persistently points to the destruction of Narnia. Indeed, the book begins sadly and bleakly with the words, 'In the last days of Narnia' (LB 7). It is not surprising, then, to find evil depicted on the first page of the narrative. There it is confined to one circumstance; but from there it proliferates exponentially in accordance with what Lewis expounds all through his fiction, the belief that once evil contaminates a human life or a human society, if it is not hindered, it will grow and flourish at an alarming rate.

Although each of the Narnian stories can be read as a parable with some Biblical referent, none derives so much from Christian apocalyptic writing as *The Last Battle*. Since it deals with Narnian eschatology, it seems reasonable that a parallel apocalyptic might apply; but another model for some of the elements in this book is possibly George Orwell's *Animal Farm*, a novel Lewis admired ('George Orwell', OTOW 136). *Animal Farm* is, in Lewis's view, an effective dystopian beast-fable because of its mythic quality, and since 'the greed and the cunning of the pigs is tragic (not merely odious) because we are made to care about all the honest, well-meaning, or even heroic beasts whom they exploit' (136). *The Last Battle* has the same kind of mythic appeal as *Animal Farm*: instead of a pig, Lewis's crafty tyrant is an ape, but the resemblance between Orwell's Boxer the Horse and Lewis's donkey, Puzzle, is surely more than coincidental. (I shall discuss in detail these and other correspondences between Lewis's polemic and Orwell's in Chapter 4, which deals with Lewis's political vision.)

'Puzzle' is a symbolic name for the donkey. He serves the ape, but (like all others in Lewis's fiction who are enslaved by evil), he fails to see the logical outcome of his actions: 'I see now,' said Puzzle, 'that I really have been a very bad donkey. I ought never to have listened to Shift' (LB 81). Eustace rebukes the donkey, suggesting that Puzzle's preoccupation with himself (even if only with his own lack) has contributed to the conquest of Narnia by the forces of evil. Indeed, Puzzle has allowed himself to be duped into impersonating Aslan; although he protests at first (12), the Ape's hint that the donkey will be guaranteed a supply of sugar is enough to convince him. It is the same kind of trivial, yet enormously evil temptation as that offered by the White Witch in *The Lion, the Witch and the Wardrobe*—the sugary Turkish Delight.

The Ape also employs the same kind of evil *modus operandi* as Lewis's other villains: the domination of others. It is therefore quite clear that Lewis uses the same symbolic motifs throughout the *oeuvre* of his fiction, linking all the books thematically. The essential critical distinctions among Lewis's novels in terms of treatment and style are those only of genre and are not justifiable in terms of theme, message, or symbolic meaning. Since the Narnian Chronicles were written towards the end of Lewis's writing career they also serve to show how entrenched were Lewis's views on matters of morality and belief; they share precisely the same polemic purpose as his adult novels.

In *The Last Battle*, the Ape becomes the tool of evil through his self-serving and self-aggrandising manipulation of Puzzle and other Narnians, and is at last thrown to the false god Tash, in whom the Ape professes not to believe, only to be devoured by the evil he had served when he had deceived himself into thinking that he merely served himself (125). Deceit is symptomatic of the evil the Ape serves, and the narrative contains many instances of it. The Ape claims to be a Man and 'the only one Aslan is ever going to speak to' (LB 33). More significantly, the Ape tells the Narnians to work for the Calormenes and their god, Tash, because 'Tash is only another name for Aslan' (35). Lewis is arguing against the evil of deception in religion, when supernatural deity is said to be 'no more' than an idol of human artifice (37). Here, as in his ethical essays, collectively titled *The Abolition of Man*, Lewis argues for an objective reality which cannot be reduced to subjective interpretation without deception. It is a surprisingly narrow view for one who incorporates so much of paganism, Platonism, Hermeticism and Greek myth into his own fantasies; it is probably the view which appeals most to Lewis's American Fundamentalist fans, and one which possibly accounts for Lewis's own absolutism.

Throughout the Narnian Chronicles, Lewis has evil confounded by Truth. Thus in *The Lion, the Witch and the Wardrobe*, Edmund denies Lucy's account of their adventures in Narnia; in *The Voyage of the Dawn Treader*, Eustace jeers at Lucy's enjoyment of the picture of the Narnian ship, but in both instances, Lewis's authorial voice assures us that Lucy 'is a very truthful girl' (VDT 10, LWW 29). Further, the evil of the White Witch is confounded by Aslan's calling forth the 'Deeper Magic from before the Dawn of Time' and conquering death (LWW 148). In *The Silver Chair*, Puddleglum's insistence on believing in what the Green Witch insists is a 'play world' ('I'm on Aslan's side even if there isn't any Aslan to lead it' [SC 156]) leads to the defeat of evil. In *The Horse and His Boy*, the reality of Aslan confronts all those lies and distortions created about him in the land of Calormen which have so blinded Shasta and Aravis. In *The Last Battle*, the good is seen to be the ultimate reality which lies beyond the material world. Emeth, the Calormene who has loved and served Tash, is rewarded by Aslan because Emeth has seen beyond Tash to truth and has served the truth: 'all find what they truly seek' (LB 156).[2] The transformation of Puzzle after the passing of Narnia also serves Lewis's polemic purpose; the donkey has become its true self: 'He was himself now: a beautiful donkey with such a soft, grey coat and such a gentle honest face ...' (LB 158–59). Surrender to Aslan has made Puzzle a true self. He is no longer a puzzle, but an individual made whole.

Though like most fairy tales *The Last Battle* is concerned with the victory of good over evil in an abstract sense, it also deals with the question of the same kind of victory in individual lives. The donkey symbolises all those who 'mean well' despite their lapses into evil; for such individuals, Lewis has some compassion, since in his fiction, to mean well indicates future redemption. As Ransom, the Director of St Anne's, tells Jane Studdock in *That Hideous Strength*: 'this is the Courtesy of Deep Heaven: that when you mean well, He always takes you to have meant better than you know' (THS 282).

By contrast, Lewis uses stereotypes for his villains, so that, in the Narnian Chronicles, evil is symbolised by the dwarf Nikabrik (in *Prince*

Caspian) who is a necromancer; by Uncle Andrew (in *The Magician's Nephew*) who is a sorcerer; and two witches, one green, one white; while in the Ransom trilogy, Weston and Devine are the stereotypes of the evil scientist and the greedy capitalist who seek power, Weston through cosmic forces, Devine through material means. In *The Screwtape Letters* and *The Great Divorce*, evil is portrayed as petty, spiteful, dominating and devouring, and ultimately self-destructive.

In every instance, evil is seen as enslavement—to a Cause or to deception; and ultimately, to the fallen Self.

It has been said that 'Polemics generally consists in trying to maintain one's own position intact whilst blasting holes in that of one's opponent' (Leech 58), and stereotyping of the kind Lewis employs in his fiction is one way of 'blasting holes'. Lewis uses stereotypes to show the human face of evil, at least as he saw it, in terms of spiritual cannibalism and domination. Generally, however, Lewis does not seem unsympathetic to the individual who is enslaved, although such individuals are made to bear the responsibility and the odium of their own spiritual disintegration.

Lewis consistently represents evil as disease, self-centredness, domination, deception, devouring, and above all, as a mere parody of what is solid and real. He portrays good as wholeness, self-abnegation and surrender; as beauty, truth, and 'undeception', and as ultimate reality and freedom. These would seem respectively to be the things from which he personally shrank and to which he personally aspired; his fiction mirrors his continuing desire for personal wholeness, a desire which seems to have been his whole life's quest.

NOTES

1. See *The Voiage and Travayle of Sir John Maundeville Knight: Which Treateth of the way towards Hierusalem and of Marvayles of Inde with Other Hands and Countreys*, edited, annotated and illustrated in Facsimile by John Ashton (London: Pickering and Chatto, 1887); an editorial footnote to this section of Mandeville's work points out that like other instances in Mandeville's *Travels*, the monopods are derived from Pliny's *Natural History*, Book 7, Chapter 11.

2. According to *Strong's Exhaustive Concordance to the Bible*, the name 'Emeth' in Hebrew means 'truth and faith'.

COLIN MANLOVE

The Lion, the Witch and the Wardrobe

*T*he *Lion, the Witch and the Wardrobe*, probably the best known of the Narnia books, stands alone perhaps more than any other book of the *Chronicles*. It is true that several of the other stories are "finished" in the sense of being self-contained: a rightful king or prince is restored in *Prince Caspian*, *The Silver Chair*, and *The Horse and His Boy*; a voyage to the end of the world is completed in *The Voyage of the "Dawn Treader."* Yet we know that these narratives are excerpts from the history of Narnia, with a before and after, where the first book is our first account of the country. (We know too that Lewis originally wrote it with no thought to a sequel.[1]) Lewis struck in *The Lion, the Witch and the Wardrobe* a blend of fantasy and the everyday that he was not again to match. The book is an extraordinary mixture of diverse things, from a lion who is a Narnian Christ to a witch out of fairy tale, from a Father Christmas out of myth to a female beaver with a sewing machine drawn from Beatrix Potter, from a society of articulate beasts and animate trees to a group of strongly characterized children partly derived from Edith Nesbit. This is the only book in which the children themselves become kings and queens of Narnia. In all the others they are relative outsiders, and in all but *The Magician's Nephew* the rulers of Narnia come from within the fantastic realm. This separation adds to the sense of a Narnia that goes on without them. The "proximity" of the children to Narnia in *The Lion*, their

---

From *The Chronicles of Narnia: The Patterning of a Fantastic World*. © 1993 by Twayne Publishers.

close involvement in its transformation from deathly winter to the spring of new life, gives that book a special poignancy: the children do not come so close to the innocence of a fantastic world again, not even in *The Magician's Nephew*, where Narnia is created by Aslan. In *The Voyage of the "Dawn Treader,"* the image of spiritual longing realized in the risen life of Aslan, and the victory and enthronement of the children as Sons of Adam and Daughters of Eve, is found only by going out of the world, by journeying across the seas to its end and *beyond*: what was "immanent" in *The Lion* is there found only by a process of transcendence. Narnia in *The Lion* is increasingly and uniquely shot through with holiness, embodied in the coming and eventual victory of Aslan. In the later books it is a much more secular world, with Aslan's presence more limited. *The Lion* seems to contain a pattern of spiritual renewal sufficient to itself: the winter of the White Witch is turned to spring, the cold laws of the Stone Table are transcended by the grace of Aslan's sacrifice, the sin of man is washed away in the restoration of Adam and Eve's lineage to their rightful thrones, the devil in the shape of the White Witch is finally slain, the paradise that was lost is regained. The whole seems to encapsulate something of the primal rhythm of Christian history, within the idiom of another world.

Lewis's method of introducing us to the realm of Narnia is, perhaps naturally, much more gradual in *The Lion* than in the later books, where the children are suddenly whisked away from a railway station where they are waiting to go their several ways to boarding school (*Prince Caspian*), or fall into a picture of an ancient sailing ship (*The Voyage of the "Dawn Treader"*), or are transported to Narnia via their deaths in a railway crash (*The Last Battle*). *The Lion, the Witch and the Wardrobe* portrays the gradual joining of two worlds. The emphasis in this novel, as in *The Magician's Nephew* and *The Last Battle*, which respectively describe the creation and eventual "uncreation" of Narnia, is on the permeability of Narnia (there through its fragility of being, here as part of a divine plan): it is entered, variously, by the children (on three different occasions), by Father Christmas, and by Aslan himself. It is of course a place that needs stimulus from the outside if it is to regain life at all, for it is a world frozen to perpetual winter by an evil witch, and nothing will change so long as she and her ice have power over it. But more than this, the book describes a gradual *incarnating*: not only Aslan's actions but the children's presence, long prophesied, in making themselves part of this world, will overthrow the witch and restore Narnia to its true nature.

For the moment let us deal with the first point, the gradualness of the approach. First the children are withdrawn from society by being sent away from the London air raids in wartime to their uncle's house in the remote country, "ten miles from the nearest railway station and two miles from the nearest post office" (9). This uncle is odd-looking; he has so much white hair that it "grew over most of his face as well as on his head" (9). The servants of the house are mentioned only to be dismissed as of no consequence to the story. The children are left free to do as they wish. All the time, identity and boundaries are melting away. The house is vast and uncharted. The world outside it seems a wilderness of mountains and woods, with the possibility of eagles, stags, and hawks among them, as well as the more domestic badgers, foxes, and rabbits (10). There is a hint here of likeness to the landscape of the world the children are to enter.

The discovery of Narnia, too, is gradual. One rainy day the children set out to explore the house, and one of them, Lucy (from *lux* meaning "light" or "perception"), investigates the inside of an old wardrobe in an otherwise empty room. It is a casual-seeming occurrence that turns to something quite other. Beyond one line of fur coats in the wardrobe Lucy finds another, and then as she pushes through that and feels the ground begin to crunch under her feet, fur turns to fir and she finds herself in a pine forest with the snow falling. The gradualism here is a marvelous tapering of everyday world into fantastic realm.

Once in this strange new world, Lucy meets a faun, Mr. Tumnus, in the forest, and it emerges, as she takes tea with him in his home, that he is a spy for the wicked White Witch. Having remorsefully confessed this, he ushers Lucy back through the wardrobe into her own world. Lucy is amazed to find that no time has passed in her absence—which could make her experience seem a dream. She tells the others of her adventure but they do not believe her, least of all the scoffing Edmund; and the wardrobe when examined by the children is now obstinately nothing but a wardrobe. Aslan's purposes transcend human wish and will. After some days, during a game of hide-and-seek on another wet day, Lucy has hidden in the wardrobe and Edmund pursues her there, only to find himself in Narnia. He then meets the White Watch herself, and she, mindful of the menace to her if the prophecy should come true and four humans become rightful kings and queens of Narnia, bribes Edmund to bring his brother and sisters to her castle. Edmund finds Lucy on his way back to the wardrobe in the Narnian wood (she has been with Mr. Tumnus again), but when they return to their uncle's house and Lucy looks to Edmund for support, he tells the others that he has only been humoring Lucy's delusion. The next move occurs one day when all four children are trying to escape a group of visitors who are being given a tour through the house. They are eventually driven to the room with the wardrobe and through the wardrobe itself into Narnia. Now all believe, and what is believed in has shifted from an indefinite place to another world in which they are set. First one, then two, then four children have entered Narnia.

Once there, there are further gradations. At first visitors, the children are brought to realize that they are in part the focus of the hopes of the Narnian creatures. What seemed accident is part of a larger pattern, if they will play their part, and if Aslan comes to help. Initially guests of the Beavers, the three children (Edmund having sneaked away to the witch) are soon active agents in the cause of Narnia. And what Narnia is and means continually deepens. At first perhaps a fairy-tale world, it does not stop being that while also being a landscape of the spirit frozen in primal sin; and the witch, who seems something straight out of Hans Christian Andersen, retains something of this fairy-tale "lightness" while at the same time becoming an agent of ultimate evil, daughter of Lilith and the giants, and ancient enemy of Aslan. Then, too, we have what seem to be layers of magic, with the witch's evil wand that turns creatures to stone at one level, and the "Deep Magic" by which Aslan may through sacrificial death rise again, at quite another. Aslan himself is lion and much more than lion. As for the children, they do not till the end stop being themselves even when accomplishing heroic deeds. The Peter who slays Maugrim, the witch's great wolf, is still a frightened but resolute boy, and the Edmund who, reformed, hinders the witch from final victory in the battle by breaking her wand, is awarded plaudits which make him at once heroic and the brightest boy in the class.

But by this point the children are very "far in" (to use one of Lewis's favorite phrases). Just as the story has taken them to a world inside a wardrobe inside a room in a house within the heart of beleaguered England, so they have penetrated to the center of Narnia and in the end become its cynosures, as they sit dispensing justice and largess on the four thrones at the castle of Cair Paravel. They are the sovereign human element long missing from the hierarchy of rational or "Talking Beasts" of Narnia, and in that sense they belong most fully to that world. At that point things have changed: they are no longer children but young adults, they have forgotten their own world, and they speak the elevated language of medieval romance. That loss of former self, and the length of sojourn in Narnia, is found with no other of the children of the *Chronicles*: Lewis has steadily moved the children away from their old selves and understandings until they become wholly part of another world. Even the style that describes them has changed: "And they entered into friendship and alliance with countries beyond the sea and paid them visits of state and received visits of state from them. And they themselves grew and changed as the years passed over them" (166); "So they lived in great joy and if ever they remembered their life in this world it was only as one remembers a dream" (167). And then having accomplished this, Lewis briskly returns the children to their own world through their pursuit of a white stag that leads them to a thicket wherein is the wardrobe; through which they return to England, abruptly restored to child form and their present-day clothes, having been absent, by the time of this world, for not one moment. This perhaps serves as an exercise in humility and a reminder that nothing that is mortal is permanent (a point to be made much more openly concerning Narnia itself in *The Last Battle*).

To some extent what is portrayed in this process is a form of spiritual development on the part of the children. They are asked to develop out of an old awareness into a new. They must show faith, trust, compassion, perception, and courage in transforming Narnia. It may be mistaken to see what happens too much from Narnia's point of view, with the children its promised saviors. It might be better to recall also that Lewis was steeped in allegory, and particularly in Spenser's *The Faerie Queene*, in which the landscape of Fairy Land is that of the soul. Narnia is, in one sense at least, a country within a wardrobe; a wardrobe seems an appropriate conveyance to Narnia, as it is a place for different clothes. If, too, we were to think of the children not just as four individuals, but also potentially as four parts of the one spirit, we might not always be wide of the mark. When the children first see Mr. Beaver surreptitiously beckoning to them from among the Narnian trees, the following exchange ensues:

> "It wants us to go to it," said Susan, "and it is warning us not to make a noise."
> "I know," said Peter. "The question is, are we to go to it or not? What do you think, Lu?"
> "I think it's a nice beaver," said Lucy.
> "Yes, but how do we *know*?" said Edmund.
> "Shan't we have to risk it?" said Susan. "I mean, it's no good just standing here and I feel I want some dinner." (62)

It is possible to see Susan as "the body" here, simply observing and registering physical needs, with Peter as "reason," Lucy as the enlightened soul, and Edmund as the evil side of the self. Such a reading is certainly too stark, and the characters do play other roles elsewhere in the narrative. But the story as a whole can be seen as a spiritual journey through a landscape of the soul, from the frost of original sin to the flowers of the redeemed spirit; one in which the kingship and queenship reached at the end, and the completion of the hierarchy of creation in Narnia by the humans, suggest the integration and potential perfection of the soul in Christ. Such a reading might explain why in this book, the children are frequently isolated from one another (just as, say, Una and Redcrosse are divided in the first book of *The*

Faerie Queene): Lucy alone, then Edmund alone, then Edmund away from the other three, then the girls absent from their brothers, and finally all four united. It is as though the spirit is broken up to be reconstituted. This reading at the very least shows how no single understanding of Narnia or the characters in it is adequate—there are multiple possibilities.

Either way, literally or allegorically, what is portrayed in *The Lion, the Witch and the Wardrobe* is growth away from the old self. Growth out of death is a theme central to the book, as Aslan dies to bring new life and winter turns to spring: that is the allegorical and anagogical level of the book (to use Dante's terms), where with the children the development is at the moral or tropological level. The antitype here is of course the witch. She is concerned only with maintaining her power over Narnia. She does nothing with it, exists for no other reason than to keep it (in contrast to the multiple activities of the children when they are kings and queens of Narnia). And Narnia expresses the nature of her spirit: frozen, uniform, static. For all life that thinks to exist independently of her will she has one answer: turn it to stone. Her castle seems to have nothing in it, and she herself in the end is nothing. That was the course Edmund would have gone. Drawn to her by his own self-conceit (where Lucy meets Mr. Tumnus, he "happens" upon the witch), he is tempted to bring his brother and sisters into her power to satisfy his appetites in the form of the Turkish Delight she offers him.

Where those whose allegiance is to the witch take, those whose allegiance is to Aslan give. The children are the long-awaited gift to Narnia. Aslan is a gift beyond telling, his coming turning winter to spring. He gives his life for Edmund's. Even Narnia itself, as a place of recovered innocence, is a gift of high adventure to the children. Right at the center of the narrative, not the anomaly he has sometimes been seen,[2] is the arrival of Father Christmas, with a sackful of gifts for everyone. And *The Lion, the Witch and the Wardrobe* as a whole is a "box of delights" full for the reader of the most wonderful creatures and events, which become still richer as one "opens" them. The book, as a progressive revelation of Aslan's nature and of the deepest potential of the children, is like a gift gradually arrived at.

The narrowness of the self is "answered" in the character of the narrative of the book. Its title, *The Lion, the Witch and the Wardrobe*, suggests its creation out of at least three separate acts of the imagination. But all come together to make a pattern long foreseen: each "separate" item is part of a larger unity. So it is with the plot itself, which is really a series of "microplots." At first there is the issue of whether or not Narnia is real. Then there is the plan of the witch to seize the children and their escape from her. With Aslan's arrival, and spring's, the witch seems defeated, especially when Edmund is rescued from death at her hands. But then there is a new plot begun by her claim to Edmund's life through an old law that makes traitors forfeit to her. The later stages of conflict with the witch involve two plots: in one Peter, Edmund, and the Narnians fight her and her forces, while in the other Aslan breathes new life into the Narnians who were made statues at the witch's castle so that they may come to the aid of the others. All these little plots amalgamate to bring about the realization of the grand design, like little selves cooperating with others. And this idea of cooperation, of society, is central. The children themselves are constituents of Narnian society, to which we are progressively introduced throughout. This particular use of microplots is unique to *The Lion, the Witch and the Wardrobe*. Other books (apart from *The Magician's Nephew*) have a much more clear-cut quest or objective from the outset, but here a series of apparently local and unconnected doings together provide the key to unlock Narnia. In a sense, too, these isolated doings might in some cases suggest the benightedness of the soul amid evil: conditions under the witch in Narnia are such that incoherence is inevitable. Then the nighttime setting of many of the scenes in Narnia is also significant; and that Father Christmas arrives, Aslan rises again, and final victory over the witch is won in the morning.

Other features of the book seem to belong to this rejection of narrowness. For one thing, there is, as already partly seen, the theme of growing and of expansion. Growth is inherent in the story itself, which from apparently small beginnings involving a girl and a faun becomes an epic on which the fate of an entire world depends. Narnia is wakened from its sleep, the talking animals from their hiding-places, the spellbound creatures from stone, Aslan from death itself. The adventure begins through a "narrow" wardrobe that turns out to open onto a whole world. Inside Narnia the perspective gradually expands. At first the omnipresence of the snow makes the adventures relatively local: Mr. Tumnus here, the Beavers there, the White Witch beyond. Gradually creatures congregate, and we begin to get a sense of Narnia as a whole and of the issues at stake. The Stone Table commands a view of all Narnia. Cair Paravel, the ultimate destination of the children, is in an open place by the shore of a sea that stretches to the world's end. The witch's castle however, is set in a hollow among hills, shut in on itself. She lives alone, but for the children the whole story involves an increase of friends: they themselves become the centers of a whole society.

We might extrapolate from the way that the White Witch has converted Narnia to a mirror image of herself in the form of one monotonous dead white, the mode by which Lewis refuses to let us settle to one view of a thing. Throughout, the children continually have their assumptions displaced. Mr. Tumnus is not just the jolly domestic host he appears to be; the wardrobe is more than a wardrobe; Narnia is not an illusion; Edmund is not rewarded by the witch; Edmund's rescue from the witch is not final; Aslan is not dead, but even more alive than before; they who were kings and queens of Narnia are in an instant returned to being modern children. Reality is not to be appropriated; its richness and depth elude ready absorption by mind. Our idea of Narnia is continually altered: at first apparently a little "play" world, it becomes more threatening with the witch, more metaphysical with Aslan, more holy in its ultimate foundation through Aslan's journey. Even then we are not to know the true and further realities until the afterworlds of *The Last Battle* are revealed, and Narnia upon Narnia lead us "farther up and farther in." Nothing is "mere": Lewis chose children as heroic protagonists to demonstrate that fact.

The object of the witch is to reduce all things to one dead level, to draw them back into herself. But the object of the story is in part to show how different, how "other" from one another things can be. To our minds Narnia may suggest the world of Andersen's "Snow Queen," of Kenneth Grahame or of traditional Christmas, but such a stereotype is swiftly dispelled as we find that this is a world in which the struggle between good and evil is between God and the devil. And if we then proceed to see similarities between Aslan's sacrifice and that of Christ in our world, we at once see that they are also quite different. Aslan is a lion in another world called Narnia. His voluntary death as a substitute for Edmund is not the same as Christ's less-chosen Crucifixion, nor His effective death on behalf of all men. Even the special sordid intimacy of Aslan's stabbing by the witch is quite different from Christ's more solitary and drawn-out bodily pain on the cross. Nor is it Aslan alone who saves Narnia: he does that through the mortal agency of the children and the Narnians themselves. The Deep Magic ordained by the "Emperor," whereby all traitors are forfeit to the witch or else all Narnia will be destroyed, is quite different in form from the "magic" that binds our world. Of course there are similarities. The process whereby Aslan dies only to rise again transfigured, is like Christ's death and resurrection. The breaking of the great Stone Table on which he is sacrificed is perhaps like the breaking of the power of the grave: as he tells the children, the witch did not know the "Deeper Magic" that "when a willing victim who had committed no treachery was killed in a traitor's stead, the Table would crack and Death itself would start working backwards" (148). In terms of ultimate metaphysics, this is what Christ's death brought about in our world: though in Narnia the idea of death working backward has much more immediate and absolute import, in the sense that the deathlike winter of the witch's power over Narnia is now destroyed, and with the children enthroned Narnia will for the time become a recovered paradise. The basic pattern of the magic that Aslan enacts, because it is a spiritual rhythm based on divine reality, will be the same in all worlds; but in all worlds it will also be uniquely manifested.

The Lion, the Witch and the Wardrobe, then, dramatizes the difference between good and evil. There is more attention to the good, because it is more real. The witch as yet has no name, nor has her dwarf; she and her agents are present much less than the Narnians, Aslan, and the children. Where she is separate from Narnia, the children become progressively more involved, "farther in." She can only reduce things—Narnia to stasis, the rational creatures of Narnia to stone, Aslan to a shorn cat—even herself, at Edmund's rescue, to a mere formless boulder. In opposition to her the book is full of selves and "things." In no other of the Narnia books are the children so distinguished from one another: the impetuous, loving and perceptive Lucy, the rather more stolid and self-regarding Susan, the cynical and jealous Edmund, the rational and brave Peter. In themselves they are complex, a varying compound of good and evil that the witch can never be; and as a group they form a multiple nature. Further, they all change and develop through the narrative. Then there is the variety of creatures in Narnia, and of the objects that surround them. There are a faun, a pair of beavers, Father Christmas, a great lion who is more than lion, and a group of modern children. The variety is heightened by juxtapositions—fur coats and fir trees, a lamppost in a wood, a faun with an umbrella, a female beaver with a sewing machine. The book conveys a gradual increase of population—first one faun, then two beavers, then a party of Narnians at a table; by the time the children and the beavers reach the hill of the Stone Table where a pavilion is pitched, the pace of creation seems suddenly to leap, as they find Aslan surrounded by a whole group of Narnians as though they had been begotten by him—which, since he has released them from the Narnian winter, is in part true. Still more it is true later when he recreates more of the Narnians out of the stone to which the witch has turned them by the even more deadly winter of her wand. For Aslan death "is only more life."[3] Everything that is good grows, and grows still more like its true nature.

At the center is Aslan. We see the witch early, but he is long heralded before his appearance. When first we see him the first words are, "Aslan stood." He is the creator, not the created; he is supreme being, *Yahweh*, "I am" (Exodus 3:14), to the witch's negativity. He radiates being to all about him. In him oppositions are not at war, as in most mortals, but are brought into energetic unity: he is both god and lion, both lovable and fearful. "People who have not been in Narnia sometimes think that a thing cannot be good and terrible at the same time. If the children had ever thought so, they were cured of it now. For when they tried to look at Aslan's face they just caught a glimpse of the golden mane and the great, royal, solemn, overwhelming eyes; and then they found they couldn't look at him and went all trembly" (117). In the wake of the shame and humiliation of his death he can still play with the children in a romp at which "whether it was more like playing with a thunderstorm or playing with a kitten Lucy could never make up her mind" (148–49).

*   *   *

The theme of growth and expansion that we have seen in this story is one that will be found throughout the *Chronicles of Narnia*; the enemy will always be that which shuts in, isolates, or immobilizes. Every story will have a variation on the idea of no time at all passing in our world while the children have their adventures in Narnia, so that they return to waiting at a railway station, looking at a picture in a bedroom, or to a school where they are being pursued by bullies, at exactly the moment they left. Every book will show a gradual increase in society, from more or less isolated figures at the start, to gathering groups and then often meetings with whole peoples. Space, too, will grow, just as in *The Lion* a wardrobe opened into a forest, and that forest was found to be part of a whole country, and that country of a world.... There will be a similar process in *Prince Caspian*. In *The Voyage of the "Dawn Treader"* a picture of a ship will turn into an actual ship on a wide ocean, and a voyage to the east will extend through realm after realm until it reaches the truest realm of all. In *The Silver Chair* we will begin to explore the lands to the west of Narnia. In *The Horse and His Boy* we will be outside Narnia, in the land of Calormen, traveling back. In *The Magician's Nephew* we will enter three different worlds by magic. And in *The Last Battle* the Narnia we know will give way to larger and ever more real Narnias beyond it. And all this enlargement will be preparing us for the final journey to Aslan's country at the end of *The Last Battle*, a place of living paradox where the smaller contains the greater, where true progression is found where there is no time, where to go "farther up and farther in" is to go farther out, and where one's true identity exists beyond the loss of self in death. Meanwhile, throughout, the *Chronicles of Narnia* will be telling a story, a chronicle, of the birth, life, and death of Narnia: but they will also passingly embody, through paradox, reversals of narrative and often-felt Divine Providence behind the action, a sense within each "net of successive moments" of "something that is not successive," the eternity that is Aslan ablaze about the coiled filament of Narnian time.

NOTES

1. "When I wrote the *Lion* I had no notion of writing the others" (Letter of 2 December 1962 in *Letters of C.S. Lewis*, 307).

2. As by Green and Hooper, *C.S. Lewis*, 241; Peter Schakel, *Reading with the Heart*, 140 n. 24; Donald E. Glover, *C.S. Lewis*, 241. Compare, however, Wilson, *C.S. Lewis*, 221.

3. George MacDonald, "The Golden Key" (1867), in *The Light Princess and Other Tales* (London: Victor Gollancz, 1967), 238.

LIONEL ADEY

Children's Storyteller

Of all the books by Lewis, the Chronicles of Narnia have attracted and retained the largest readership. Critics have explored their plots, characters, and genre, religious and moral teaching, language, biblical and literary sources, structural devices, symbols, and motifs, not to mention the geography of their imagined worlds.[1] Just as it seemed that nothing new could be said about them, I read David Holbrook's *Skeleton in the Wardrobe*.[2] After so many encomia on the stories, this book acted as a shot of adrenalin, but when a Leavisite critic attempts assassination by psychoanalysis, no friend of Narnia can stand by and do nothing.

Holbrook gives two reasons for thinking the tales unfit for children. The first is that Lewis was insufficiently mature to handle the "deeply disturbing material" (Holbrook, 173) that welled up from his unconscious as he wrote. Queen Jadis the White Witch (*Magician's Nephew, The Lion, the Witch and the Wardrobe*) and the Witch of the Green Kirtle (*Silver Chair*) emanated from Lewis's mother, who had not only rejected him by dying but had earlier failed to confer a secure identity through creative play. Aslan, the Christ of Narnia (whose name Lewis derived from the euphonious Turkish word for lion),[3] bounded into Narnia "out of Lewis's own unconscious" (Holbrook, 55), originating in Rev. Robert Capron, the flagellating principal of Wynyard School ("Belsen"). Having identified with the aggressor, the

From *C.S. Lewis: Writer, Dreamer, and Mentor.* © 1998 by William B. Eerdmans Publishing, Co.

"unhappy child" (Holbrook, 11) surviving within the distinguished academic turned Capron into a punitive deity.

Holbrook goes on with the happy freedom of an amateur psychoanalyst to convert Mrs. Lewis's "cheerful and tranquil affection" (*Surprised by Joy*, 9) into maternal coldness and inadequacy, and her nine-year-old son's grief into a castration complex (Holbrook, 36, 48–49). He infers a presumption that her cancer had resulted from marital intercourse (Holbrook, 65), that her "Bad Breast" is represented in the spires and turrets of the White Witch's castle (Holbrook, 36, 68, 73), and that a Narnian lamp-post represents the paternal penis (Holbrook, 67). In response to such an interpretation, the uninventive scholar can only protest that from at one time daily readings of Wordsworth's *Prelude* Lewis was fully conscious of the maternal role in forming a child's identity, and that he nowhere wrote of being thrashed at Wynyard, only of his unsought status as Capron's "pet."[4]

Admittedly the most convincing villains in the tales are female, and the heroes include three orphan princes. Compared to Queen Jadis, King Miraz (*Prince Caspian*) is a paper cutout of Hamlet's wicked uncle, and Uncle Andrew (*Magician's Nephew*) a clown. Since Jadis the Queen-Witch existed from before the creation of Narnia, her name probably derives from the French word *jadis* ("formerly," "once upon a time") rather than from "jade" ("nightmare") as Holbrook suggests (Holbrook, 65). She brought about the ruin of the ancient city of Charn, introduced evil into the world on the day of Narnia's creation (*Magician's Nephew*), and practiced "Deep Magic from the dawn of time" (*The Lion, the Witch and the Wardrobe*, chap. 13). As I have argued, Lewis's antifeminism and need of a surrogate mother did result from his childish perception of being abandoned by his mother and the added shock of being sent so soon to boarding school. But this does not license conjectures about his babyhood for which neither *Surprised by Joy* nor the letters of Mrs. Lewis offer any support, so as to turn her into a witch. Nor will supposed parallels with psychiatric patients prove much about Lewis.

There is more to support Holbrook's belief that Capron's cruelty inflicted lasting damage. Lewis describes with horror seeing a classmate caned (*Surprised by Joy*, 28), an experience I recall as being more distressing than being caned in person. But Lewis's own attribution of his first religious convictions—and terrors—to the faith of clergy at the Anglo-Catholic church near the school (*Surprised by Joy*, 33) implies an identification with them rather than with the clerical sadist Capron.

As regards the "minatory" (Holbrook, 34 et al.) figure of Aslan, it is important to note that punishments in the tales usually involve religious symbolism. Thus the metamorphosis of Eustace into a dragon (*Voyage of the "Dawn Treader"*) alludes to a biblical image of the devil (Revelation 12:3–9).

The peeling of the dragon skin down to the boy's heart, which Holbrook converts from singular to plural (Aslan "lacerates and unpeels people": Holbrook, 30), represents conversion and repentance. Its good effects can be seen in Eustace's satisfaction in helping his fellow voyagers while still a dragon and in his newly developed sense of humor once restored to human shape. Aslan's mauling of Aravis (*The Horse and His Boy*) is also an external sign of a need for inward change, for it brings home to her the punishment of the slave-girl she deceived into abetting her escape. When Shasta comes to her defense, Aslan at once departs. In the same book, Prince Rabadash's transformation into a donkey is reversed on condition of good behavior, a fact that Holbrook conveniently ignores. Like the dwarf's taunting of Edmund, "'Turkish delight for the little prince'" (*The Lion, the Witch and the Wardrobe*, chap. 11), it represents reform by ridicule. To call Aslan a "minatory figure" is to miss much that children love about him: the golden mane and silky fur, the playful rolls and graceful steps.

Holbrook's second major criticism is that Lewis acts duplicitously in presenting his own nightmares as fairy tales, his own misogyny and paranoid view of the world as Christian teaching. If, as Lewis maintained, his fictions grew out of mental images[5] (as Holbrook adds, from his unconscious), he had no hidden agenda. If he found the world a cruel place through which his characters needed guidance, so do many children in tough schools or adults outside the secure enclaves of the prosperous. On Lewis's own submission, the win-or-lose situation of Britain in the 1940s was what his experience had led him to expect (*Surprised by Joy*, 32), but that says as much about his battle experience in 1918 as about his schooldays at Wynyard. By combining his antipathy to "coarse, brainless" boys at Malvern who had inflicted "abject misery, terrorism and hopelessness" (*They Stand Together*, 47, 55) with his tirades about homosexuality between "Bloods" and "tarts" (*Surprised by Joy*, chaps. 7–8), one might guess at sexual abuse that an adolescent would be too embarrassed to report yet surely too grownup to repress into his unconscious, but that would be only conjecture.

Although Lewis was worried by a headmistress's prediction that his *Lion, the Witch and the Wardrobe* would confuse and terrify children,[6] in fifteen years of teaching the stories to students who mostly read them first as children, I recall not one complaint of their inspiring fear or hatred. Some objected to talking animals and some, justifiably, to the strictures on coeducation in the *Silver Chair*, a book dated by its author's prejudice against "progressive" schooling and parenting, not to mention the absurd headmistress of Experiment House. Such, however, is often the case with children's classics. Consider the Victorian idea of a healthy diet in *The Secret Garden*: eggs, butter, and lashings of cream. Or compare the "delight and joy" that Isaac Watts's *Divine and Moral Songs* gave eighteenth-century children with their denunciation by a twentieth-century historian appalled by their images of hell.[7] Indeed, that Lewis himself received countless enquiries from both children and adults is a tribute in itself.

To judge the Chronicles of Narnia from figures and symbols taken out of context is to distort them. To read the tales as wholes, whether individually or in sequence, is to realize the equal importance of symbols that originated in mid-twentieth-century life, in medieval and Renaissance literature, and in Lewis's own past.[8] Captain Maugrim the wolf (*The Lion, the Witch and the Wardrobe*) may embody a castrating mother-figure, as Holbrook claims (Holbrook, 65), but as head of a tyrant's secret police he signified a very real threat when Lewis began the tale (1939), or even when he published it (1951). The medieval swords and arrows of Narnian warfare are even less likely to terrify or brutalize children than the six-shooters of old-time westerns. As with the final slaughter in Homer's *Odyssey*, obsolete weaponry and the written word filter violence through the reader's imagination. It may be of interest to note that the villainess of Morris's *Water of the Wondrous Isles* is also called a "Witch," and the heroine addressed as "Daughter of Adam" (Morris, 469). In the case of educational or racial prejudices, as in the portrayal of dark-skinned, garlic-smelling Calormenes (*Last Battle*), such elements risk provoking protest and so spoiling the illusion for adult readers, but whether they annoy or puzzle the young one must vary with the individual.

It may be useful to consider the Chronicles' probable meaning, influence on, and attraction for young readers. Details noticed by young readers may depend on whether the books are read at random, as must often happen, or in a deliberate order: either the order in which the books were completed (*The Lion, the Witch and the Wardrobe*; *Prince Caspian*; *Voyage of the "Dawn Treader"*; *Horse and His Boy*; *Silver Chair*; *Last Battle*; *Magician's Nephew*); the order of their publication (*The Lion, the Witch and the Wardrobe*; *Prince Caspian*; *Voyage of the "Dawn Treader"*; *Silver Chair*; *Horse and His Boy*; *Magician's Nephew*; *Last Battle*); or the order of chronology from the creation to the end of Narnia (*Magician's Nephew*; *The Lion, the Witch and the Wardrobe*; *Horse and His Boy*; *Prince Caspian*; *Voyage of the "Dawn Treader"*, *Silver Chair*; *Last Battle*).[9]

Those who read in the order of writing are more likely to perceive the progression from early childhood to old age in the protagonists and in the Narnian landscape.[10] Having briefly begun writing *The Lion, the Witch and the Wardrobe* late in 1939, Lewis resumed in the summer of 1948. From that point, the whole series took him six years, long enough for some changes of perspective to emerge. In *The Horse and His Boy*, written in 1950, the

Calormene sovereign, Prince Rabadash, and the Grand Vizier use the rhetorical formulae of the Arabian Nights. In *The Last Battle*, written two years later, the worshipers of Tash bow to the ground like Muslims, yet the Calormene officer Emeth uses plain English and is welcome in Aslan's country because he has obeyed the universal moral law that Lewis elsewhere called "the Tao." Imagination and, no doubt, reflection on the author's own *Abolition of Man* have modified a stereotype and a dogma. The continuing concern in the Chronicles with the effects on children's values of positivist conditioning has been very fully explored by Myers.[11]

In *The Lion, the Witch and the Wardrobe*, the four Pevensie children are evacuated from London during the war to the house of an old bachelor known as "the Professor." While hiding in a wardrobe to escape a tour of the house led by the housekeeper, they find it to be a passage into another world and so stumble into Narnia by seeming accident. Yet in Aslan's good time they find themselves to be Narnia's long-expected sovereigns.[12] The youngest of the children, and the first to enter Narnia, is named after Lucy Barfield, to whom the book is dedicated, whose first name has the root meaning "light."[13] Lewis concluded the book by anticipating "further adventures" in Narnia, and at once began *Prince Caspian*. As that book opens, the Pevensies are waiting at a junction for the trains that will take the girls to one school and the boys to another, when they are summoned back to Narnia by a horn blast. The horn signals a cross-over not only from childhood to pubescence but also from present time to the author's inner journey, for Prince Caspian's medieval education is analogous to Lewis's own development from predilection for folklore and romance to rejection of modernism and secular humanism. When finally returned to the station platform, Peter and Susan have grown too old to visit Narnia again.

The past in the enchanting *Voyage of the "Dawn Treader"* is more cultural than personal. The two youngest Pevensies, Edmund and Lucy, are spending the summer with their aunt and uncle. Their cousin Eustace has had a modern, permissive upbringing by parents who taught him to call them by their first names instead of "Mother" and "Father" and has attended a school resembling Summerhill or Dartington Hall. While discussing a picture of a Narnian ship that is hanging in a back bedroom, all three children suddenly find themselves aboard the ship, which is called the *Dawn Treader* (a name signifying discovery and enlightenment). Once at sea, Eustace is reeducated by experience in a world that is predominantly symbolic and mythological. Transformed in the "Lone" Isles into a dragon, he suffers the isolation that awaits a spoilt child, then has his dragon skin peeled off down to his heart, so as to become a caring and sharing person. Lewis attributes the boy's greed and egoism to his permissive upbringing. The more spoiled the child, the deeper and more painful his reformation.

Following Eustace's transformation, the voyage takes us even further into a timeless world of myth and symbol. The finding of a Narnian lord's corpse on the isle called Goldwater by King Caspian but Deathwater by the idealist Reepicheep (chap. 8) doubtless originated in the Midas myth but represents opposed values. A psychological symbol, the rescue from Dark Island of an exiled Narnian lord nearly driven mad by the terror of nightmares coming true (chap. 12) implies a lack of trust remarked by Bacon: "Men fear death as children fear to go in the dark."[14] When the *Dawn Treader* approaches the Utter East to set Reepicheep down near Aslan's country, Caspian's lust to follow recalls Sir Percival's obsessive quest for the Grail in Tennyson's *Idylls of the King*.

In the next tale Lewis wrote, *The Horse and His Boy*, which features an adolescent boy and girl who break free of wicked stepparents, discover their true identities, and eventually become King and Queen of Archenland, Lewis juxtaposed three cultures. In the southern empire of Calormen, the ruler, crown prince, and Grand Vizier address each other in the language of the *Arabian Nights*. In Archenland, law and custom rule even its king, who hunts like a medieval monarch. The free-spoken Narnians who accompany their Pevensie sovereigns from the north seem idealized Vikings.

The ensuing *Silver Chair* draws upon the medieval quest-romances, and beyond them the myth of Orpheus. The "Underland" inhabited by the Witch's inhibited and silent subjects blends elements from the Greek Underworld, the Judaic Sheol, and the modern totalitarian state. Once liberated, Prince Rilian experiences a compulsion to descend to the still lower region of Bism, a desire compounded of curiosity about an alien world and a momentary death-wish. This overcome, his ascent to Narnia blends liberation from confinement by a possessive foster mother with joyous awakening to life and freedom. His confinement explains both his outbreaks of violence[15] and the general rejoicing at the Green Witch's death. His relief resembles that of Lewis when Mrs. Moore died, shortly before he began this book.[16]

At the beginning of the book, Eustace Scrubb and Jill Pole have entered Narnia from a shrubbery where they hid from Jill's tormentors at Experiment House. The sea voyage in the *Dawn Treader* that has changed Eustace forever took place during the recent school holidays, so he is still about nine years old. At first, his classmate Jill behaves like a schoolchild, posturing at the cliff edge until Eustace tries to rescue her. When Eustace falls off himself, Aslan blows him down to Narnia (21–22).[17] Unaware that the lion is Aslan, Jill is terrified of him. She tries to excuse herself for her part in Eustace's fall but soon bursts into tears. Isolated and thirsty, she has no choice but to follow Aslan's direction to drink from the only stream. Humbled and submissive because of her recent fear and guilt, she accepts the quest to search for the lost Prince Rilian and listens carefully to Aslan's explanation of four signs to follow. Jill and Eustace mature quickly during the journey and adventures that follow. Imprisoned in the giants' castle, Jill simulates childish giggles and behavior to deceive the Queen and attendants into allowing her to explore the castle and find an escape route.

Since even children so mature for their age could not have coped alone with the Queen-Witch in Underland, Lewis gave them a mentor. The transformation of his gardener Fred Paxford and perhaps his old tutor Kirkpatrick[18] into Puddleglum the Marsh-wiggle was a stroke of genius. As with Dickens's Mark Tapley, Puddleglum's demeanor varies with his circumstances. He is pessimistic when all seems well, soberly confident in Aslan's instructions when the children are bewildered, and prompt and courageous in stamping on the Witch's fire as its hypnotic fumes begin to lull the Prince and children into acquiescence. Already the drug has made them deny the sun's existence, just as secularism and materialism dispose moderns to deny God. In that sense, Underland signifies the post-Christian culture.

The remaining books have both theological and personal meaning, the latter more affecting for young readers. Having ended his first story with the resurrection of Aslan and the defeat of the Witch, Lewis relates Narnia's apocalypse in the most fully theological story, the *Last Battle*, which he began last and finished in the summer of 1953. In the next few months he finished *The Magician's Nephew*, begun in 1949 and resumed for part of 1951. He probably wrote the central chapter of *Magician's Nephew*, relating Narnia's creation and fall, before starting the *Last Battle*. The opening and closing episodes of *The Magician's Nephew* are saturated in his personal history, from the attic passage and "end room" of Little Lea and the magic rings of Nesbit's *Amulet*,[19] through the occultism of the "adept" Uncle Andrew, which recalls the "Great War" against Steinerism (though the would-be magician also combines the ruthlessness of Weston with the greed of Devine),[20] to the poignant episode of Digory healing his mother by feeding her the apple. The last fulfills a wish not granted Lewis in childhood. Was he right to grant it to Digory, whom Aslan has prepared to live without his mother? Yet child-readers might be depressed by a conclusion so inconsistent with the mercy of Aslan, who has invited the prayer he grants. Her death would, moreover, make nonsense of the quest for the apple of life or, as the Witch claims, eternal youth. Lewis concluded the tale as Nesbit concluded her *Amulet*, for no sooner has Digory healed his mother than his father returns rich from the East.

Thus the Chronicles take the Pevensies from Lucy's first entry into Narnia in *The Lion, the Witch and the Wardrobe* to their final entry into the "real Narnia" in Aslan's country in *The Last Battle*, via a stable that alludes to the Nativity. After the final destruction of the old Narnia, the creatures who love Aslan enter the new Narnia through the doorway, while the others disappear into Aslan's dark shadow. Among those who enter the door are a Calormene and many creatures from folk-literature, all of whom have in common good hearts and the power of speech. But only three of the four Pevensie children join the rush "farther up and farther in," for Susan has succumbed to the lure of teenage pleasures and fashions and is "no longer a friend of Narnia." After their first adventures in Narnia, the only collective undertaking by all four is the rescue of Prince Caspian. This completed, the adolescents Peter and Susan can no longer return to Narnia. At the end of *The Voyage of the "Dawn Treader,"* Edmund and Lucy are told that they will not visit Narnia again, and Eustace and Jill take the central roles in *The Silver Chair* and *The Last Battle*. Aslan's explanation to the three Pevensies at the end of *The Last Battle* that they and their parents left the "Shadowlands" of earth by means of a railway accident may have been suggested to Lewis by a pile-up of three trains at Harrow on 8 October 1952 in which more than a hundred passengers died.[21]

In representing puberty as closing the door to Narnia, Lewis seems to have had in mind the teenager's rejection of fairy tales as "kids' stuff."[22] Narnia resembles the worlds of myth and fairy tale in which everything, whether Narnian or English, is alive and existentially meaningful for the central figures. Aslan's country includes a "real" Narnia but also a "real England," thus uniting imagination and reality as in the Platonism Professor Digory Kirke commends in his old age, or the Neoplatonism of Steiner and Barfield.[23] When the creatures of Narnia enter Aslan's country with their human visitants, all distinction between fact and imagination disappears.

Looking at the tales in the order of the chronology of Narnia, one begins with its creation in *The Magician's Nephew*, continues with its redemption in *The Lion, the Witch and the Wardrobe* and its golden age under the four Pevensie sovereigns in *The Horse and His Boy*, and proceeds through the quest-voyages to its decay and apocalypse in *The Last Battle*. In keeping with Lewis's principle of smuggling in Christian doctrine, this sequence approximates the Christian mythos,[24] beginning with the creation and fall (*Magician's Nephew*), continuing with the sacrifice of Aslan on the Stone Table and his resurrection (*The Lion, the Witch and the Wardrobe*), followed by the Narnian equivalent of Exodus (*The Horse and His Boy*),[25] then by a mission to retrieve lost lords and journey toward heaven (*Voyage of the "Dawn Treader"*), a descent into Sheol (*Silver Chair*), and the apocalypse (*Last Battle*).

This order would self-evidently put more weight on Lewis's theological overthought than on his personal underthought. How much of it is gathered upon a first reading must vary with the reader's age, education, and acquaintance with the Bible.

Only readers well-versed in English literature and recent history will discern some sources and allusions. To illustrate from his creation and apocalypse narratives, in the *Magician's Nephew* the Deplorable Word of Jadis, a female equivalent of the Dolorous Stroke in Malory's *Morte d'Arthur*, turns the city of Charn into a charnel house and is the antithesis of God's creative word "Let there be light." The story proceeds from the undoing of creation within the Witch's world to her failure to tempt Digory to disobey Aslan and take an apple to revive his mother with the forbidden fruit. As Aslan later explains, this would have been giving it to her "at the wrong time, in the wrong way" (chap. 14). After eating the apple, Digory's mother falls into a sweet, drug-free sleep, but she is pronounced cured only after Digory has buried the apple core in the garden (chap. 15). To understand why Digory would have brought disaster upon himself by eating the apple we must combine several passages, from the rhyme over the golden gates (chap. 13) to Aslan's explanation. According to the rhyme, those who enter the garden over the wall to "steal" apples will find their "heart's desire" but also "despair." This implicitly echoes the contrast in *Paradise Lost* between the Devil's climb into Eden over the wall and a pilgrim's entry into Heaven through the golden gates. The injunction breached by the Witch, "Take of my fruit for others or forbear," helps Digory resist her temptation to eat an apple himself and share eternal youth and power with her, as king and queen of Narnia or Earth. Digory prefers to "go to Heaven" after his allotted span. The Witch then tempts him to steal an apple and take it immediately to cure his mother. If he does not, she argues, he will always feel guilty for having failed her—the charlatan's argument to a cancer patient's relative. Though hesitantly responding that his mother has taught him to keep promises and not to steal, Digory finally refuses when urged to abandon Polly (his Eve).

Aslan's "Well done" (as to the faithful servant in Matthew 25:21) remains Digory's sole reward until he has planted the apple that will protect Narnia and seen the misery of his Uncle Andrew, the would-be magician, who has endured being planted and watered by animals who think him a type of tree. As the astonished boy sees a perfumed tree grow from the apple, Aslan explains that its smell nauseates the Witch, just as long life and power bring misery upon the evil-hearted. Had someone plucked the fruit and sown the seed unasked, he would have made Narnia into a cruel world like Charn. In the same way, it is the apple Digory plucks at Aslan's direction from the new-grown tree that heals his mother. The text both upholds religion against amoral magic and implicitly contrasts the divine order with slave empires from the Egypt of the Pharaohs to the Soviet Union under Stalin.

The framework of the *Last Battle* consists mainly of theological symbols. We may dismiss as gothic machinery the thunderclap when Shift assures Puzzle that 'Aslan never turns up nowadays" (chap. 1), yet the figures of the ancient ape and his ass combine a glancing blow at Darwinism with an allusion to the bestiary characterization of the ape (simius) as deceitfully imitative.[26] The name "Shift" connotes a fraudulent stratagem, a change of clothing, and the shifts of front Lewis thought characteristic of evil. Shift is often referred to as "the Ape" to emphasize both his subhuman status and the pretense implied in our verb "to ape." Shift's announcement that "true freedom" consists in obedience to him is his version of the "glorious liberty of the children of God" (Romans 8:21). It is also comparable to the enslavement by the Pigs in Orwell's *Animal Farm*.[27] The context becomes unambiguously theological when jewel the unicorn calls on seven adherents of Aslan to proclaim the truth at Stable Hill and King Tirian commands the Narnians to make a stand by the "great Rock" whence they drink refreshing water (Isaiah 32:2).

The dream of Tirian, who is the seventh in descent from King Rilian, in which he sees the seven friends of Narnia dining together, is meat and drink to the numerologist. Since the Pevensies had been told that they cannot return to Narnia, they realize that they must have entered Aslan's country. The final entry to the "real "Narnia through the stable door, Aslan's "Well done!" to Tirian, the giant squeezing the sun that has swallowed the moon, and Aslan's order "Now make an end" complete the apocalypse.[28]

Why the Chronicles have attracted so many readers is a question best considered with regard to individual books, but first we should note two reasons evident from reading them in the order of their writing. The first is the progression from childhood to old age noted earlier, which would obviously extend the age-range of readers and reward rereading. The second is an increasing subtlety in narration.

Lewis uses the narrator most explicitly in the first book completed (*The Lion, the Witch and the Wardrobe*). The narrator warns readers of the foolishness of shutting oneself in a wardrobe, explains the White Witch's descent from Lilith, announces Edmund's desertion, partly blames his bad behavior on his schooling, hopes readers will not suffer the misery of Lucy and Susan after Aslan's death but will understand the quiet that follows their storms of tears, asks them to imagine the jubilant rides on Aslan's back, and promises further adventures in Narnia.

The events of *Prince Caspian* are conveyed by more varied means and with less use of the narrator. By describing Prince Caspian's childhood, education, and escape from King Miraz from Trumpkin's view point (chaps. 4–8), Lewis compels the reader to contrast the dwarf's skepticism with Lucy's faith that the trees might speak again, as in Narnia's "good old days" (chap. 9). Conversely, Trumpkin displays alertness and promptitude in shooting the bear who would have eaten the contemplative girl. Yet Lucy and her convert Edmund wisely counsel the group to take Aslan's suggested way, while the practical Peter decides on the wrong one. All this is accomplished without authorial comment. Not until the thirteenth chapter does the narrator intrude, by explaining that it was stranger for the Prince to meet the great kings out of the old stories than for them to meet him. The narrator becomes omniscient only later in that chapter when reporting King Miraz's manipulation by his advisers into accepting Peter's challenge to single combat.

In *The Voyage of the "Dawn Treader"*, "the narrator explains "port" and "starboard" and blames Eustace's "greedy, dragonish thoughts" for his transformation into a dragon, but otherwise merely adds details, as in the brief conclusion. Apart from the beauty of its imagined scenes and the intense longing communicated by the description of the sea near Aslan's country, the delight of this tale largely results from skillful use of Eustace as diarist, of Edmund as interpreter of Eustace's encounter with Aslan and transformation back into human form, of the magician Coriakin as cartographer, and of Ramandu's daughter as exponent of festal symbols and the means of disenchanting the sleeping lords.

The reader is expected to exercise judgment in reading the two portions of Eustace's diary. In the first portion, the "facts" he notes are always negative and the other voyagers always at fault. In the second, though Eustace still complains of his "unanswerable" arguments being ignored by Caspian, he records attempting to steal water and later receiving some from Lucy. Even young readers should see through her face-saving excuse that boys get thirstier than girls.

After his restoration to human shape, Eustace conforms to Todorov's theory of fantasy as "hesitation," wondering whether his nightmarish experience had been real or a dream, until Edmund assures him of its reality and identifies the lion as Aslan. Like Lucy, he saves the boy's self-respect by confessing his own treason in Narnia.

By unobtrusive shifts of viewpoint—to those of Eustace on Dragon Island and Lucy in the magician's library—Lewis provides constant variety without sacrificing clarity of outline. But the chief pleasure of the Voyage lies in the marvelous descriptions of the scenes through which the ship journeys and in Lewis's unobtrusive use of motifs by Malory, Tennyson, and Morris.[29]

In the next completed tale, the *Horse and His Boy*, Lewis makes skillful use of viewpoint. After the overheard conversation between the Tisroc and

Ahoshta he departs from this well-worn convention by recording the very different reactions of the eavesdroppers. Implored to abandon her plan of escape, Aravis shakes her panic-stricken companion, threatens to rush screaming from the room to ensure their capture, and declares she would rather "be killed" than marry Ahoshta (chap. 9). As they part, that superficial socialite Lasaraleen, who might be any "flapper" of the 1920s, urges her to change her mind now that she has seen "what a very great man" her prospective husband is. In calling him a "grovelling slave" who has encouraged the Tisroc to send his son to certain death, Aravis articulates the likely response of young readers not bemused by rhetorical formulae.

Lewis is most inventive when using the Hermit to narrate the battle by interpreting its shapes reflected in his pool and the questions or comments of his listeners to flesh out his report. As he describes "a tall Tarkaan with a crimson beard," Bree interjects, "My old master Anradin!" When the Hermit says he sees "Cats" rushing forward, Aravis repeats, "Cats?" and the Hermit hastily explains, "Great cats, leopards and such" (159). His illustration of Edmund's "marvelous" swordplay, "He's just slashed Corradin's head off" (161), is too insensitive from the Hermit in his present way of life. Lewis regresses to his soldiering days in his commentary:

> Oh, the fool! ... Poor, brave little fool. He knows nothing about this work. He's making no use at all of his shield. His whole side's exposed. He hasn't the faintest idea what to do with his sword. Oh, he's remembered it now. He's waving it wildly about.... It's been knocked out of his hand now. It's mere murder sending a child into the battle; he can't live five minutes. Duck, you fool— oh, he's down. (160)

When the breathless listeners cry, "Killed?" the Hermit replies, "How can I tell?" and continues to relate what he sees of the rest of the battle, leaving us in suspense until the narrative resumes with the words "When Shasta fell off his horse, he gave himself up for lost" (161). When last in Shasta's viewpoint, we shared his realization "If you funk this, you'll funk every battle all your life" (157). In a rare intrusion warranted by personal experience, Lewis justifies the switch to the Hermit's viewpoint by pointing to the futility of describing a battle from that of a single combatant.

The award-winning *Last Battle* shows Lewis at his best and worst as a storyteller. Introduced as the "last King of Narnia," Tirian is soon bound to an ash tree by Calormenes in league with the Ape. Watching the goings-on in front of the stable from afar, even Tirian wonders whether the stiff, silent creature shown to the frightened Narnians might after all be Aslan, until he recalls the Ape's "nonsense" about Tash and Aslan being identical (42). He recollects Narnia's past glories, recalling how children from another world had appeared in Narnia at every crisis. His reverie, amounting to a brief retrospect of the Chronicles, leads him to call out a plea for help for Narnia, even at the cost of his own life. Dawning hope prompts his appeal to all "friends of Narnia," upon which he is plunged into his dream or vision of the Seven Diners. When Peter challenges him, "If you are from Narnia, I charge you ... speak to me," Tirian finds that he is unable to speak (45). Tirian's disillusionment as he wakes at dawn stiff with cold is among Lewis's subtlest touches; his misery is relieved almost at once by the appearance of Eustace and Jill, who untie him.

Peter's self-announcement as "High King" contrasts with the colloquial speech of Jill and Eustace and with Tirian's medieval salutation of Jill as "fair maid" (46). The ash tree and King Tirian's pronouncement "Narnia is no more" (85) on hearing of the death of Roonwit the Centaur link the Christian and pagan mythologies; in the Norse sagas the world is supported by an ash tree, and Tirian's pronouncement recalls the death of Baldir. The reporting of Roonwit's death by Farsight the Eagle echoes another Norse motif.

Too often, however, Lewis indulges in personal and contemporary intrusions. We can accept the children's entry to Narnia via the railway accident, which Eustace perceives as a "frightful jerk" (51) and later identifies as a collision (89), but when Jill says she would rather be killed fighting for Narnia than to "grow old and stupid at home ... and then die in the end just the same" and Eustace replies, "Or be smashed up by British Railways!" (88), Lewis's apparent allusion to the Harrow accident has no place in the fantasy. In addition, at times his word choices can be misleading. As a working-class term for colored immigrants, the Dwarf's epithet "Darkies" for the Calormenes (116) has unintended overtones of racism.

An odd feature of *The Last Battle*, the Ape's retreat into alcoholism and his replacement as leader by the Ginger Cat, at first seems a mere contrivance for using his sad experience of Warnie's dipsomania and a mental image of a cat bolting from a stable. The cat motif, however, probably originated in the talking animals of the Boxen tales, for the surname of a pleasure-loving bear, the rakish Lieutenant James Bar,[30] was reused in *The Horse and His Boy* for the lord who set Shasta adrift. The motif involving the Ginger Cat shows a subtle irony in that the Cat agrees with the Calormene captain Rishda that Aslan and Tash are only figments of the imagination, tells the Narnians that Aslan has swallowed up King Tirian, cynically persuades the dwarfs that there is no real Aslan (73–74), coolly offers to enter the stable, stalks in with feline primness (99), then moments later bolts into oblivion when confronted by Tash (100). Disbelief evaporates in the presence of evil.

While occasionally involving uncertainty (Todorov's "hesitation") as to the reality of an event or person, the fantasy more often uses reversal of ground rules, or what Manlove calls "upset expectations."[31] Thus Tirian, who talks and thinks as a medieval monarch, is struck by the strange, drab garments of the twentieth-century children. Combining reversal with word-play, Aslan explains that the hard-bitten dwarfs are so anxious to avoid being taken in that they cannot be taken out of this world and brought into a better one (135).[32] Their satisfaction that "the Dwarfs are for the Dwarfs" is more than a simple takeoff on communism or the triumphalism that accompanied the Labour landslide in the 1945 election. In contrast to Edmund, who attained "a kind of greatness" when breathed on by Aslan in Prince Caspian (153), these godless dwarfs, having forsworn the means of growth, must remain forever dwarfish.

A more fundamental reversal takes place in the final chapters. In "Night Falls on Narnia" (chap. 14), the falling stars, red moon near the sun, and creatures heading for the doorway to Aslan's country echo Revelation and the Flood myth. As in pagan myths, the falling and vanishing stars are people. As in what Lewis called the "myth" of evolutionary progress,[33] dragons and lizards inhabit Narnia—but at the end of time, not the beginning.

In chapter 15, as in his *Great Divorce*, Lewis endeavors to reverse the stereotype of heaven as a state of eternal torpor. Having reversed the dark and lonely cosmos of post-Newtonian astronomers by encountering warmth and daylight beyond the stable door, the children find themselves caught up with creatures factual and fabulous in a westward, not eastward, rush when the Unicorn calls them "farther up and farther in" (*Last Battle*, 155), a refrain that one critic has suggested might otherwise connote returning to the womb.[34] The refrain is repeated and the rush intensified in the final chapter, called (with Platonic implication) "Farewell to Shadowlands." Here Lewis reverses the image of heaven as a city, for the voyagers pass waterfalls and climb mountains. The self-reflexive image that ends the Chronicles of Narnia, the story in which every chapter is better than the last, suggests that heavenly stasis is a conclusion never to be reached.

In these stories a childless academic managed to communicate with children throughout and beyond the English-speaking world. What proportion of child readers belong to his own social class has never been determined. Nor to my knowledge has reader research established why the Chronicles have been found such compulsive reading. For that matter, we do not know whether more children have first heard them read by parents or read them independently. The following suggestions, therefore, are merely speculative.

First, the attraction may derive from the narrator's identification with children. In *The Silver Chair* the narrator presumes that his readers attend better-disciplined schools than Experiment House, where the need for just authority is appreciated. Presuming impatience with discipline near the end of term, he presents in *The Last Battle* the entry into Aslan's country, where life resembles an everlasting holiday, as a joyous running and bounding akin to the end-of-term fever at a hard-working school. Second, the narrator assumes agreement on principles that do not need to be justified to children: loyalty to schoolmates, brothers, and sisters; dislike of bullies or tyrants, sycophants or flatterers. Many an impoverished author must wish that to uphold such principles would automatically guarantee sales in the millions.

Looking for inducements to read on, we find some in elements common to all the cafes. Two or more children of both sexes enter an enchanted world via a door, or its equivalent—a picture that comes alive, or magic rings they must learn to manage.[35] In each tale, the children depend upon a nonhuman counselor, perhaps mythical, but always full-grown: a beaver, raven, horse, or centaur. Sometimes they depend on an observer, but—whether eagle or hermit—not one they would meet at home. Notably, apart from Aslan, the animal companions change with the implied reader's age. In the first tale Mr. Tumnus the faun and Mr. and Mrs. Beaver are roughly the same size as the children, who can eat and converse in the Beavers' cozy home. In the *Horse and His Boy*, Bree and Hwin require riders well into their teens; and the owl, eagle, or centaur who advise the protagonists of later books are clearly distanced by their size and/or mythological associations. In the first tales the children meet no parents, teachers, or other adult humans they can respect in the enchanted world, but only the witches, magicians, or sovereigns of fairy tales; in the later tales they begin to encounter good human adults, such as the Hermit and the large-hearted King of Archenland in *The Horse and His Boy* or Drinian and Lord Bern in the *Voyage of the "Dawn Treader."* In war, they use medieval weapons and tactics. They depend immediately on signs and omens but ultimately on Aslan the lion-god, a figure derived partly from Christ the Lion of Judah and perhaps partly from Richard the Lion-heart, but also from Lewis's dream of a lion. As in medieval romance, the stories always involve a quest, which takes them to an island, a castle, a subterranean prison, and ultimately a stable.

The enchanted world differs from their real one in its time-frame. During a school vacation, centuries of Narnian time can pass, a dynasty can rise and fall, children can function as adults[36]—kings or queens, generals or discoverers—yet never attain independence. In seeking self-sufficiency,

Eustace finds loneliness and misery on Dragon Island, his precursor death. The enchanted world of Lewis offers escape, not only from childhood subservience to parents and teachers and from city life in an industrial country, but also from the whole notion of carving out one's own path in life. So in the author's view do myth, literary fantasy, and the Christian life. Yet the boy or girl character drawn into Narnia finally depends on Aslan, who with one exception[37] will interpret only his or her own life story.

In other ways the fantasy depends on reversal of normal distinctions between humans and animals, reality and imagination. Folklore becomes practical, and the folly or wickedness of practical people—Uncle Andrew, King Miraz, Nikabrik, the bureaucrat Gumpas, or the wily Tisroc—is sometimes cruelly exposed. The outdated education by Dr. Cornelius stands Prince Caspian in good stead, while Eustace has to unlearn his "progressive" education at Experiment House. The key elements of Narnian education are ethical and ecological: courage in battle, comradeship, cooperation with other species, and care of trees and plants threatened by commercial exploitation. The approaching end of Narnia is signaled by religious uncertainty or disbelief and a ruined environment.[38] Above all, the child characters play a crucial role in the enchanted world; instead of being marginal because of their inexperience and simplistic view of life, children affect the whole future of that world by making plans or decisions at places adults would consider marginal, historical, or imaginary: animal lairs; islands; castles; a subterranean, real, or remote wood.

The moral ground rules are those of the child reader's normal world, in that actions are always right or wrong, information trite or untrue. At times, Lewis appears to share that simplicity. In this sense, his much-remarked immaturity enabled him to communicate with children. Consider, for example, Professor (Digory) Kirke's reasoning on Lucy's account of her first entry to Narnia:

> Either your sister is telling lies, or she is mad, or she is telling the truth. You know she does not tell lies and it is obvious that she is not mad. For the moment then and unless any other evidence turns up, we must assume that she is telling the truth. (*The Lion, the Witch and the Wardrobe*, 47)

Elsewhere Lewis used a similar argument to justify belief in the divinity of Christ. Further alternatives—daydream, wish-fulfillment, hallucination—would have taken him beyond the child reader's register and the context of the episode.

The increasingly subtle switching between viewpoint characters, as compared with the obtrusive switching in *That Hideous Strength*, may blind us to the fact that the viewpoint character is nearly always a juvenile extending his or her experience. The principal learner is Lucy, followed by Edmund, Eustace, and Jill. We enjoy the viewpoints of Narnian characters within single novels, *Prince Caspian*, the *Horse and His Boy*, or the *Last Battle*. Save for occasional passages in the viewpoint of Susan or Peter—or gap-filling by Trumpkin, the Hermit, or a nonhuman observer—the viewpoint character is of the child reader's presumed age. Thus, as Doris Myers remarks, the reader vicariously experiences life at different stages: young childhood with Lucy, middle or late adolescence with Shasta, the consciousness of age and impending death with King Tirian and Jewel.[39]

In one sense, the Narnian Chronicles are the medievalist's revenge upon the modernist; in another, as Kath Filmer notes,[40] they anticipate a civilization that still lies ahead. As in medieval stories, events and situations often conform to literary patterns or analogues. We have noticed the parallel between Caspian's urge to follow Reepicheep into Aslan's country and the Grail obsession. What is acceptable in a mouse or hermit would be neglect of duty in King Caspian. In his boyhood, Caspian, like Hamlet, disliked his usurping uncle, but without knowing why. Lewis departs from Shakespeare by making the Queen a wicked stepmother and the birth of her son the incentive for the now-redundant Prince to flee the court.

Near the end of *Prince Caspian*, Aslan, Bacchus, and the Maenads disrupt a dull history lesson. After transforming the girls' school into a "forest glade," its ceiling into tree branches, and the teacher's desk into a rose bush, they put to flight the teacher and all the pupils except for the inattentive Gwendolen, whom two Maenads whirl in a dance and help remove the "unnecessary and uncomfortable" parts of her school uniform (171). Lewis told Greeves of the joy and vitality he found in pagan mythology.[41] Though rightly condemning the ridicule of the woman teacher and schoolgirls, David Holbrook misses the point of the episode. Less convincingly than D. H. Lawrence, Lewis exposes the lifelessness of a culture bereft of the gods who infused pagan societies with energy and joy in life. To avoid the appearance of misogyny, in the following episode "pig-like" schoolboys are unconvincingly put to flight.

Lewis shows originality in blending derived with invented incidents. The baptismal bath of Eustace is preceded by the unpeeling of his dragon skin, and Lucy's magical restoration of the Dufflepuds to visibility takes place only after she eavesdrops on her schoolmates' conversation about herself. Mystery or enchantment attaches to figures and incidents drawn from literature or mythology, while invented elements are literal, even prosaic.

Turkish Delight makes far more sense literally, as an inducement to betrayal at a time when candies were rationed in England, than in Holbrook's gloss of it as a disguised form of breast milk.[42] When Prince Rilian laments his ten-year subjection to the Witch as surrogate mother, surely any autobiographical reference is much more likely to involve Lewis's subjection to Mrs. Moore than the maternal inadequacy presumed by Holbrook.

Will the Chronicles continue to be relevant to the lives of children? A case can be made either way. Whether future generations of children will enjoy battles with swords and bows and arrows may be doubted, but they will unquestionably condemn clear-cut logging and slavery. The influence of Tolkien's readings to the Inklings from the *Lord of the Rings* is patent in episodes of *Prince Caspian* and the *Last Battle* that feature trees as combatants.[43] The popularity of Tolkien's trilogy at the dawn of the ecological movement was by no means coincidental. As yesterday's protest becomes tomorrow's orthodoxy, more and more stories are likely to involve preservation of the natural environment.

Whether instant and miraculous answers to prayers will endear the Chronicles to tomorrow's children is again doubtful. In alluding in *The Last Battle* to Aslan's nonappearance "nowadays" Lewis acknowledges the declining influence of religion. C. N. Manlove remarks that Lewis "was unusual among Christian writers in admitting the draught from outside [Christianity]."[44] In order of completion, the Chronicles show Aslan a central figure in the first two (*The Lion, the Witch and the Wardrobe*; *Prince Caspian*), absent for long periods in the next three (*Voyage of the "Dawn Reader"*; *Silver Chair*; *Horse and His Boy*), and returning to center stage in the conclusions of the final two (*Magician's Nephew*; *Last Battle*). In their christological reference, they begin with the crucifixion and resurrection, continue with discipleship, the following of Aslan's path, the baptism and conversion of a modern spoiled child, and the renewed vision of eternal life, and end with the routing of secular magicians and gurus, Aslan's second coming, the ridicule of godless class-consciousness, and (skeptical Dwarfs excepted) the general entry into Aslan's country. There is no mention of Hell, for Calormenes killed in battle simply vanish. In the finale, the lost simply disappear into Aslan's shadow, while the saved from all seven books undergo no Last Judgment but a kind of evolution. Their eternal life perpetually unfolds, the root meaning of "evolve."[45] The metaphor of a book that improves chapter by chapter implies design by an Author warming to his subject matter. In this way Lewis marries an age-old Christian metaphor with a conception of divinely planned evolution common in his childhood[46] and extends to eternity the progressive revelation evident in the Old Testament.

As regards the moral "upshot" of the Chronicles, isolated incidents or phrases can be used to demonstrate antifeminism and a veneer of male toughness covering the unhealed wounds, but it is sounder to note the purport and emphasis of a whole story or major episode. The child reader cannot but condemn the willingness of Edmund to betray his brother and sisters to the Witch in *The Lion, the Witch and the Wardrobe*, still more his pretended disbelief in Narnia, from which he has just returned. The virtues of family loyalty and sincerity require no huddling together of schoolmates at Wynyard to explain them. Again, readers attuned to Lucy's love of Aslan will understand her pity at his humiliation and delight in his resurrection without recourse to Lewis's grief for his mother.

The upshot of *Prince Caspian* is less clear. Arguably, Caspian's love of old Narnian folklore and his happiness when with animals could promote an immature response to the troubles of adolescence. In a wider perspective, Dr. Cornelius saves Caspian's life both literally in urging him to flee the palace and metaphorically in nourishing his imagination with a cultural tradition that forearms him against the withering reductiveness of the commercially minded Telmarines, whose very name connotes both marring of earth (*tellus*) and skepticism ("tell it to the marines"). If the youngest readers see how the courtiers of the vain King Miraz manipulate him into accepting Peter's challenge, or even decipher the meaning of "Sopespian," the name "Glozelle" (liar) will surely escape any readers unfamiliar with medieval or Renaissance English. If death seems too harsh a judgment on Nikabrik for wishing to use the White Witch as an ally against Miraz, the author surely asserts principle against expediency. But nothing in the behavior or feelings of characters in *Prince Caspian* is so morally compelling as the treason of Edmund or the faith and love of Lucy.

In the *Voyage of the "Dawn Treader"* the reformation of a spoilt child and the assertion of common sense against excesses of chivalry and self-centered mysticism carry more conviction than any moral "upshot" in the *Silver Chair*. Instead, the latter story sheds light into the mind darkened by positivist conditioning against religion. In fact, later stories show a distinct shift in emphasis, for the practical sagacity commended in Puddleglum appears in Jill, Shasta, Aravis, and Lucy. What is rebuked is lack of empathy—by Aravis with the deceived slave girl, or by Jill when her posturing draws Eustace to the cliff edge. Yet Jill's devising of an escape from the castle of the giants (*Silver Chair*) and her shrewdly compassionate treatment of Puzzle (*Last Battle*) rebut Holbrook's charge of authorial misogyny based on passing references to tears spoiling bowstrings and blood wiped from swords.[47]

The final issue between hostile and sympathetic readers of the Chronicles concerns the quality of the writing. In condemning a passage on the pleasure of eating freshly caught fish as being insensitive to children's feelings (*The Lion, the Witch and the Wardrobe*, 70), Holbrook puts his finger on the central difficulty of an Edwardian-reared adult writing for mid-twentieth-century children of any class.[48] The problem may be highlighted with his contrast between Lewis's "paternal respect" and "admiration of the children's energy and courage" when describing their regal appearance in fur coats and his "prep-school language"[49] when Peter calls the treasonous Edmund a "poisonous little" beast and Edmund thinks the others "stuck-up, self-satisfied prigs" (*The Lion, the Witch and the Wardrobe*, 55). Both use the Edwardian public-school argot perpetuated in magazine stories up to the Second World War. Reared in an era and class that wore fur coats and used such terms (as he sometimes did to Greeves), Lewis could not plausibly have employed the diction of children from any class in the 1940s. Instead, he kept author-to-reader address to a minimum by staying within viewpoints. For example, this description follows Peter's suggestion to the others that they spend the rainy morning exploring the house:

> Everyone agreed to this and that was how the adventures began. It was the sort of house that you never seem to come to the end of... full of unexpected places. The first few doors ... led only into spare bedrooms, as everyone had expected ... but soon they came to a very long room filled with pictures and there they found a suit of armour; and after that there was a room all hung with green, with a harp in one corner; and then came three steps down and five steps up, and then a kind of little upstairs hall and a door that led out on to a balcony, and then a whole series of rooms that led into each other and were lined with books—most of them very old books and bigger than a Bible in a church. (*The Lion, the Witch and the Wardrobe*, 11)

This atomistic account of a house conceivably inspired by Little Lea sets the tone of medieval romance and ends with an illustration that all readers can picture.

A little later, as Lucy enters the wardrobe, advice is given from her viewpoint. She leaves the door ajar "because she knew that it is very foolish to shut oneself into any wardrobe" (12). When Edmund goes in, he closes the door, "forgetting what a very foolish thing this is to do" (30). Lewis uses advice probably drawn from experience with evacuees at The Kilns to suggest prudence in the girl with second sight and willfulness in the skeptical boy.

In the stories the narrator sometimes takes sides, with unfortunate results. In *Prince Caspian*, Lewis's forgivable hit at a modern materialist history lesson contributes nothing to the story; in addition, as Holbrook says, the partial stripping of Gwendolen may strike readers as indelicate, while the transformation of disorderly schoolboys into pigs (172–73) is pointlessly petulant. The same may be said of Polly's aspersions upon Susan:

> I wish she *would* grow up. She wasted all her school time wanting to be the age she is now, and she'll waste all the rest of her life trying to stay that age. Her whole idea is to race on to the silliest time of one's life as quick as she can and then stop there as long as she can. (*Last Battle*, 124)

A far more important aspect of Lewis's writing, one unremarked by Holbrook, is Lewis's use of a repertoire of styles to fit incidents and speakers. He shifts at will from plain speech for Peter to Morrisian medieval language for Reepicheep or Tirian ("Hast any skill with the bow, maiden?" [*Last Battle*, 55]) or *Arabian Nights* rhetoric for the Tisroc and Grand Vizier (*Horse and His Boy*). The array of styles is most dazzling in the *Voyage of the "Dawn Treader"*, "which shifts within a page from hierarchic-feudal language to announce King Caspian "come to visit his trusty and well-beloved servant the governor of the Lone Islands" (51) to mumbled bureaucratese by the porter ("No interview without 'pointments 'cept 'tween nine 'n' ten p.m. second Saturday every month") to stage cockney ("'Ere? Wot's it all about?'") at Bern's Shakespearean reproof "Uncover before Narnia, you dog" (51). In the next few pages (52–57), the bureaucratese of Gumpas ("Nothing about it in the correspondence.... Nothing in the minutes.... All irregular. Happy to consider any applications"), laced with economic jargon in support of the slave trade, alternates with plain but increasingly abrupt orders from Caspian. The slave auctioneer's sales-pitch swings sympathy away from the unseated governor, no longer "His Sufficiency."

Eustace's record of the resumed voyage, written in a plain style, betrays egotism in every "I" and self-righteousness in every account of a disregarded suggestion. When Caspian dismisses his idea of rowing back to Doorn on account of the water shortage, Eustace writes, "I tried to explain that perspiration really cools people down, so the men would need less water if they were working. He [Caspian] didn't take any notice of this, which is always his way when he can't think of an answer" (65–66).

Near the end of the *Voyage*, the style shifts to the plain but solemn phrases of the ancient star Ramandu, recalling those of the "Great Dance" episode in Perelandra:[50] "And when I have become as young as the child that was born yesterday, then I shall take my rising again ... and once more tread the great dance" (177), punctuated by the chivalric speech of

Reepicheep. As the ship nears the world's end, the style changes to the romantic, northern expressions of Lucy, exhilarated by the sea's "fresh, wild, lonely smell" (201).

How long children will continue to read the Chronicles of Narnia may depend on considerations unrelated to their artistic merits: reception of stories via electronic media rather than books; the religion or irreligion of parents and school librarians; social or educational changes rendering some episodes less comprehensible. Already schoolchildren must find the animus against coeducation difficult to understand. While at present Holbrook's view of the tales as unfit for children seems as perverse as Eliot's judgment of *Hamlet* ("an artistic failure"), many incidents or passages that Holbrook finds morally or stylistically objectionable do show a lack of restraint in the author. Lewis's achievement as a storyteller was limited by over-hasty production and unwillingness to take his fiction as seriously as his major critical works. As novelists, the perfectionist Tolkien and the boyishly eager Lewis represent opposed extremes.

While the images and values of the Chronicles had been in Lewis's mind for decades, the energy that enabled Lewis to complete the Chronicles within seven years (1948–54) may well have been generated by personal stresses: Mrs. Moore's senility, his entanglement with Joy Davidman, the denial of promotion at Oxford, and the campaign to defeat his ill-judged candidacy for the Professorship of Poetry. Undoubtedly anxiety or anger from these stresses as well as his bereavement and exile in childhood affect a number of episodes. What I have tried to show is that, so far from distorting or blurring the impact of a story, such "speaking pictures" (to quote Sidney) and moral attitudes at times enhance it. Even Holbrook appears moved by Digory's anxiety to heal his mother and finds the *Silver Chair* a well-told tale of adventure. Yet of all the stories the latter is most susceptible to the now dated academic game of psychoanalytic reductionism: the Witch as Mrs. Lewis turned nasty, or Prince Lewis unable to mate because he never got over the Queen's death. As Freud maintained, most if not all works of art spring from some trauma—in Edmund Wilson's phrase, a creative "wound." The only issue that should concern a critic is the quality of craftsmanship evident in the resultant works. The late John Peter, himself a Leavisite critic and Pulitzer Prize-winning novelist, once told me that while he detested Lewis and "everything he stood for," when reading the stories with his children he discerned "quality." For all their imperfections, they constitute a body of fiction worthy of their immense and sustained readership.

NOTES

1. Among others, Donald E. Glover, *C.S. Lewis: The Art of Enchantment*, and Evan Gibson, *C.S. Lewis: Spinner of Tales*, discuss plots and characters; Michael Murrin, "The Multiple Worlds of the Narnia Stories," in Peter J. Schakel and Charles A. Huttar, eds., *Word and Story*, 232–55, examines the Narnia stories in connection with German art fairy-tale genre; and Dabney A. Hart, *Through the Open Door: A New Look at C.S. Lewis*, discusses Lewis's use of myth. Among those writers who examine religion, ethics, and language in Lewis are Doris T. Myers, *C.S. Lewis in Context*, 112–81; Jim Pietrusz, "Rites of Passages"; John D. Cox, "Epistemological Release in *The Silver Chair*," in Peter J. Schakel, ed., *The Longing for a Form*, 159–70. Charles A. Huttar, "C.S. Lewis's Narnia and the Grand Design," in Schakel, ed., *Longing for a Form*, 119–35, and Kathryn Lindskoog, *The Lion of Judah in Never-Neverland*, examine Lewis's use of motifs, especially biblical motifs. More comprehensive studies of the Chronicles include C. N. Manlove, "'Caught Up into the Larger Pattern,'" in Schakel and Huttar, eds., *Word and Story*, 256–?6; Paul F. Ford, *A Companion to Narnia*; Hooper, *Past Watchful Dragons: The Narnian Chronicles of C.S. Lewis*; and Peter J. Schakel, *Reading with the Heart: The Way into Narnia*.

2. David Holbrook, *The Skeleton in the Wardrobe*. Page references will be given parenthetically in the text.

3. Letter to W. L. Kinter, 28 October 1954.

4. See *Surprised by Joy*, 26; *Letters to an American Lady*, 117 (6 July 1963).

5. Lewis, "Sometimes Fairy Stories Say What's Best to Be Said."

6. Letter to Ruth Pitter, 28 November 1950.

7. Frances Hodgson Burnett, *The Secret Garden*; Isaac Watts, *Works*, 1:xix; Esmé Wingfield-Stratford, *A Victorian Tragedy*, 57–58.

8. In *C.S. Lewis: His Literary Achievement*, 120–86, C. N. Manlove traces allusions in the Chronicles to literary sources in all periods.

9. All information concerning the order and dates of the stories is taken from tables in Ford, *A Companion to Narnia*.

10. Myers, *C.S. Lewis in Context*, esp. 125.

11. Myers, *C.S. Lewis in Context*, 112–81.

12. On the blurred distinction between accident and design, see Manlove, "'Caught Up into the Larger Pattern,'" 262.

13. Manlove, *C.S. Lewis: His Literary Achievement*, 135.

14. Francis Bacon, "Of Death," in *Essays*, 4–6.

15. Cf. the violent outbreaks of Knight in William Morris, *Water of the Wondrous Isles*, 258. It may also be noted that in Morris's book as well as in *Silver Chair* the villainess is called "Witch" (Morris, 343, etc.) and the heroine is addressed as "Adam's Daughter" (Morris, 469).

16. George Sayer points to Lewis's inviting friends to stay at Kilns again, resuming exercise, and improving in health (*Jack: C.S. Lewis and His Times*, 203–4).

17. Page references given parenthetically in the text for all of the Narnian Chronicles refer to the editions cited in the bibliography.

18. Respectively, Hooper, *Past Watchful Dragons*, 81–83; Myers, *C.S. Lewis in Context*, 151.

19. Cf. Manlove, *C.S. Lewis: His Literary Achievement*, 170.

20. Myers, *C.S. Lewis in Context*, 171.

21. Armin Schneider and Ascanio Mase, *Railway Accidents of Great Britain and Europe*, 67–73. The enquiry into the accident resulted in the installation of automatic signaling.

22. In "On Three Ways of Writing for Children," Lewis blames modernist critics for promoting this attitude.

23. On Platonism in the Chronicles, see Myers, *C.S. Lewis in Context*, 151, 180–81, and Murrin, "The Multiple Worlds of the Narnia Stories," 232.

24. Cf. Manlove, *C.S. Lewis: His Literary Achievement*, 124, where he describes the Chronicles as "Christian history."

25. Manlove, "'Caught Up into the Larger Pattern,'" 267.

26. Myers, *C.S. Lewis in Context*, 177.

27. Manlove, *C.S. Lewis: His Literary Achievement*, 182.

28. Manlove provides a list of apocalypse signs that appear in *The Last Battle* in *C.S. Lewis: His Literary Achievement*, 182.

29. For example, compare the Isles of Nothing, Kings and Queens, Young and Old, and Increase Unsought in Morris, *Water of the Wondrous Isles*, with the islands in *Voyage of the "Dawn Treader"*, and Utter Hay in Morris's book with the Utter East in the *Voyage*.

30. In "Littera Scripta Manet" (unpublished) and "The Sailor" (in *Boxen*, 153–94).

31. Manlove, "'Caught Up into the Larger Pattern,'" 262.

32. Manlove (*C.S. Lewis: His Literary Achievement*, 136) mentions changing ground rules in *Prince Caspian* and fantasy as paradox plus reversal (185), but he sees this within extraterrestrial episodes rather than between real and imagined worlds.

33. Lewis, "The Funeral of a Great Myth," in *Christian Reflections*, 110–23.

34. Glover, *C.S. Lewis: The Art of Enchantment*, 56.

35. On entrances, see Murrin, "The Multiple Worlds of the Narnia Stories."

36. Manlove points out that the child-heroes of MacDonald and Nesbit remain children (*C.S. Lewis: His Literary Achievement*, 122).

37. The one exception Aslan makes to this rule is telling Digory what would have happened had he given his mother the forbidden apple (Myers, *C.S. Lewis in Context*, 168).

38. Myers, *C.S. Lewis in Context*, 132–33; Lindskoog, *The Lion of Judah in Never-Never Land*, 46.

39. Myers, *C.S. Lewis in Context*, 125.

40. Kath Filmer, *The Fiction of C.S. Lewis: Mask and Minor*, 73, 83–86.

41. E.g., *They Stand Together*, 433 (Dec. 1931) Lewis writes of Morris: "his treatment of love is so undisguisedly physical and yet so perfectly sane and healthy—real paganism at its best, which is the next best thing to Christianity."

42. Holbrook, *The Skeleton in the Wardrobe*, 42.

43. Cf. Manlove, *C.S. Lewis: His Literary Achievement*, 142.

44. Manlove, *Christian Fantasy from 1200 to the Present*, 261.

45. A. Owen Barfield, *History in English Words*, 190.

46. The popularity of this concept of divinely planned evolution is attested to by a *Daily Telegraph* reader survey of 1904, cited in Hugh McLeod, *Class and Religion in the Late-Victorian City*, 155, 229–31.

47. Holbrook, *The Skeleton in the Wardrobe*, 248.

48. Holbrook, *The Skeleton in the Wardrobe*, 39.

49. Holbrook, *The Skeleton in the Wardrobe*, 45–46.

50. The similarity was pointed out to me by Dr. Edwards.

NICOLE M. DuPLESSIS

ecoLewis:
Conservationism and Anticolonialism in
The Chronicles of Narnia

In 1993, reflecting on the state of criticism on C.S. Lewis, Colin Manlove indicated that much Lewis criticism is thematic in nature, dealing primarily with the presence of Lewis's Christian beliefs in his texts (11). In the decade since the publication of Manlove's *"The Chronicles of Narnia": Patterning of a Fantastic World*, very little has changed: critics evaluate Lewis's *Chronicles of Narnia* largely on the basis of their agreement or disagreement with the moral views, often conflated with "worldview," expressed in his fantasies for children. However, the rhetorical force of a text may reach beyond the strict intentions of its author to connect with contemporary issues—in this case, issues of justice that involve humankind and nature. Close examination of C.S. Lewis's diaries and his scholarly writing demonstrate his appreciation of the beauty of nature and his concern for the transience of nature—and often for humanity's part in nature's demise.[1]

In *The Chronicles of Narnia*, the "worldview" embodied in the fantasy world of Narnia may productively be considered from an ecocritical perspective. Such a perspective connects the interest Lewis had in issues of his day, including vivisection and colonialism, to his use of "enchanted woods" as a metaphor for the human experience of nature in his criticism of fantasy and his children's fiction, demonstrating that while Narnia is utopian, its environmental troubles are meant to translate to the real world. *The*

From *Wild Things: Children's Culture and Ecocriticism*. © 2004 by Wayne State University Press.

Chronicles variously depict deforestation, exploitation of natural resources, and the political and social evils of colonialism, which have implicit ecological consequences because the indigenous population of Narnia are talking animals. Although Lewis would not have allied himself explicitly with protoenvironmental movements, his work thus anticipates the theories of ecoanarchist Murray Bookchin, who argues that "the very notion of the domination of nature by man stems from the very real domination of human by human" (1), as well as the work of more recent ecofeminists and advocates of environmental justice, who identify destruction of the earth with the modern industrialist obsession with power that leads to the exercise of control over both nature and fellow humans.[2]

While C.S. Lewis is seldom considered an environmentalist by his critics and biographers, his connection with nature is never denied. In the past decade, Kath Filmer's *The Fiction of C.S. Lewis* has addressed the political implications of Lewis's children's fiction, including his "conservationist views" (79), and articles by Nancy-Lou Patterson (1994) and John Laurent (1993) have explored Lewis as a "nature mystic" and an early animal rights advocate interested in evolutionary theory, respectively. Laurent, whose work focuses on Lewis's *Space Trilogy*, sees Lewis's concern for animal experimentation, which has sometimes been taken as an affront to science, as a belief in soulfulness in animals, specifically in regard to the "kindliness of one species toward another: the very antithesis of self-centeredness, and surely having something to do with morality" (49). Patterson traces Lewis's "nature mysticism" primarily through his nonfiction writing and the *Space Trilogy*, demonstrating Lewis's anticipation of twentieth-century "Green theology" (7), also known as ecotheology or the Christian "stewardship" movement. *The Chronicles of Narnia* are not addressed at length in either Laurent's or Patterson's article, though each contributes admirably to an understanding of Lewis's concern for nature and how this is demonstrated in his writings for adults.

Similarly, discussions of *The Chronicles* themselves do not treat the representations of nature or animals as such. As anthropomorphic beasts are a standard feature of fables, fairy tales, and children's fantasy, the presence of talking animals in Lewis's stories does not automatically lend the novels to an ecocritical reading. Rather, many environmentalist critics might find this treatment of nature suspect, as making animals more like humans, in the case of a fairy tale or fable, may effectively diminish their affinity with the natural world, promoting an anthropocentric rather than biocentric view of existence. It is necessary to consider how nonhuman creatures function in Narnia in order to understand that Narnians, who include talking animals and supernatural creatures (such as naiads, dryads, fauns, and centaurs) traditionally linked to nature and the natural, are not simply "not nature." Although they are natural and anthropomorphic, their status as part of nature is not compromised by their having human and nonhuman characteristics; rather, they are doubly endangered by this synthesis as demonstrated by the contact they have with human conquerors.

In *The Magician's Nephew* and, to a lesser extent, *The Lion, the Witch, and the Wardrobe*, Lewis establishes that the legitimate monarchs of Narnia are humans; however, the indigenous population of Narnia is not used for the benefit of humans as colonizer. Indeed, there is no sanctioned "colonization" of Narnia by its original human inhabitants, who provide a model of stewardship by protecting the indigenous inhabitants without subjugation while Narnia remains largely wild. Nevertheless, in several of *The Chronicles*, specific characters may be identified with colonial or imperial impulses, and in *The Lion, the Witch, and the Wardrobe*, *Prince Caspian*, and *The Silver Chair*, Narnia must be rescued from illegitimate rulers, usurpers, and colonial rule. In *The Last Battle*, colonization is finally the instrument of Narnia's destruction, as the Talking Beasts are sold into slavery to the tyrannical Calormenes.

Kath Filmer, who devotes a chapter in *The Fiction of C.S. Lewis* to a discussion of the politics of Lewis's children's fiction, mentions colonialism in her treatment of *Prince Caspian* and *The Voyage of the Dawn Treader* in particular. A recent biographer notes that having grown up in Ulster, Lewis was familiar with postcolonial Irish politics from an early age, even writing a school essay on "Home Rule," in which "he states that he will defend home rule when he grows up while also acknowledging that it is a 'matter of mighty weight not to be answered in a moment'" (Bresland 16). That Ireland was still a part of Lewis's consciousness when he wrote *The Chronicles of Narnia* is evident from *The Lion, the Witch, and the Wardrobe*: there is a room in the Professor's house that is "all hung in green, with a harp in one corner" (3).

Lewis introduces colonial control of nature as early as the first published book, also the most widely read, of *The Chronicles*: *The Lion, the Witch, and the Wardrobe*.[3] The White Witch practices a particularly environmental form of evil, controlling the inhabitants by making it "always winter but never Christmas" (14) in Narnia; her evil power resides in her ability to interrupt the cycle of the seasons. However, the first fully developed character who can be clearly identified with a colonial impulse is Eustace in *The Voyage of the Dawn Treader*. An obnoxious—though not fully evil—character, Eustace participates in the "experimentation on animals simply out of curiosity" (Laurent 46). The product of "very up-to-date and advanced people .... [Eustace] liked animals, especially beetles, if they were dead and pinned to a card" (*Dawn Treader* 1). This initial description of

Eustace establishes that he is "a young proto-vivisectionist" (Filmer 80). Filmer notes that "vivisection is not only included in the activities which Lewis condemns in his non-fictional polemical writing, it is also associated with the devilry of the 'modernist' political structure of the NICE [N.I.C.E., National Institute of Coordinated Experiments] in *That Hideous Strength*, and the demon-possessed Un-Man in *Perelandra* who mutilates small creatures in a manner which differs from Eustace's only in degree." The negative portrayal of Eustace in the first chapter of the book illustrates Lewis's pro-animal leanings; however, Eustace's enjoyment of bullying those over whom he has an advantage also suggests Lewis's antipathy toward colonialism. "Eustace extends his cruelties (albeit petty ones) to humans of a particular religious and ethical persuasion antipathetic to his own ... the cruelty with which Eustace treats his beetles extends to humans of a particular kind—that is, those who do not pander to him" (Filmer 81). This condemnation of Eustace's behavior in *The Voyage of the Dawn Treader* suggests toleration of differences and an admonition not to bully—that is, not to exercise unfair authority over others simply because one has the advantage.

Eustace's taste in books becomes bound up with the idea of colonialism: "He liked books if they were books of information and had pictures of grain elevators or of fat foreign children doing exercises in model schools" (*Dawn Treader* 1). The mention of grain elevators suggests general food production, but may be interpreted as the product of a colony, which would then be consumed by the wealthy colonial power. In his discussion of Eustace, Dabney Adams Hart asserts: "Surely Lewis meant that pictures of foreign countries should portray something unusual and fascinating about them rather than illustrate what propagandists have identified as progress: the Great Wall of China or the golden domes of Samarkand, rather than mass calisthenics for Communist youth" (90). Hart suggests that rather than being interested in consumerism or what a country or culture could become through the influence of progress and a colonial power, Eustace should have been interested in the culture of a people: who they were rather than what they produced. It is notable that, although Eustace claims to be a "Republican" (25), he aligns himself ideologically with the country of Calormen, which is a tyranny rather than a benign monarchy like Narnia.

What is mere bad breeding and childishness in Eustace, who has the possibility of redemption, emerges as a fatal flaw in Digory's Uncle Andrew in *The Magician's Nephew*. Uncle Andrew, a "greedy capitalist" (Filmer 86), has colonial designs on Narnia on the day of its creation. Andrew Ketterley is a petty, evil magician who feels himself to be above moral and natural law. Through him, "Lewis provides a frightening suggestion of the destruction that can occur if power is given over to the hands of immoral experimenters" (Ford 6). His experimentation on guinea pigs, "some of [which] only died. Some of [which] exploded like little bombs" (*Magician's Nephew* 21), allies him with those scientists and vivisectionists who, disrespectful of animals, experiment with them out of mere curiosity. Like many Lewis villains, Uncle Andrew's lack of respect for living things extends to humans, which he demonstrates when he sends a little girl, Polly, and his nephew Digory into the unknown where he himself is afraid to venture.

Uncle Andrew's treatment of Polly more than justifies an ecofeminist critique. Uncle Andrew relies on the cultural perception of females as weaker and in need of protection, exercising his control over her by exploiting her "natural" vanity,[4] relying on his nephew's sense of social convention and gallantry to rescue her from the unknown. In his experimentation, he makes no distinction between human and animal; nevertheless, the initial human object of his experimentation is gendered female. Lewis reveals that Uncle Andrew suffers psychologically for his experiments: "He had never liked animals at the best of times, being usually rather afraid of them; and of course years of doing cruel experiments on animals had made him hate and fear them far more" (*Magician's Nephew* 128). However, he remains largely unaware of this mental suffering or its connection to his "high and lonely destiny" (18) as a magician. Because of his instinctive fear and rejection of the animals, he is "estranged from the Narnian creatures, whose speech he cannot understand" (Manlove 91). As a result, Uncle Andrew's experience of Narnia is mainly a traumatic one.

Lewis also translates Andrew's greed for magical power and hatred for animals into a capitalistic desire to exploit Narnian resources for personal gain at the expense of its inhabitants. Ford notes Uncle Andrew's "inability to understand anything that doesn't directly relate to his own needs" (8): hence his inability to understand the talking beasts. However, this characteristic also relates to his discovery of the commercial possibility of a land where everything grows. After seeing the bar of a London lamppost "grow" into a whole lamppost, Uncle Andrew exclaims: "I have discovered a world where everything is bursting with life and growth. Columbus, now, they talk about Columbus. But what is America to this? The commercial possibilities of this country are unbounded. Bring a few old bits of strab iron here, bury 'em, and they come up as brand new railway engines, battleships, anything you please" (111–12). This invocation of Columbus evokes America as a colony; critics (Meilaender; Filmer) also see a connection between Uncle Andrew's desire to exploit Narnia and the designs of Lewis's Devine, "the greedy capitalist from *Out of the Silent Planet*" (Filmer 86). Because he fears the lion, Aslan, who is the creator of Narnia, his first order of business will be "to get that *brute* [Aslan] shot" (*Magician's Nephew 112*; emphasis added). Like Devine's, Uncle Andrew's fear and hatred of the "other," here the animals, combined with his inability to relate to or understand anything beyond selfish gain, lend a particular violence to his designs of exploitation, and he plots the destruction of the creator of Narnia and, presumably, any other creatures of Narnia who hinder his objective.

In addition to connecting capitalistic impulses to negative views of nature in specific human characters, Lewis introduces his readers to notions of exploitation and oppression of indigenous peoples through the "silencing" of nature in *Prince Caspian*. Arguably the most overtly political of *The Chronicles, Prince Caspian* deals not only with usurpation versus legal—indeed, divinely bestowed—kingship, but also gives thorough treatment to the concepts of colonization, suppression, and the fear of the environment that both results from and perpetuates mistreatment of animals and other beings. The Telmarines, an ethnic group that is sociopolitically dominant, function in the same way as Uncle Andrew, but on a larger scale. As with Uncle Andrew, whose fear of animals is the result of cruel experimentation, the Telmarines' fear of the sea and the woods surrounding it is related to their tyranny and suppression of true Narnia. Their suppression of the spirits of the water (Naiads) and trees (Dryads) provides examples of the environmental damage resulting from their illegitimate rule: "In the divided Narnia to which Prince Caspian is heir in the second of the Narnian *Chronicles*, humans under the rule of the usurping King Miraz have been 'felling forests and defiling streams' so that the Dryads and Naiads have 'sunk into a deep sleep'" (Filmer 79). In her discussion of the political nature of Lewis's fiction for children, Filmer notes that "Lewis clearly associates such activities with evil; they take place in a state of enslavement" (79). One might extend this further to note that these actions are the result of enslavement, and that the actions of the dominant group in turn enslave the oppressors, who are unable to function effectively, even as oppressors, because of their fear of nature.

A useful way to describe the political situation in *Prince Caspian* is Colin Manlove's term *displacement*, which he recognizes in the transportation of the children from London into Narnia as well as in their displacement from the scene of the conflict when they arrive in Narnia. More important, he uses *displacement* to refer to "the way the Old Narnians have been conquered by the invading Telmarines; [and] the rightful King Caspian's flight from court into exile" (46–47). This displacement involves the environment, which includes, and is, the indigenous population of Narnia, since the Talking Beasts are unknown to the human inhabitants of Narnia except through legends. "The Telmarines are levelers of forests and builders of towns, roads, bridges, and schools—not out of a desire to civilize, but out of the more negative urge to suppress wildness, that characteristic of Old Narnia" (Manlove 49). Motivated by fear, the Telmarines, by separating themselves from nature, allow the wilderness to become wilder and deny the existence of beings who blend wildness and sentience.

Like historical conquerors, colonizers and imperialists who use "cultural programming" to "promote the occupiers' ... culture" (Kiberd 5), the Telmarines use education as part of their strategy of suppression/oppression. Caspian has been taught by his uncle, King Miraz, and his traditional Telmarine tutors that there were no inhabitants of Narnia before the Telmarines, Caspian's people. Doctor Cornelius, Caspian's half-dwarf, half-human tutor, teaches Caspian the true history of Narnia, revealing Caspian's ancestors as colonial conquerors and tyrants:

> All you have heard about Old Narnia is true. It is not the land of men. It is the country of Aslan, and the country of the waking trees and visible naiads, of fauns and satyrs, of dwarfs and giants, of the gods and the centaurs, of talking beasts. It was against these that the first Caspian fought. It is you Telmarines who silence the beasts and the trees and the fountains, and who killed and drove away the dwarfs and fauns, and are now trying to cover up even the memory of them. The King does not allow them to be spoken of. (*Prince Caspian* 41–42)

The environmental element of Telmarine domination is emphasized in Doctor Cornelius's lecture. The word *silence* is an appropriate description of a conquering people's invalidation of native culture by forbidding indigenous peoples the practice of their traditions, which often includes the suppression of a tongue. However, a "silencing" of nature describes human encroachment upon the environment so that the animals are forced either to adapt to sudden changes in the environment, migrate, or become extinct. Because the Old Narnians function as both animals and indigenous population, both readings of the Telmarine conquest are applicable.

Doctor Cornelius himself represents the racial tension produced by colonization. When Caspian guesses his dwarf ancestry, he reveals himself as racially mixed, suggesting the social problems of colonialism as they exist in human contexts. Dwarfs are shown to be privileged in this construct; though they have lost their community—and, in a sense, their identity—through normalization, they have survived in a sentient form and can remember. Talking beasts, who could not become "normalized" in human society, could only revert to their nontalking state, thereby losing sentience. The less anthropomorphic sentient beings, therefore, have less chance for survival. This suggests the need to respect nature and beasts in our own world, and may be used to show the responsibility humans have to preserve from extinction those species affected by human encroachment upon their territory.

The displacement of Old Narnians by the Telmarines has created imbalance, fear, and hatred. To achieve order and reconciliation in *Prince Caspian*, Manlove argues, further displacement must occur: "Miraz must be deposed and Caspian enthroned in his stead" (47). Likewise, human "civilization" must give way to wild nature, and the two must become productively integrated. "The Narnia that has been seized and 'civilized' into bridges, roads, and towns must be released to find its own equilibrium once more: the river god asks to be freed from his chains, and is so by the destruction of the bridge over Beruna by the disjointing power of Bacchus and his ivy." In this instance, the wild liberates itself—as presumably, over time, the traces of man's domination are destroyed by natural forces such as the ivy. Lewis redefines "civilization" by creating a human culture in Narnia that is free from signifiers of domination: as "maps"—markers of "civilization"—are reevaluated in postcolonial criticism, so one must question the appropriateness of Telmarine "bridges" and "roads"—things that can be mapped by the colonizer—as appropriate markers of civilization. Silenced nature in Narnia must be awakened by divine agency and not the actions of humans. This is made clear in the case of the Dryads. Although she calls to them and is able to feel a faint stirring, Lucy is unable to awaken the spirit of the trees (*Prince Caspian* 96–97). Aslan's intervention is necessary to liberate them and restore their speech. Although it is not explicit in the text, this may suggest that conservation is necessary *before* the trees are silenced— since in this world, unlike in Narnia, there is no magic that may bring them back. The theme of displacement, found throughout *The Chronicles*, "is a means always of shaking loose the self from settled assumptions, of undercutting human appropriations of reality" (Manlove 47). In *Prince Caspian*, the settled assumption is the "natural" domination of humans over nature. Though it is established by Aslan that correct, just rule in Narnia is human rule, respect for the Talking Beasts and other natural forces is an understood condition of this rule. When Caspian, with his respect and appreciation for "Old Narnia," is restored to the throne, as when the trees are wakened and the bridges removed, the natural order is restored: with humans and wild and sentient nature harmonized under a benign monarchy.

Lewis continues the theme of unjust treatment of indigenous peoples in *The Silver Chair*. The fourth book in the series involves an attempted attack on Narnia which, if successful, would result in an enslavement of the

Narnian population. It is different from *Prince Caspian*: the attack is thwarted, and the Narnians face exploitation, not eradication, by their would-be ruler. The agent of evil in *The Silver Chair*, as in *The Lion, the Witch, and the Wardrobe*, is a northern witch. Her plan involves the capture and magical enslavement of Prince Rilian of Narnia, son of Caspian X. "Rilian is to be the witch's tool for gaining power in Overland, which is actually, unbeknown to him, his own country of Narnia, the realm he in any case has the lineal authority to govern" (Manlove 70). In *The Silver Chair*, Lewis shows the domination and exploitation of indigenous peoples in the witch's control of the Underland and its inhabitants, gnomes. She plans to lead the gnomes, who labor under her command, to conquer Narnia, in spite of the gnomes' intense fear of the Overland. These figures suggest the fate of Narnia under the witch's rule: "Loss of power characterizes the Underland. The Earthmen there work silently, without animation, in virtual darkness, the vegetation is sickly, and whole caverns are full of motionless, sleeping creatures" (Manlove 70). The glumness that characterizes the Underland gnomes is revealed as a by-product of their enslavement. When Rilian kills the witch, the Earthmen begin to mobilize, presumably to avenge her. However, it is soon revealed that the Earthmen were not willing servants of the witch, and, unaware that she has been killed, are mobilizing for an attack against the witch, in order to return to their homes in the deeper land of Bism. Her control, which Manlove defines as tyranny, had effectively robbed them of their selfhood; the witch "destroys selves and allows no free will" (Manlove 70). Though, unlike the Telmarines, the witch does not seek to populate either Narnia or the Underland, her exploitation of the inhabitants of Bism and her intended exploitation of Narnia point to the establishment of rule so that the controlling power may reap the benefits of labor as a natural resource.

Environmental exploitation, including mistreatment of animals, is more often mentioned than portrayed in *The Chronicles*, although Lewis demonstrates repeatedly that harming animals is wrong, as in the examples of Eustace and Uncle Andrew. Only in *The Last Battle*, which chronicles the "last days of Narnia," does colonial exploitation reach its extreme. The rightful ruler, King Tirian, must confront the infiltration of his country by a hostile power, the deforestation of the land by these invaders, and the enslavement of Narnia's free inhabitants. Early in the book, King Tirian learns of the deforestation, the murder of talking trees, which may truly be termed Narnian genocide:

> "Woe, woe, woe!" called the voice. "Woe for my brothers and sisters! Woe for the holy trees! The woods are laid waste. The ax

is loosed against us. We are being felled. Great trees are falling, falling, falling."

With the last "falling," the speaker came in sight. She was like a woman but so tall that her head was on a level with the Centaur's; yet she was like a tree, too....

"A-a-a-h," gasped the Dryad, shuddering as if in pain—shuddering time after time as if under repeated blows. Then all at once she fell sideways as suddenly as if both her feet had been cut from under her. For a second they saw her lying dead on the grass and then she vanished. They knew what had happened. Her tree, miles away, had been cut down. (16–17)

This highly emotional and graphic portrayal of the destruction of nature is unparalleled except perhaps for the White Witch's execution of Aslan in *The Lion, the Witch, and the Wardrobe*. However, the murder of the Dryad lacks the underlying religious purpose of Aslan's death, while the sad tranquility of Aslan's sacrifice is replaced by violence and meaninglessness. Here the tree, representative at once of wild nature and sentience, calls on Tirian for assistance. This emphasizes humanity's role as protectors of the natural environment, while the felling of the trees represents humanity's role in the destruction of nature. The anthropomorphism here is particularly effective. The anguish of the Dryad at seeing her "brothers and sisters" murdered and the pain of her own death provide a vividly human perspective on the horror of deforestation.[5] The tree, a living being, is cut down before the reader's eyes—and unlike the silencing of the trees by the Telmarines, this evil cannot be reversed. In *The Last Battle*, as in the real world, the environmental corruption is absolute.

Lewis again links destruction of the environment with colonial issues in *The Last Battle* when King Tirian goes to investigate this atrocity and discovers that his people have been sold into slavery to the Calormenes by the false Aslan. Lewis adds an additional dimension to this injustice by contrasting the beauty of the forest with the ugliness of the clearing made by deforestation, emphasizing that the Calormenes' actions violate moral and aesthetic sensibilities: "Right through the middle of that ancient forest—that forest where the trees of gold and of silver had once grown and where a child from our world had once planted the Tree of Protection—a broad lane had already been opened. It was a hideous lane like a raw gash in the land, full of muddy ruts where felled trees had been dragged down to the river" (20). This is not a unique image in Lewis's fiction; he uses similar imagery to describe the N.I.C.E.'s alteration of an English country landscape in *That Hideous Strength*. The violence of this particular opening of earth, described as a "raw gash" with "muddy ruts," may be contrasted with the image of the earth bursting open during the creation of the animals in *The Magician's Nephew* and the harvesting of earth for the Dryads' feast in *Prince Caspian*. Lewis demonstrates that there are proper and improper ways of using the earth, as the dwarfs' mining is presumably environmentally friendly, while this Calormene industry is a violation.

Children's and adolescent literature, at their best, may be said to pave the way for certain kinds of consciousness in their readers. By emphasizing ecological aspects of *The Chronicles* that perhaps are not as explicit as their Christian imagery, it is possible to introduce to their study concepts that ultimately expand the relevance of the texts. Throughout *The Chronicles*, the negative effects of colonial exploitation and the themes of animal rights and human responsibility to the environment are emphasized in Lewis's construction of a community of living things. Through the negative examples of illegitimate rulers, Lewis constructs the "correct" relationship between humans and nature, providing examples of rulers like Caspian who fulfill their responsibilities to the environment.

Several factors indicate that C.S. Lewis would not have been an environmentalist by today's standards. Although Lewis approaches concepts that are dear to contemporary environmentalists, because his worldview is hierarchical, emphasizing one's proper place in the scheme of things, his work is at odds with many contemporary perspectives, although it can be argued that by favoring a hierarchical vision Lewis is approximating the concept of the ecosphere or the food chain. Many theorists argue that the realization of "responsible stewardship" may only mature in a democratic society (Binde 23). By implication, the harmonious coexistence of humanity and nature is incompatible with monarchy and other forms of government, though this may require further investigation. Karin Lesnik-Oberstein exposes an impulse toward hierarchy that seems inherent in children's literature while arguing that "ideological, political and moral issues are asserted with concentrated force with regard to the 'child,' and find their clearest articulation in books assigned to a child-audience in the prevalent belief (right or wrong) that those books have a unique capacity to affect, and therefore enlighten, their child-readers" (216). Toward this end, Lewis provides a model of human interaction with nature in his *Chronicles*, creating an environmental ideal in the fantasy world of Narnia that reaches for social harmony, though this is necessarily limited by the time period in which Lewis was writing and the sociopolitical factors that influenced the production of the texts. Lewis's love of nature infuses his books for children, illustrating that humans are responsible for nature's continuity and providing examples of human and nonhuman nature existing harmoniously in a community of living things, perhaps stimulating similar appreciation and concern for the wonder of nature in his young readers.

NOTES

1. For example, Lewis devotes a large part of his discussion in *Studies on Words* to the implications of the word *nature* and the evolution of its meaning.

2. See, for example, Killingsworth and Palmer.

3. For a discussion of reading order of *The Chronicles*, see Ford (xxxiv–xxxv).

4. In his discussion of the word *nature* in *Studies in Words*, Lewis, invoking Aristotle, cites historical social injustices to define *nature* as what really is, as opposed to what is ordained purely by law, custom, or society: "The claims made by women when the suffragist movement began, or by native Africans in parts of Africa, could in traditional language have taken the form 'Our inferiority to you (men or whites) is legal or conventional, not *natural*'" (58). Here Lewis analyzes the term *natural* as it is used rhetorically by oppressed groups, including women. In *The Chronicles*, he actualizes this rhetoric, demonstrating by his use of animal nature that oppression is not natural, and that nature is disrupted by oppressive control and coercion.

5. This scene is also interesting in comparison to Whitman's "Song of the Redwood-Tree" (1874), which contains the implicit argument that the departure of the spirit of the forests (dryads and hamadryads) as the great forest meets the ax is a necessary tragedy, making way for the superior human race. See M. Jimmie Killingsworth.

WORKS CITED

Binde, Per. "Nature in Roman Catholic Tradition." *Anthropological Quarterly* 74 (2001): 15–27.

Bookchin, Murray. *The Ecology of Freedom*. Palo Alto, Calif: Cheshire, 1982.

Bresland, Ronald W. *The Backward Glance: C.S. Lewis in Ireland*. Antrim, Northern Ireland: W. and G. Baird, 1999.

Filmer, Kath. *The Fiction of C.S. Lewis: Mask and Mirror*. New York: St. Martin's, 1993.

Ford, Paul. *Companion to Narnia*. San Francisco: Harper San Francisco, 1994.

Hart, Dabney Adams. *Through the Open Door: A New Look at C.S. Lewis*. Tuscaloosa: University of Alabama Press, 1984.

Kiberd, Declan. *Inventing Ireland*. Cambridge: Harvard University Press, 1996.

Killingsworth, M. Jimmie. "The Voluptuous Earth and the Fall of the Redwood Tree: Whitman's Personifications of Nature." In *Walt Whitman, East and West*. Ed. Ed Folsom. Iowa City: University of Iowa Press, 2002.

Killingsworth, M. Jimmie, and Jacqueline S. Palmer. "Ecopolitics and the Literature of the Borderlands: The Frontiers of Environmental Justice in Latina and Native American Writing." In *Writing the Environment Ecocriticism and Literature*. Ed. Richard Kerridge and Neil Sammells. London: Zed, 1998, 196–207.

Laurent, John. "C.S. Lewis and Animal Rights." *Mythlore* 71 (1993): 46–51.

Lesnik-Oberstein, Karin. "Children's Literature and the Environment." In *Writing the Environment: Ecocriticism and Literature*. Ed. Richard Kerridge and Neil Sammells. London: Zed, 1998, 208–38.

Lewis, C.S. *The Last Battle*. 1956. New York: Macmillan, 1986.

———. *The Lion, the Witch, and the Wardrobe*. 1950. New York: Macmillan, 1988.

———. *The Magician's Nephew*. 1955. New York: Scholastic, 1988.

———. *Prince Caspian*. 1951. New York: Macmillan, 1986.

———. *The Silver Chair*. 1953. New York: Macmillan, 1986.

———. *Studies in Words*. 1960. Cambridge: Cambridge University Press, 1967.

———. *The Voyage of the Dawn Treader*. 1952. New York: Macmillan, 1986.

Manlove, Colin. *"The Chronicles of Narnia": Patterning of a Fantastic World*. New York: Twayne, 1993.

Meilaender, Gilbert. *The Taste for the Other: The Social and Ethical Thought of C.S. Lewis*. Grand Rapids, Mich.: Eerdmans, 1978.

Patterson, Nancy-Lou. "The Green Lewis: Inklings of Environmentalism in the Writings of C.S. Lewis." *Lamp-Post of the Southern California C.S. Lewis Society* 18 (1994): 4–14.

Chronology

1898	Clive Staples Lewis is born November 29 in Belfast, Northern Ireland, to Albert James Lewis and Flora Augusta Hamilton Lewis. His brother, Warren Hamilton Lewis, was born on June 16, 1895.
1905	The Lewis family moves to their new home, "Little Lea," on the outskirts of Belfast.
1908	Mother, Flora, dies of cancer; C.S. Lewis and brother are sent to Wynard School in England.
1910	Attends Campbell College boarding school in Belfast.
1911–1913	Lewis studies at Cherbourg School, Malvern, England.
1914	Under the private tutoring of William Kirkpatrick, Lewis begins extensive literary and philosophical studies (Latin, Greek, French, German, and Italian).
1916	Wins scholarship to University College, Oxford.
1917	Lewis attends University College, Oxford, but enlists in the British army during World War I.
1919	Returns to his studies at Oxford. Publishes *Spirits in Bondage*, his first book.
1921	Lewis's mentor, William Kirkpatrick, dies.
1924	Serves as philosophy tutor at University College.
1925	Elected a Fellow of Magdalen College, Oxford, where he will serve as tutor in English Language and Literature for 29 years.

1926	Publishes *Dymer*.
1929	Father, Albert, dies on September 24.
1930	The Inklings, a sort of literary society, first meets in Oxford. Members, who will continue to meet for the next sixteen years, include J.R.R. Tolkien, Hugo Dyson, Charles Williams, Dr. Robert Harvard, Owen Barfield, Neville Coghill, and others.
1931	Lewis returns to belief in Christianity.
1933	*The Pilgrim's Regress* is published.
1936	*The Allegory of Love: A Study in Medieval Tradition* is published.
1938	*Out of the Silent Planet*, the first novel in the Ransom Trilogy, is published.
1940	*The Problem of Pain* is published.
1941	Gives radio addresses on "Right and Wrong: A Clue to the Meaning of the Universe?" From May 2 until November 28, *The Guardian* publishes 31 *Screwtape Letters* in weekly installments.
1942	The first meeting of the Socratic Club is held in Oxford. *The Screwtape Letters* published.
1943	*Perelandra*, the second novel in the Ransom Trilogy, is published.
1944	*The Abolition of Man* is published.
1945	*That Hideous Strength*, the final novel in the Ransom Trilogy, is published. *The Great Divorce* is published.
1947	Lewis appears on the cover of *Time* magazine.
1950	*The Lion, the Witch and the Wardrobe*, the first of seven books in *The Chronicles of Narnia*, is published.
1951	*Prince Caspian* is published.
1952	*Mere Christianity* is published. *The Voyage of the Dawn Treader* is published.
1953	*The Silver Chair* is published.
1954	*The Horse and His Boy* is published. In June, Lewis accepts the Chair of Medieval and Renaissance Literature at Cambridge.
1955	*The Magician's Nephew*, the sixth of the seven Chronicles of Narnia, is published; *Surprised by Joy* is published.
1956	*The Last Battle*, the seventh and final book in *The Chronicles of Narnia*, is published; Lewis receives the Carnegie Medal

	in recognition of it. *Till We Have Faces* is published. Lewis and Joy Gresham are married in a civil ceremony in Oxford. Joy is diagnosed with cancer.
1957	Lewis and Gresham have a religious wedding ceremony at her hospital bed.
1958–59	Joy's cancer goes into remission. Lewis is elected an Honorary Fellow of University College, Oxford. *Reflections on the Psalms* is published.
1960	Joy dies on July 13 at the age of 45. *Studies in Words* and *The Four Loves* are published.
1961	*A Grief Observed* is published under the pseudonym of N.W. Clerk. *An Experiment in Criticism* is published.
1963	Lewis dies one week before his 65th birthday on Friday, November 22, after a variety of illnesses, including a heart attack and kidney problems.

Contributors

HAROLD BLOOM is Sterling Professor of the Humanities at Yale University. He is the author of 30 books, including *Shelley's Mythmaking* (1959), *The Visionary Company* (1961), *Blake's Apocalypse* (1963), *Yeats* (1970), *A Map of Misreading* (1975), *Kabbalah and Criticism* (1975), *Agon: Toward a Theory of Revisionism* (1982), *The American Religion* (1992), *The Western Canon* (1994), and *Omens of Millennium: The Gnosis of Angels, Dreams, and Resurrection* (1996). *The Anxiety of Influence* (1973) sets forth Professor Bloom's provocative theory of the literary relationships between the great writers and their predecessors. His most recent books include *Shakespeare: The Invention of the Human* (1998), a 1998 National Book Award finalist, *How to Read and Why* (2000), *Genius: A Mosaic of One Hundred Exemplary Creative Minds* (2002), *Hamlet: Poem Unlimited* (2003), *Where Shall Wisdom Be Found?* (2004), and *Jesus and Yahweh: The Names Divine* (2005). In 1999, Professor Bloom received the prestigious American Academy of Arts and Letters Gold Medal for Criticism. He has also received the International Prize of Catalonia, the Alfonso Reyes Prize of Mexico, and the Hans Christian Andersen Bicentennial Prize of Denmark.

KATHRYN ANN LINDSKOOG, who died in 2003, was the author of *The Lion of Judah in Never-Never Land; The C.S. Lewis Hoax; Light in the Shadowlands;* and *Dante's Divine Comedy: Journey to Joy.*

CHARLES A. HUTTAR is emeritus professor of English who taught at Hope College in Michigan for thirty years.

CHAD WALSH is the author of several books, including *C.S. Lewis: Apostle to the Skeptics* and *The Literary Legacy of C.S. Lewis*. One of the original founders of the *Beloit Poetry Journal*, a national literary quarterly, Walsh was also a professor at Beloit College.

MARGARET PATTERSON HANNAY is the author of *C.S. Lewis* and the editor of *Silent But for the Word: Tudor Women as Patrons, Translators, and Writers of Religious Works* and *As Her Whimsey Took Her: Critical Essays on the Work of Dorothy L. Sayers*.

DONALD E. GLOVER is Professor Emeritus at Mary Washington College, where he was the founding director of the Master of Arts in Liberal Studies program. His the author of *C.S. Lewis: The Art of Enchantment*.

LEE D. ROSSI is the author of *The Politics of Fantasy: C.S. Lewis and J.R.R. Tolkien*.

JOE R. CHRISTOPHER is the author of C.S. *Lewis: An Annotated Checklist of Writings About Him and His Work* and *C.S. Lewis*. He teaches at Tarleton State University.

KATH FILMER is a Celtic researcher and two-time winner of the Mythopoeic Society's Scholarship Award in Myth and Fantasy Studies. She is the author of *The Fiction of C.S. Lewis: Mask and Mirror*; *Skepticism and Hope in Twentieth Century Fantasy Literature*; and *Fantasy Fiction and Welsh Myth: Tales of Belonging*.

COLIN MANLOVE taught English literature at the University of Edinburgh until 1993. He is the author of *Modern Fantasy: Five Studies*; *Literature and Reality, 1600–1800*; *The Gap in Shakespeare: The Motif of Division From "Richard II" to "The Tempest*; *The Impulse of Fantasy Literature*; *Science Fiction: Ten Explorations*; *C.S. Lewis: His Literary Achievement*; *Critical Thinking: A Guide to Interpreting Literary Texts*; *Christian Fantasy: From 1200 to the Present*; and *From Alice to Harry Potter: Children's Fantasy in England*.

LIONEL ADEY is a Professor Emeritus for the Department of English at the University of Victoria. He is the author of *C.S. Lewis' "Great War" with Owen Barfield*; *Hymns and the Christian "Myth"*; *Class and Idol in the English Hymn*; and *C.S. Lewis: Writer, Dreamer, and Mentor*.

NICOLE M. DuPLESSIS received her bachelor's degree from the University of New Orleans in 1997 and her master's in 2001 from Texas A&M University, where she is currently enrolled in the Ph.D. program in English.

Bibliography

Adey, Lionel. *C.S. Lewis' 'Great War' with Owen Barfield*. Univ. of Victoria, B.C.: ELS Monographs, 1978.

———. *C.S. Lewis: Writer, Dreamer, and Mentor*. Grand Rapids, MI: Eerdmans, 1998.

Alexander, Joy. "'The Whole Art and Joy of Words': Aslan's Speech in the *Chronicles of Narnia*." *Mythlore: A Journal of J. R. R. Tolkien, C.S. Lewis, Charles Williams, and Mythopoeic Literature* 24: 1.91 (Summer 2003): 37–48.

Beetz, Kirk. H. *Exploring C.S. Lewis' The Chronicles of Narnia*. Osprey, FL: Beacham Pub., 2001.

Blount, Margaret. *Animal Land: The Creatures of Children's Fiction*. London: Hutchinson, 1974.

Bowman, Mary R. "'A Darker Ignorance': C.S. Lewis and the Nature of the Fall." *Mythlore: A Journal of J.R.R. Tolkien, C.S. Lewis, Charles Williams, and Mythopoeic Literature* 24:1.91 (Summer 2003): 62–78.

Carpenter, Humphrey. *The Inklings: C.S. Lewis, J.R.R. Tolkien, Charles Williams, and Their Friends*. London: Allen & Unwin, 1978.

Christopher, Joe R., and Joan K. Ostling. *C.S. Lewis: An Annotated Checklist of Writings about Him and His Works*. Kent, OH: Kent State University Press, 1973.

Cooper, Helen. "C.S. Lewis and Animals." *Bulletin of the New York C.S. Lewis Society* 3.8 (1972): 2–4.

DuPlessis, Nicole M. "EcoLewis: Conservationism and Anticolonialism in *The Chronicles of Narnia.*" *Wild Things: Children's Culture and Ecocriticism.* Eds: Sidney I. Dobrin and Kenneth B. Kidd. Detroit, MI: Wayne State University Press, 2004.

Duriez, Colin. *The C.S. Lewis Encyclopedia: A Complete Guide to His Life, Thought, and Writings.* Wheaton, IL: Crossway Books, 2000.

Edwards, Bruce L. *Taste of the Pineapple: Essays on C.S. Lewis as Reader, Critic, and Imaginative Writer.* Bowling Green, OH: Bowling Green State University Popular Press, 1988.

Filmer, Kath. *The Fiction of C.S. Lewis: Mask and Mirror.* New York: Macmillan, 1993.

Ford, Paul F. *A Companion to Narnia.* San Francisco, CA: HarperCollins Publishing Company, 1994.

Fredrick, Candice, and Sam McBride. *Women Among the Inklings: Gender, C.S. Lewis, J.R.R. Tolkien, and Charles Williams.* Westport, Conn: Greenwood Press, 2001.

Gibson, Evan K. *C.S. Lewis, Spinner of Tales: A Guide to His Fiction.* Grand Rapids, MI: Eerdmans, 1980.

Gilbert, Douglas, and Clyde S. Kilby. *C.S. Lewis: Images of His World.* Grand Rapids, MI: Eerdmans, 1973.

Glover, Donald. *C.S. Lewis: The Art of Enchantment.* Athens, Ohio: Ohio University Press, 1981.

Graham, Jean E. "Women, Sex, and Power: Circe and Lilith in Narnia" *Children's Literature Association Quarterly (CLAQ)* 29 1–2 (Spring-Summer 2004): 32–44.

Green, Roger L., and Walter Hooper. *C.S. Lewis: A Biography.* New York: Harcourt Brace Jovanovich, 1974.

Griffin, William. *Clive Staples Lewis: A Dramatic Life.* New York: Harper and Row, 1986.

Hannay, Margaret Patterson. *C.S. Lewis.* New York: Ungar, 1981.

Hart, Dabney Adams. *Through the Open Door: A New Look at C.S. Lewis.* Montgomery: University of Alabama Press, 1984.

Holbrook, D. *The Skeleton in the Wardrobe: C.S. Lewis' Fantasies, a Phenomenological Study.* Lewisburg, PA: Bucknell University Press, 1991.

Holmer, Paul L. *C.S. Lewis: The Shape of His Faith and Thought.* New York: Harper, 1976.

Hooper, Walter *C.S. Lewis: A Companion and Guide.* San Francisco: Harper, 1996.

————. *Past Watchful Dragons: The Narnian Chronicles of C.S. Lewis*. New York: Collier Books, 1979.

Howard, Thomas. *The Achievement of C.S. Lewis: A Reading of His Fiction*. Wheaton, IL: Harold Shaw Publishers, 1980.

Johnson, William C. and Marcia K Houtman. "Platonic Shadows in C.S. Lewis' *Narnia Chronicles*." *MFS: C* 32.1 (Spring 1986): 75–87.

Keefe, Carolyn, ed. *C.S. Lewis: Speaker and Teacher*. Grand Rapids, MI: Zondervan, 1971.

King, Don. *C.S. Lewis, Poet: The Legacy of His Poetic Impulse*. Kent, Ohio: Kent State University Press, 2001.

Kreeft, Peter. *C.S. Lewis: A Critical Essay*. Grand Rapids, MI: Eerdmans, 1969.

Lindskoog, Kathryn A. *The Lion of Judah in Never-Never Land: The Theology of C.S. Lewis Expressed in His Fantasies for Children*. Grand Rapids, MI: Eerdmans, 1973.

Manlove, Colin. *The Chronicles of Narnia: The Patterning of a Fantastic World*. New York: Twayne, 1993.

————. *C.S. Lewis: His Literary Achievement*. Basingstoke, Hampshire: Macmillan Press, 1987.

Mills, David, ed. *The Pilgrim's Guide: C.S. Lewis and the Art of Witness*. Grand Rapids, MI: Eerdmans, 1998.

Myers, Doris T. *C.S. Lewis in Context*. Kent, OH: Kent State University Press, 1994.

Nagakura, Reiko. "Aslan the Lion in C.S. Lewis' Narnia." *Sophia English Studies* 4 (1979): 23–33.

Patterson, Nancy-Lou. "The Visionary Woman in C.S. Lewis' *Chronicles of Narnia* and *That Hideous Strength*." *Mythlore: A Journal of J.R.R. Tolkien, C.S. Lewis, Charles Williams, and the Genres of Myth and Fantasy Studies* 6 (Summer 1979): 6–10.

Reilly, R.J. *Romantic Religion: A Study of Barfield, Lewis, Williams, and Tolkien*. Athens: University of Georgia Press, 1971.

Rossi, Lee D. *The Politics of Fantasy: C.S. Lewis and J.R.R. Tolkien*. Ann Arbor: University of Michigan Press, 1984.

Rudd, David. "Myth-Making—or Just Taking the Myth? The Dangers of Myth Becoming Fact in Lewis's Narnia series." *Papers: Explorations into Children's Literature* 2002 Apr; 12 (1): 30–39.

Sammons, Martha C. *A Guide Through Narnia*. Wheaton, IL: Harold Shaw Publishers, 1979.

Schakel, Peter J., ed. *The Longing for a Form: Essays on the Fiction of C.S. Lewis*. Kent, OH: Kent State University Press, 1977.

Schakel, Peter J., and C.A. Huttar, eds. *Word and Story in C.S. Lewis.* Columbia, MO: University of Missouri Press, 1991.

Sibley, Brian. *Shadowlands.* London: Hodder, 1985.

Smith, Robert Houston. *Patches of Godlight: The Patterns of Thought of C.S. Lewis.* Athens: University of Georgia Press, 1981.

Walsh, Chad. *C.S. Lewis: Apostle to the Skeptics.* New York: Macmillan, 1949.

———. *The Literary Legacy of C.S. Lewis.* New York: Harcourt, 1979.

Ward, Michael. "Through the Wardrobe: A Famous Image Explored." *Seven: An Anglo-American Literary Review* 15 (1998): 55–71.

Wilson, A.N. *C.S. Lewis: A Biography.* London: Collins, 1990.

Acknowledgments

"Spoiled Goodness: Lewis's Concept of Nature" by Kathryn A. Lindskoog. *The Lion of Judah in Never-Never Land: The Theology of C.S. Lewis.* © 1973 by William B. Eerdmans Publishing Company. Reprinted by permission.

"C.S. Lewis's Narnia and the "Grand Design" by Charles A. Huttar. *The Longing for a Form: Essays on the Fiction of C.S. Lewis.* Peter J. Schakel, ed. © 1977 by The Kent State University Press. Reprinted by permission.

"The Parallel World of Narnia" by Chad Walsh. *The Literary Legacy of C.S. Lewis.* © 1979 by Chad Walsh. Reprinted by permission.

"Further Up and Further In: Chronicles of Narnia" by Margaret Patterson Hannay. *C.S. Lewis.* © 1981 by Frederick Ungar Publishing Co., Inc. Reprinted by permission.

"The Chronicles of Narnia, 1950–1956: An Introduction" by Donald Glover. *C.S. Lewis: The Art of Enchantment.* © 1981 by Donald Glover. Reprinted by permission.

"C.S. Lewis: The Later Fantasies" by Lee D. Rossi. *The Politics of Fantasy: C.S. Lewis and J.R.R. Tolkien.* © 1984 by Lee D. Rossi. Reprinted by permission.

"The Romancer (II) The Chronicles of Narnia (1950–56)" by Joe R. Christopher. *C.S. Lewis: Twaynes English Authors Series.* © 1987 by G.K. Hall & Co. Reprinted by permission.

"Images of Good and Evil in the Narnian Chronicles" by Kath Filmer. *The Fiction of C.S. Lewis: Mask and Mirror.* © 1993 by Kath Filmer. Reprinted by permission.

"The Lion, the Witch and the Wardrobe" by Colin Manlove. *The Chronicles of Narnia: The Patterning of a Fantastic World.* © 1993 by Twayne Publishers. Reprinted by permission.

"Children's Storyteller" by Lionel Adey. *C.S. Lewis: Writer, Dreamer, and Mentor.* © 1998 by William B. Eerdmans Publishing Co. Reprinted by permission.

"ecoLewis: Conservationism and Anticolonialism in *The Chronicles of Narnia*" by Nicole M. DuPlessis. *Wild Things: Children's Culture and Ecocriticism.* © 2004 by Wayne State University Press. Reprinted by permission.

Index

Characters in literary works are indexed by first name (if any), followed by the name of the work in parentheses